The World's Fastest Trains

Patrick Stephens Limited, a member of the Haynes Publishing Group, has published authoritative, quality books for enthusiasts for more than 20 years. During that time the company has established a reputation as one of the world's leading publishers of books on aviation, maritime, military, model-making, motor cycling, motoring, motor racing, railway and railway modelling subjects. Readers or authors with suggestions for books they would like to see published are invited to write to: The Editorial Director, Patrick Stephens Limited, Sparkford, Nr Yeovil, Somerset, BA22 7JJ.

The World's Fastest Trains

From the Age of Steam to the TGV

2nd edition

Geoffrey Freeman Allen

Patrick Stephens Limited

First published as *The Fastest Trains in the World* by Ian Allan Ltd in 1978
Second edition published by Patrick Stephens Limited in 1992

British Library Cataloguing in Publication Data

Allen, Geoffrey Freeman
The world's fastest trains — 2nd ed.
I. Title
625.2

ISBN 1-85260-380-1

Patrick Stephens Limited is a member of the Haynes Publishing Group P.L.C., Sparkford, Nr Yeovil, Somerset, BA22 7JJ.

Designed & typeset by G&M, Raunds, Northamptonshire
Printed by J. H. Haynes & Co. Ltd.

1   3   5   7   9   10   8   6   4   2

Contents

Introduction

The first edition of this book was written with the construction of France's first high-speed line, the TGV-PSE, still two years from completion. Given the decades of methodical research and development which the French had previously dedicated to perfecting the synergy of high-speed traction, vehicles and infrastructure, the immediate technical fulfilment of the first TGV was predictable. Less foreseeable was its extraordinary commercial success. Or, largely because of that, completion by the end of 1990 of a second TGV (operating, moreover, at 300 kmph, not the 250 kmph which I then took to be the realistic speed ceiling for the immediate future); and a start on three more TGV routes. Least of all did I anticipate that within a dozen years of the first edition's publication the world wheel-on-rail speed record would be thrust beyond 300 mph and 500 kmph by a specially-prepared TGV unit.

France has a claim to top billing in the drama of rail speed advance during the 1980s. But there were other stars, plus a considerable supporting cast, few of which had the equipment or performance to warrant attention in the first edition. In this edition, generally speaking, I have set current or shortly anticipated regular operation at 125 mph or 200 kmph as the minimum to justify a latter-day development's discussion. Even so, the amount of new text required — as well as revision of the original — has been so considerable that some of the first edition's descriptions of early rail speed exploits have had to be curtailed to keep the book within manageable proportions. Some of the original illustration, too, has had to make way for the extensive photographic coverage of 1980s innovation. But none of the milestones in rail speed history recorded in the first edition are omitted.

This is not, as I stressed in the first edition, a book for students of engineering. It deals only in technicalities that are basic to a layman's understanding of how the steady advance of day-to-day passenger train speed has been achieved. It is, I hope, not only a compact 20th-century history of rail speed, but also a narrative that brings to life the chronicle's more venturesome exploits.

Geoffrey Freeman Allen
Blockley, Glos

1
Steam's quest for the hundred

In the second half of the last century and the first half of this there was only one rail speed mark that counted. If you dealt in traditional Anglo-Saxon terms it was 100 miles per hour, and if you worked in metrics, 160 kilometres per hour. No one imagined that the orthodox steam locomotive could be pushed much faster.

The 100 mph-160 kmph barrier was probably broken for the first time around the turn of the century. One has to write `probably' because, *pace* the chauvinists on both sides of the Atlantic, scarcely any of the early claims are backed by watertight evidence that defies analysis. None of the American exploits was scientifically timed. The solitary British `hundred' was certainly timed by a respected recorder on the train. But subsequent dissection of his statistics has suggested that he may have been momentarily distracted and jotted down an exaggerated peak speed.

Some of the records alleged were plainly incredible. For instance, there was the ludicrous tale of a freight engine, commandeered to replace a failed locomotive on the `Florida Mail' of the one-time Plant system, later the US Atlantic Coast line, which was supposed to have hurtled over the final 5 miles (8.04 km) of its run to a dead stand at Jacksonville, Fla, in just $2^1/_2$ minutes. Allowing for deceleration, that would have meant the engine careering into this stretch at a peak of around 140 mph (225 kmph)!

Even the two runs that are revered as authentic in all North American record books (if not in Europe, because fully-timed data in support is lacking) are open to question in the hindsight of latter-day steam locomotive science. That the late 19th century techniques of steam passage layout and valve-setting were advanced enough to allow an engine to apply and exhaust steam at anywhere near the rapidity essential to hold the 120 mph (193.08 kmph) claimed is hard to credit. Obviously, though, speeds exceptional for the period were attained.

The first of the two earliest American record claims that are most widely accepted was posted in May 1893. In that last decade of the 19th century the New York Central was effectively run by the dynamic diarchy of its General Passenger Agent, a patent medicine salesman-turned-railroader named George H. Daniels, and its Superintendent of Motive Power & Rolling Stock, a Scot named William Buchanan, who had started on the railroad workshop floor at 17 and then, without a day of formal training, worked his way up via both engine cab and lathe to the top engineering spot on Vanderbilt's railroad.

Daniels was a born showman with a flair for promotion way ahead of his time. Intent on revolutionizing the New York-Chicago rail service, he seized on the 1893 staging of the Columbian Exhibition in Chicago as the opportunity for a short-term proving of equipment potential. That summer and autumn he put on the 'Empire State Express' to run New York Fair visitors to the Chicago fair in a hitherto unheard-of 20 hours for the 980 miles via Central's Lake Shore route. A splendorous overnight train-set was turned out for the service by the Wagner Palace Car Company, the last-surviving Pullman rival.

For Daniels' brainchild Buchanan had his West Albany shops build a one-off 4-4-0 that was especially styled for pace. No 999's driving wheels were a striking 7 ft 2 in (2.184 m) in diameter, so that the leading one had — unusually for an American engine — to be modestly splashered above the running plate; and she was air-braked on every wheel, those of her bogie tender included.

The first surge through the rail speed barrier was claimed for No 999 on 9 May 1893. The 'Empire State Express' was lagging behind the tight schedule — for those days — of 8 hours 40 minutes for the 440 miles (708 km) from New York to Buffalo, four stops *en route* included. In an energetic time-recovery effort, so the conductor claimed, No 999 had whipped its four-car train up to a peak of 102.8 mph (165.4 kmph) in the course of covering 69 miles (111 km) in 68 minutes.

Only two days later, on 11 May, the conductor maintained that he had timed No 999's driver, Charlie Hogan, to do better still. As they stormed down a gentle 1 in 350 grade to Buffalo in the region of Batavia, NY, he had reckoned Hogan to cover a measured mile in 32 seconds flat by his watch. That was 112.5 mph (181 kmph). However vulnerable the evidence, on the strength of it the ebullient Daniels managed to persuade the US Postmaster General to display No 999 and train on a bi-coloured two-cent postage stamp. No 999 won herself eventual preservation and permanent display in Chicago's Museum of Science and Industry, even though some years later the New York Central management itself conceded to sceptical foreign critics that the top speed on 11 May might have been no higher than 81 mph.

In June 1902 George Daniels inaugurated

Buchanan's 4-4-0 No 999, claimed to have worked New York Central's 'Empire State Express' up to a peak of 112.5 mph (181 kmph) on 11 May 1893. (Locomotive Publishing Co)

his 'Twentieth Century Limited' and crystallized the 20-hour New York-Chicago timing as a daily service all year round. 'Surely,' editorialized one incredulous English newspaper, 'it is only a experiment? There are over 900 miles between the two American cities. Can so high a rate of speed as will be necessary to accomplish the feat be maintained daily without injury to the engine, the rails and the coaches? The operators will soon find that they are wasting fortunes in keeping their property in condition and then, loving money better than notoriety, the 20 hour project will be abandoned.' It wasn't, of course; even with steam, whole hours were to be cut from the timing before diesels reduced the schedule to an ultimate 16 hours.

'America's Greatest Railroad' was Daniels's cherished tag for his New York Central. But the Pennsylvania topped that with the boast that it was 'The Standard Railroad of the World'. By the dawn of this century they were in fierce contention, above all in the long-haul New York-Chicago passenger business. Pennsylvania's route between the two cities was shorter, 908 miles (1,461 km) against Central's 960 miles (1,545 km), but west of Philadelphia its grading was severe, whereas the Central made much promotionally of its easier 'Water Level Route'. But if Central could make Chicago in 20 hours, so could Pennsylvania, even though the latter's best train was dragging out as much as 28 hours on the run before the premiere of Central's 'Twentieth Century Limited'.

Americans were astounded when the Pennsylvania announced that from 15 June 1902, the very day of the rival 'Century's' debut, it would lop a whole 8 hours from its New York-Chicago schedule and run a new 'Pennsylvania Special' between the two cities in 20 hours. The press blazoned a 'Great Speed War' in banner headlines, and the public lapped it up as avidly as a World Series. Pennsylvania's 'Red Rippers', as they were popularly dubbed in the Eastern US by virtue of their traditional Pennsylvania Tuscan red livery, ran for just over a year and a half, until February 1904, when they were written out of the timetables because rising freight traffic in the Pittsburgh area was making hay of the 'Special's' timekeeping

day after day.

But in 1905 the Pennsylvania swung back into the attack. Since mid-1902 it had been steadily modifying its layout in the Pittsburgh area, creating new freight cut-off routes and switching traffic flows. Now it could dare even bolder schedules.

On 8 June 1905 the eastern US was astounded by a display advertisement in the *New York Daily Tribune* proclaiming: '18 Hours to Chicago — The Fastest Long Distance Train in the World — "The Pennsylvania Special"'. Just three days later the 'Red Rippers' were to be dashingly reincarnated, an incredible 2 hours faster than before.

The gauntlet was scarcely grounded before Central grabbed it. The same 2 hours were slashed from the 'Century's' timecard; and Central, too, brazenly splashed its train with the identical slogan to that of Pennsylvania's 'Fastest Long Distance Train in the World', though granted they had possibly more right to the title in view of the greater mileage of the 'Water Level Route'. The speed war had been rejoined *con brio* and the public was enthralled.

Four cars made up the 'Pennsylvania Special': a combination baggage car and Pullman smoking saloon, draped with ornate tapestries and furnished with deep leather armchairs; a diner decked out in fine linen and gleaming silver where the catering was sumptuously elaborate; a 12-section Pullman sleeper that included a drawing room and a state room, staffed by both porter and maid; and a combined six-compartment and observation Pullman car, the saloon staff including a shorthand typist whose services were free.

At the head end would be one of Pennsylvania's latest Class 'E2' 'Atlantics'. The Pennsylvania had started to build 4-4-2s in 1899, beginning with centre-cab 'camelbacks' but soon switching to several series of orthodox engines. With these handsome machines Pennsylvania could at last match up to the neighbouring Philadelphia & Reading, with which it was in strenuous contention for the lucrative short-haul New Jersey passenger business from Camden to Atlantic City. In the last few years of the 19th century the pacy exploits of Reading's Baldwin-built four-cylinder Vauclain compound 4-4-2s, vigorously publicized by the Reading management and happily rehearsed by the press, had badly scarred Pennsylvania pride. Mind you, the most striking feats claimed for the Reading `Atlantics' at this time lack any data to encourage credulity. On its booked times the Reading's Camden-Atlantic City `Seashore Flyer' was certainly the world's fastest daily scheduled train in the late 1890s. Whether its Atlantic No 1027 did once, as alleged, reel off the 55.5 miles (89.3 km) in 44³/₄ minutes with six cars and 285 passengers, or on another occasion hit a top speed of 106 mph (170.6 kmph) is something else.

It was the inaugural day's westbound `Pennsylvania Special' which took posterity's headlines. Some 20 miles east of Manfield, Ohio, its 4-4-2 was lamed by a hot box. The engine of a freight train in the vicinity was hurriedly coupled in the cripple's place and trundled the `Special' the next 30 miles or so to Crestline. There Engineer Jerry McCarthy and 4-4-2 No 7002 had been readied to take over. McCarthy had been ordered to recoup as much as possible of the 26 minute deficit on schedule — and of the Pennsylvania's threatened reputation.

He drove like Jehu. From Crestline to Fort Wayne is 131.4 miles (211.4 km) and they were gobbled up, according to the day's operating records, in 115 minutes. That alone, representing a start to stop average speed of 68.56 mph (110.31 kmph), was way above contemporary par for such a distance in any part of the world. But over the 3 miles (4.83 km) from AY Tower to Elida in Ohio, they asserted, McCarthy had whipped his engine up to 127.1 mph (204.5 kmph).

A fantastic achievement — but perhaps literally so. What was the evidence? Just the passing times recorded by operating staff at each end of the section as the train flashed by them. The gulf between average speeds over the whole Crestline-Fort Wayne distance is so wide and the timing data so rudimentary that, taking into account the technological considerations I outlined earlier, one can only record that famously equivocal verdict of Scottish jurisprudence: not proven.

A year ahead of these North American excitements, the first 100 mph had been claimed for European steam traction (as will

Another early American speed record claimant: four-cylinder Vauclain compound 4-4-2 No 1027 of the Philadelphia & Reading Railroad, with `camelback' cab. It was said to have reached 106 mph on the tightly-scheduled Camden-Atlantic City `Seashore Flyer' in the late 1890s.

be recounted in a later chapter, the first European 'hundreds' by any form of power are credited to German electric traction).

At the turn of the century England's Great Western and London & South Western Railways were battling it out for transatlantic liner traffic from Plymouth to London. In 1903 the North German Lloyd and Hamburg-America lines, then the fastest on the North Atlantic route, elected to make Plymouth their English port. Although Plymouth was served by both the GWR and the LSWR, the GWR was far better prepared to pick the new plum, and initially it monopolized both passenger and mail traffic off the transatlantic ships.

But the LSWR, licking its lips at the income from its fine new Ocean Terminal at Southampton, was not about to be shut out of another money-spinning maritime business. It hastened to establish another new marine terminal at Plymouth, which was ready in 1904. That was the starting gun. True, both railways made the ensuing contest something of a 'friendly' by mutual agreement that the LSWR should carry the passengers, the GWR the mails: but even so, prestige hung on whether passengers or mails reached London first.

With its fiery locomotive superintendent Dugald Drummond riding the passenger boat trains to screw endeavour up to the tightest pitch, the LSWR wasn't long in overtaking the GWR's head start. By the end of April 1904, in fact, the LSWR train showed a very neat pair of heels to the Great Western mail. They would have been cleaner still but for the GWR's ace in the hole — the intersection of the GWR and LSWR routes at Exeter, where the LSWR had to use GWR tracks for over a mile through St Davids station. The GWR had a statutory right to halt every LSWR train in the station — and they rigorously exercised it. Nevertheless, on 23 April 1904 the LSWR train rolled into its Waterloo terminus in London in a record 4 hours 3 minutes from Plymouth, well clear of the GWR mail train's arrival in the capital.

Exactly seven days later the mail train reached the GWR's Paddington terminus in London just 3 hours 54 minutes after departing Plymouth — and that with two engine changes *en route*, against the LSWR's one. But it was just a trailer for 9 May 1904. Not

The 'Pennsylvania Special' on the one-time steel truss bridge over the Schuylkill River at Philadelphia, headed by a Pennsylvania Class 'E2' 4-4-2.

only was every Great Western man on the ground involved in the mail train operation keyed up, but also the mighty George Jackson Churchward, the railway's revered locomotive chief. The track was in fine fettle and the operating organisation finely tuned, he told his enginemen: so let them go forth and `break their bloody necks'. And what better pretext than a goodly cargo of gold, due to be transhipped to the mail train connecting with the German liner docking at Plymouth on 9 May?

Both railways from Plymouth to Exeter, the LSWR round the northern fringe and the GWR skirting the south of bleak Dartmoor, were nastily curved as the original engineers fought to take advantage of every contour of the hilly terrain to keep gradients in check. Even so, gradients were extremely severe. On the outskirts of Plymouth the GWR line soon strikes the steady 1 in 41 of Hemerdon bank. Beyond that it still climbs, but not so steeply, to Wrangaton, then dips, easily at first, until at Rattery signal box the slope sharpens to a precipitate 1 in 46-57 into the delightful valley town of Totnes. From Totnes trains curve into the famous climb to Dainton summit, which steepens eventually to 1 in 37 before the tunnel crowning the summit. Then follows an equally swift downhill descent to Newton Abbot, after which it is level pegging along the sea wall from Teignmouth to Starcross and up the Exe Valley to Exeter. Because of the curvature the whole Plymouth-Exeter section is stringently speed-restricted and there is little scope to exploit the down grades.

On 9 May 1904 Driver Clements thrashed his elegant inside-cylinder 4-4-0 *City of Truro* up the slopes and round the curves with such abandon that the gold-bearing GWR mail train dismissed the 31.85 miles (51.25 km) from Plymouth to Exeter in an extraordinary 33^1/$_2$ minutes. Risking an average of nearly 70 mph (112.6 kmph) down the winding track from Wrangaton to Totnes, he gave his five-coach, 150-tonne train such a flying start up Dainton bank that they negotiated its serpentine curves at an overall average of 57.5 mph (92.5 kmph), despite grades steeper than 1 in 100 the whole way.

Thus far, though, the buccaneering

Clements had just been flexing his muscles. The other side of Exeter he flogged *City of Truro* so remorselessly up the 20 miles of almost unbroken grind to Whiteball summit, which finishes at 1 in 115, that they were still making a mile a minute at the top. And when the track began to fall away on the initial 1 in 80-90 of the descent to Taunton he left the throttle alone. Exhaust still roaring, *City of Truro* steadily accelerated until, 3 miles (4.8 km) below the summit, a dedicated recorder of locomotive performance in the train, who had been specially invited by the GWR to observe the run, claimed that his stopwatch had clicked on a peak speed of 102.3 mph (164.6 kmph).

But at that instant Clements had to throw out the anchors. A track gang was on nonchalant patrol right in his path. A rapid succession of frantic whistles didn't budge them. There was nothing for it but to yank the throttle shut and slam on the brakes until at last the gang realised that a train was bearing down on them and ambled out of the way.

Clements had been balked only a third of the way down the hill. Unchecked, he may well have established a peak speed proof against any critical analysis. But although the record claimed by the respected observer on the train, Charles Rous-Marten, is widely accepted and *City of Truro* is honourably preserved on the strength of it, some experts subsequently ran a meticulous rule over the timings and alleged inconsistencies. Rous-Marten, they suggested, may have been distracted by the violent braking and Clements' petrifying whistles into misreading his watch by a few seconds. Give or take those disputed seconds, Clements had certainly come close enough to 100 mph to make this an epic run for the times.

The race from Plymouth was ended by abrupt tragedy. Such might so easily have occurred that same year of 1904, when it was common gossip that both contenders were grossly exceeding speed restrictions and taking extravagant risks. Knowledgeable Americans off the transatlantic liners, it was said, were frequently pressing a fistful of dollars on the LSWR drivers in hopes of a record sprint to London; and the enginemen were

Europe's first steam claimant to 100 mph honours: The Great Western 4-4-0 City of Truro, *for which 102.3 mph was claimed on 9 May 1904.*

giving the visitors value by such excesses as hitting the sharp curves through Salisbury at twice the stipulated speed limit. Within a month or two, however, LSWR chiefs had stamped on the recklessness with some strong-worded injunctions against any attempt to improve on the already exacting boat train schedules. For two years thereafter little was heard of the boat trains. Then, on 1 July 1906, Britain awoke to disaster.

The previous evening a five-coach LSWR boat train had set off uneventfully from Plymouth to its usual engine-changing point in the heart of England's West Country at Templecombe. Here Driver Robins and 4-4-0 No 421 backed on for the second stage of the journey. Robins was an experienced man who knew the road perfectly. What's more he clearly had no dreams of glory that night — quite the reverse. Talking to one of the station staff before he coupled on, he was worried that he might be carpeted if he gained any time on the schedule to London.

The subsequent catastrophe is therefore inexplicable. It happened on the sharp curve at the London end of Salisbury station, long restricted to a maximum speed of 30 mph (48.3 kmph).

The few railwaymen about just before 02.00 reckoned that No 421 was making about 70 mph (112.6 kmph) as she came careering downhill towards Salisbury. Her whistle was shrilling, her throttle well open — and the dumbfounded bystanders gradually realised that it was going to stay that way. Through the station she stormed, lurching crazily as she hit the opening of the curve, then keeling right over at the sharpest pitch. She caught the rear of an empty milk train on the next track, cannoned off and rammed into an aged 0-6-0 goods engine in a bay platform. At that instant No 421's tender jack-knifed upwards, crushing the crew to instant death, while the following coaches strewed themselves about the layout, splintering to matchwood. In all 24 passengers and four railwaymen were killed.

The LSWR and GWR continued to contend for the Plymouth business for some years thereafter, but high speed was never again a weapon. The ghosts of Salisbury haunted both companies for a long time.

2
The Golden Age of steam speed

The First World War over, the railways did not resume their chase for 100 mph in earnest until the 1930s. By then the automobile was really challenging for their passenger business and there was menace in the sound of an aeroplane engine.

There was one historic occasion in the late 1920s, though, when a train rubbed an aeroplane's prop in the dirt. In May 1927 air-mail pilot Charles Lindbergh had engrossed the world as well as his native Americans by piloting his 200 hp Ryan monoplane *Spirit of St Louis* non-stop and solo from Roosevelt Field, Long Island, to Le Bourget, Paris, in 33 hours 8 minutes. Lindbergh had intended to stay in Europe awhile, but President Coolidge had him promptly shipped home in state on the US Navy cruiser *Memphis* to a rapturous

A Pennsylvania Class 'E6' 4-4-2 of the type that headed the Lindbergh film special of May 1927. In this picture No 61 is believed to be fronting the 'Broadway Limited'.

welcome from the President in person at the Washington Navy Yard on the Potomac.

Now film of the epoch-making affair had to be rushed off for processing, much of it to New York. Most of the agencies had hired airplanes: one even contracted a popular stunt pilot of the day to parachute film straight into laboratories at Long Island City. But the International News Reel Co had reason to know that train could beat plane if a railroad car were rigged up to process its film *en route* to New York. On Coolidge's Inauguration Day, 4 March 1925, International and Pennsylvania had laid on their first mobile film laboratory exercise — and succeeded. International's film of the ceremony was unfolding on New York cinema screens well before any that had been flown out of Washington.

For the Lindbergh operation Pennsylvania mobilized 1914-built Class `E6' `Atlantic' No 460, a standard baggage van fitted out as a darkroom and a standard day coach, the last hooked on more to add weight and braking power than anything else. No sooner had the automobile convoy with the film wheeled into Union station and its photographers literally run their precious film to the train than she was off.

The Pennsylvania had clearly determined to steal some of the day's glory. Despatchers down the track to New York had been bidden to keep freight clear; certain local authorities *en route* had been contacted and persuaded to relax speed restrictions imposed in their population zones; and an elite four-man engine crew had been mustered, with Assistant Road Foreman James Warren at the throttle as far as Baltimore, and Assistant Road Foreman Aleck Sentman from there on to New York.

From the first pull of his throttle Warren hammered the `Atlantic' relentlessly, so much so that they took the first water troughs too fast and the air-operated tender scoop picked up precious little, ploughing out a fierce spray about the train wheels instead. To make good they would have to make an unscheduled halt for water.

The footplate party decided to make the water stop at Wilmington. Already they had averaged 80 mph (128.7 kmph) for long stretches, and beyond Baltimore someone —

posterity does not record who — claimed that a mile had been tossed off in 33 seconds, which meant 110 mph (177 kmph).

The scurrying footplate crew topped up their tank at Wilmington in less than a minute and three-quarters, then stormed off towards Philadelphia, 23.3 miles (37.5 km) away. They were through Philadelphia in 17$^1/_2$ minutes, which represented an average of 79.9 mph (128.6 kmph) from a standing start, so if the passing time was accurate they must certainly have been close to 100 mph (160 kmph). Foreman Anderson reckoned that they had touched 115 mph (185 kmph). Anderson himself took over the throttle again after Philadelphia and coaxed the `Atlantic' up to its highest sustained speed of the whole remarkable run. Despite a slowing for another water pick-up from troughs, he ran 66.6 miles (107.2 km) off the reel to the outskirts of Newark in 47 minutes flat for an average of almost precisely 85 mph (136.8 kmph). When the special halted at Manhattan Transfer for the mandatory switch to electric traction over the last 8.6 miles through the Hudson River Tunnel to New York's Pennsylvania Station, the 216 miles (347.5 km) from Washington were shown to have been covered in only 175 minutes, the Wilmington water stop included, for an overall average speed of 74.05 mph (119.1 kmph). Sirens screaming, a police escort convoyed the fully processed newsreels off to Broadway cinemas; and within 15 minutes of the train's coming to rest in the city, New Yorkers had the day's rapture in Washington on their screens. It was more than an hour before any of the rival airborne film was ready for showing. Whether or not the `Atlantic's' speed did peak as high as 115 or even 110 mph, it was unquestionably a ranking run in the rail speed annals.

As the 1920s dissolved into the 1930s, the rail speed focus was taken by Britain's Great Western Railway yet again. Ever since 1923 the GWR had been steadily screwing up the Swindon-London time of its `Cheltenham Spa Express'. This was a fairly humdrum service until it had threaded the Cotswold Hills to join Brunel's superbly engineered Bristol main line at Swindon for the final 77.3 miles of near level track to London's Paddington terminus. By 1929 the GWR had cut the time for this stretch back to 70 minutes, an average of 66.2 mph (106.5 kmph), and could justifiably lay claim to operate 'The World's Fastest Daily Train'. In the public timetables the train's title was the prosaic same as ever; but to the public at large it was now the 'Cheltenham Flyer'.

The GWR was briefly robbed of its crown in 1931 by a bitter contest between Canadian National and Canadian Pacific for the Montreal-Toronto passenger business. This climaxed in a Canadian Pacific booking of 108 minutes for the 124 miles (199.5 km) from Montreal West to Smith's Falls, which on average bettered the GWR by some 2.7 mph. Within months, the GWR had taken time out of its 'Flyer's' schedule sufficiently to regain the world title. Eventually, by September 1932, the GWR was timing the 'Flyer' at an average of 71.4 mph (114.9 kmph) from Swindon to London.

The highpoint of the 'Cheltenham Flyer's' career, though, was a deliberate attempt at record-breaking on 6 June 1932. That day one of the Great Western's four-cylinder 'Castle' 4-6-0s, standard power for the 'Flyer' as for the backbone of the railway's express passenger traffic, streamed up the 77.3 miles from Swindon to Paddington in 56¾ minutes at a start to stop average of 81.7 mph (131.5 kmph). No 5006 Tregenna Castle was the engine, on a six-coach rake of

some 198 tonnes. For 28 miles (45.1 km) on end she was making never less than 90-92 mph (145-148 kmph). To the end of British steam, the start-to-stop average speed registered that afternoon was never excelled by any regular service train.

But the diesel was already growling at steam's heels when Tregenna Castle made the record books in the early summer of 1932. The Germans were just unveiling the prototype of the streamlined diesel multiple-units with which, from 1933 onwards, they were to weave a high-speed web interlacing every major population centre in the country. With these units 100 mph (160 kmph) became for the first time scheduled routine in daily passenger operation. Across the Atlantic diesel traction was to begin its conquest of North American railroads a year later. With these new tools, plus developments in electric traction, the upsurge of world rail speed was such that the 'Cheltenham Flyer' would slide to well below 100th place in the world table of fastest trains by 1939.

Steam was not to yield the pass without its own fling at regular 100 mph operation, though.

In Britain the London & North Eastern Railway was keen to set new speed standards on its East Coast main line from London to the North. The newborn German diesel train-sets looked heaven-sent for the purpose, but

*Below left: The Great Western Railway's `Cheltenham Flyer' speeds up the Thames Valley behind
`Castle' 4-6-0 No 5000 Launceston Castle in November 1934. The headboard proclaims it to be the
`World's Fastest Train'.*

*Above: 4-6-0 No 5005 Manorbier Castle, one of two GWR engines that were semi-streamlined in 1935.
Some GWR directors were far keener to take up the new fashion than the railway's engineering chief,
Collett, who is said to have done their bidding by impatiently applying plasticine to a model and ordering the result to be translated into engineering drawings. The various excrescences were gradually
removed from the engine over subsequent years, beginning with the cylinder fairings later in 1935,
because they caused overheating.*

*Below: The GWR `King' that was similarly streamlined in 1935, No 6014 King Henry VII, poses with the
new `Cornish Riviera Express' train-set of that year near Swindon. (British Rail)*

when the Germans put in their assessment of feasible schedules for the London-Newcastle route of 268.3 miles (431.7 km), the LNER was not altogether impressed. Its management had a feeling that steam could improve on the Germans' 4¼ hour end-to-end estimate. Moreover, the German train-set's seating was cramped by comparison with that of orthodox locomotive-hauled coaches and its catering limited to a cold buffet; wouldn't this be off-putting to a businessmen's clientele that now took full trainboard meal service and roomy 1st class comfort for granted?

So Nigel Gresley, the LNER's Chief Mechanical Engineer, was bidden to draft a steam alternative. As a preliminary, he tested the sustained speed potential of his existing 4-6-2 types. On 30 November 1934 his Class `A1' 4-6-2 No 4472 *Flying Scotsman* (still alive today as an active museum-piece in private ownership) was coupled to a four-coach train and despatched on a speed test from London's King's Cross to Leeds and back. The schedule was so comfortably kept going north that the load was stiffened by two coaches to 208 tonnes for the return.

Descending the 8-mile (12.9 km) Stoke bank south of Grantham, Britain's ideal rail racetrack in steam days, on this leg *Flying Scotsman* was coaxed up to 100 mph (160 kmph). This time the peak was incontrovertible, because the test train included a dynamometer car. More significant, though, was that of the day's out-and-home round of 371½ miles (597.7 km), no fewer than 250 miles (402.3 km) had been covered at an average of 80 mph (128.7 kmph) or more.

And that was with Gresley's original `Pacific' design. On 5 March 1935 one of his Class `A3s' with higher boiler pressure, superheating and improved valve and cylinder design, No 2750 *Papyrus*, was set at the full King's Cross-Newcastle course with a six-coach train and ridiculed the diesel men's prospectus by reaching the Tyneside city in 3 hours 57 minutes: then, after a 2¾ hours' servicing pause, sweeping back to London in just under 3 hours 52 minutes. The driver, a firebrand named Sparshatt, was the same as for the 1934 trial, specially selected for the job in both instances. This time he urged *Papyrus* up to a fully authenticated peak of 108 mph (173.8 kmph) down Stoke bank

In March 1935 Gresley's LNER Class `A3' 4-6-2 No 2750 Papyrus, *seen here on everyday express work at the time emerging from Hadley Wood Tunnel, was whipped up to 108 mph on a pre-streamliner trial from King's Cross to Newcastle and back.* (James R. Clark)

and had her averaging 100 mph (160 kmph) for 12 miles (19.3 km) on end. At the end of the day they had torn off around 300 miles (483 km) at an average of 80 mph (128.7 kmph).

By the date of *Papyrus's* run, however, the LNER management had already made up its mind. A new breed of streamlined 'Pacific' with train-sets to match had been ordered in March 1935.

Britain's first essay in specific high-speed train design emerged in the following September, named 'Silver Jubilee' to mark the contemporaneous royal event and liveried to match in silver-grey from end to end. Up front was Gresley's new Class 'A4' 'Pacific', the familiar upperworks of a steam locomotive shrouded in a smooth stream-lined casing — and not just for meretricious publicity effect, as was the case with a good many of the frills and furbelows draped about passenger engines around the world in the late 1930s and 1940s. Laboratory tests had persuaded Gresley that in the 70-100 mph (112-160 kmph) speed range, the air resistance of a conventionally-outlined train doubled, until at 100 mph it was absorbing

as much as 85 per cent of the traction power. Not only did he streamline his 'A4' 'Pacific', therefore, but also its train as effectively as he could, by blocking off the gaps between coach ends with rubber sheeting and dipping underframe panels between the coach bogies almost to rail level.

On 27 September 1935, three days before the 'Silver Jubilee' was opened to the public, the LNER staged on unforgettable demonstration run. The flagship of the 'A4' 'Pacifics', No 2509 *Silver Link*, was the engine, coupled to the standard seven-coach train-set of two articulated twin-sets and a restaurant-kitchen articulated triplet grossing 224 tonnes. *Silver Link's* enginemen had been instructed to give the 'Pacific' her head, so as to persuade the guests that the planned London-Newcastle schedule of 4 hours lay comfortably within the 'A4's' range; but Gresley himself, one now believes, did not fully realize before they set out that afternoon what a thoroughbred he had created.

It might have been less thrilling if the track and vehicle suspension art of the day had been on a par with Gresley's steam locomotive science. Before *Silver Link* had cleared

The record-breaking 'Silver Jubilee' demonstration run of 27 September 1935: Gresley's Class 'A4' 4-6-2 No 2509 Silver Link *storms past grandstanders at the top of Potters Bar bank, on its way out of the London suburbs to a British speed record of 112.5 mph (181 kmph). (E.R. Wethersett, Ian Allan Library)*

One of the Gresley 'A4' 'Pacifics' now preserved in working order, No 4498 Sir Nigel Gresley, *heads a special over the Settle-Carlisle line in 1977.* (Bernard McCall)

the London suburbs she was closing on 100 mph and ripping into curves and pointwork previously negotiated at not more than three-quarters of the new train's speed. The articulated suspension swung the coach bodies about, and inside the train it felt like riding a caterpillar at the steady trot. Faces paled, though not Gresley's: he was jovially unmoved as on a downgrade of 1 in 200-264 some 30 miles (48.3 km) out from King's Cross, his 'Pacific' stormed up to a peak of 112.5 mph (181 kmph). For 25 miles continuously *Silver Link*'s pace was above 100 mph (160 kmph) and the average for that distance was 107.5 mph (173 kmph).

It is worth adding that the 27 September 1935 demonstration was *Silver Link*'s only full-dress trial before tackling daily service on the 'Silver Jubilee'. She went all but straight from the Doncaster Works assembly line to head the streamliner each way for the train's inaugural fortnight — in other words to cover just over 4,500 miles (7,240 km) at an average of 70 mph (112.6 kmph). In fact, none of the first quartet of Gresley's 'A4' 'Pacifics' had a minute of lost time booked against them in the streamliner's first 100,000 miles

(160,000 km) of operation.

Once the Germans' new diesel train-sets had made their spectacular debut, it seemed highly improbable that steam would take any further share in the speed development of that country. After all, there had been precious little visible attempt to extract more speed from steam even before the diesel units' development; published records showed nothing better than the 95.7 mph (154 kmph) obtained on special test from a Bavarian Class 'S2/6' 4-4-4 way back in 1907 between Munich and Augsburg. When the German locomotive industry approached the Reichsbahn at the end of 1931 for encouragement to develop a 150 kmph (93 mph) steam locomotive design, it wasn't rebuffed, but it wasn't greeted with much enthusiasm either. Few of the top brass had any faith in the higher speed potential of steam power.

But eventually grudging assent for construction of prototypes was forthcoming. If there were to be any merit in the development, majority opinion, convinced with the diesel train-sets in mind that the high-speed inter-city passenger future lay in low-slung, limited-capacity lightweights, favoured some-

There were several French essays in steam streamlining in the mid-1930s. This PLM Railway experiment was conducted with a 28-year-old 4-4-2, No 221.A.14, which in 1935 was operated with a special streamlined train set between Paris and Lyons. In regular service, speed was limited to 75 mph (120 kmph), but on a special test run from Paris to Dijon the engine was worked up to 97 mph (156 kmph) and covered the first 159 miles (256 km) out of Paris in 136 minutes. (La Vie du Rail)

thing along the lines of two extraordinary double-deck, articulated twin-set push-pull trains, each with a streamlined 2-4-2 tank engine, that Henschel and Wegmann were building for the then privately-owned Lübeck-Büchen Railway. So it was that in 1935 Henschel turned out the impressive streamlined Class `61' 4-6-4T No 61.001, and Wegmann a splendidly furnished four-car train-set, closely resembling one of the diesel units in its external styling, to go with it. A second of these huge tank engines was built in 1939 as a 4-6-6. The Henschel tank and train took up Berlin-Dresden service, but the records hold no really outstanding performance by them.

It was the prototypes built by Borsig which made the Reichsbahn's final mark in steam speed history. The genius largely responsible for their design was Dr Richard Paul Wagner of the Reichsbahn's central office responsible for all traction.

In developing their design, Wagner and Borsig paid special attention to streamlining efficiency, conducting lengthy wind-tunnel experiments and testing some of their ideas on an existing `Pacific', No 03.154, in the summer of 1934. Eventually the project took shape as two three-cylinder 4-6-4s, Nos 05.001 and 05.002, designed for a 175 kmph (109 mph) capability with a 300-tonne train. This promised an economy in high-speed passenger service decidedly superior to that of the lightweight diesel trains.

In streamlining, Borsig and Wagner went further than Britain's Gresley. Not merely the upperworks of this pair of three-cylinder 4-6-4s but their wheels, cylinders and motion were encased down almost to rail level by sheeting windowed below the running plate with ventilation grilles. The running plate was high, for the driving wheels were of a remarkable 7 ft $6^1/_2$ in (2.30 m) diameter. The engines were outshopped in 1935, the Reichsbahn's Centennial year, but the Germans spent much of that year in methodical tests of the machines to eliminate any weaknesses before they were put on public high-speed display. At the same time they needed

to fettle up the track and modify the signalling on the streamliners' planned course between Berlin and Hamburg. By 1936 the pair were in regular use on new high-speed morning and evening business expresses of four cars and a restaurant, booked over the 178.1 miles (286.6 km) between the two cities in 145 minutes eastbound and 144 minutes westbound for end-to-end averages of 73.7 mph (118.5 kmph) and 74.2 mph (119.4 kmph) respectively.

In May of 1936 No 05.002 was taken out of public service for what were said to be special brake tests. More likely, though, another propaganda triumph for the greater glory of Hitler's Third Reich was the covert objective, since the Transport Minister, Dorpmüller, just happened to be among the four-car, 200-tonne test-train's occupants on the day that counted, 11 May 1936. On that Hamburg-Berlin trip, it was claimed, *Oberlokführer* Langhans had urged his 4-6-4 up to a top speed of 124.5 mph (200.4 kmph) on the almost imperceptible 1 in 333 downgrade to Zernitz, near Neustadt on the final states of the run in to the then German capital city.

No detailed supporting data for that record have ever been published, though the claim was based on dynamometer car readings. But not far off the same peak was certainly attained *and* irrefutably recorded later that

same month by the dean of British train timers, my father, the late Cecil J. Allen, who was in Germany with a distinguished party from Britain's Institution of Locomotive Engineers. Eager to impress the guests, the Reichsbahn naturally staged a demonstration trip from Berlin to Hamburg and back behind No 05.002. This time the load was three cars of 137 tonnes — one of them again a dynamometer car, whose comprehensive instruments confirmed my father's chronograph reading.

At the start out of Berlin the 4-6-4 was driven at about two-thirds throttle, with little more than half its rated boiler pressure of 285 lb per sq in in the steam chest and on a long cut-off. That was enough to keep speed hovering just below 100 mph (160 kmph), however. Then on dead level track after Wittenberge the *lokführer* gave her just a touch of the spur, edging the throttle open enough to raise the steam-chest pressure to 225 lb. At that, speed climbed sweetly to 118 mph (190 kmph); 7.49 miles (12 km) were timed at an average of 111.4 mph (179 kmph) and 19.4 miles (31 km) at an average of 101 mph (162.6 kmph). More eminent members of the British party had been invited to ride the 4-6-4's footplate, among them London Midland & Scottish Chief Mechanical Engineer William Stanier. They were mightily impressed by her smoothly solid riding at

Left: One of the streamlined push-pull double-deck units built for the Lübeck-Büchen Railway in the mid-1930s, the 2-4-2 tank engine by Henschel and the coaches by Wegmann. The privately-owned railway was absorbed by the Reichsbahn in the late 1930s and the engines then became Reichsbahn Class `60´.

Above: The parentage of the Lübeck-Büchen design is evident in this view, of the Reichsbahn's Henschel-Wegmann train, photographed at the Reichsbahn Centenary Exhibition at Nuremberg in 1935, headed by Class `61´ 4-6-4T No 61.001.

Below: The fully streamlined 4-6-4 `Pacific´ locomotive No 05.001 of 1935. (Deutsche Bundesbahn)

Streamlined 4-6-4 No 05 002 pauses during the 118 mph (190 kmph) demonstration laid on for the British Institution of Locomotive Engineers in May 1936. The previous year the Institution had awarded the '05' design its Gold Medal. (Cecil J. Allen)

100 mph plus: as steady as in the coaches, they said.

A third and very distinctive Class '05' was built in 1937. No 05.003 was arranged to burn pulverized coal dust and hence turned end for end, with the cab in front and the smokebox end coupled to its tender: some sources suggest that the fuel arrangements may have been adopted in part as a means to design a cab-in-front coal-burning steam engine, which would then be capable of push-pull operation despite being paired with a tender. Little more was heard of No 05.003 and it was rebuilt as an orthodox non-streamlined 4-6-4 in 1944.

Several more streamlined steam types were turned out for the Reichsbahn in its final years. The origins of most could be

Deutsche Reichsbahn's cab-in-front, pulverized-coal-burning 4-6-4 No 05 003, built in 1937. (Cecil J. Allen Collection)

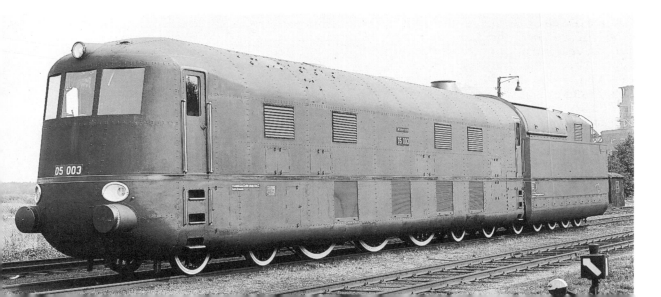

One of the two Krupp-built Class '06' streamlined 4-8-4s for heavy express passenger work introduced in 1938, seen in action at Frankfurt/Main Hbf soon after entering service.

traced to the birth period of the '05s', but although some sterling work was reported of the latter on Reichsbahn inter-city passenger services up to the outbreak of the Second World War, they had their troubles, ranging from steaming problems to track wear on curves. The Krupp-built Class '06' 4-8-4s of 1938 and the '03.10' and '01.10' 'Pacifics' of 1939, therefore, were devised with considerably lower speed ceilings in mind.

The potential implicit in the telling demonstration runs of North America's pioneer diesel streamliners in the mid-1930s did not deflect US railroads from fresh high-speed steam locomotive development for a number of years. As late as the summer of 1938, for instance, the Committee on Further Development of the Reciprocating Steam Locomotive of the Association of American Railroads was organizing track trials to determine the drawbar horsepower needed to keep a 1,000-tonne passenger train moving at a steady 100 mph on level track. The tests were conducted with a 1,005-tonne rake of standard Pennsylvania coaches on the Pennsylvania, Chicago & North Western and Union Pacific systems. Star of the show in terms of peak speed was Union Pacific's massive 4-8-4 No 815, which,

with its 300 lb per sq in boiler pressure and 6 ft 5 in (1.96 m) driving wheels, summoned up well over 4,000 drawbar hp to keep the huge train rolling at 102.4 mph (164.8 kmph) on its home ground. Far from discomfited, though, was one of the much more compact Pennsylvania Class 'K4' 'Pacifics' which were the trialists in Pennsylvania territory. On level track they managed to accelerate the same train to 92 mph (148 kmph) between Chicago and Fort Wayne.

The 'K4s', one of North America's most venerated and proficient steam passenger engine designs, were stellar performers well into the 1940s; for Pennsylvania, as will be demonstrated shortly, was among the major railroads that long resisted total dieselization. From 1936 onwards some 'K4' 'Pacifics' were subjected to the streamlining vogue of the day, supposedly in the cause of aerodynamic science. But what was scientifically valid and effective in fuel economy on engines like the British 'A4' 'Pacifics' and German '05' 4-6-4s, routinely driven in the 90-100 mph speed range, was pure flummery where speed restrictions of 80 mph officially prevailed, as they did on most US main lines in the 1930s. In those conditions streamlining was quite unproductive

Renowned US speed performer of the mid-1930s — the Pennsylvania Class `K4' 4-6-2. This pair is heading the Chicago-New York `Rainbow' out of Canton, Ohio. (Cecil J. Allen Collection)

economically. Whatever publicity value it may have had was negated by its inconvenient shrouding of vital parts, the casing's extra weight and even, sometimes, its reverse aerodynamic effect if the engine was buffeted by a strong side wind. Not surprisingly, many railroads persuaded by their salesmen to jump on the streamlining bandwagon didn't take long to unfrock the engines they had dressed up, all too often in a pretty tawdry gear. Much more significant was the refinement of steam locomotive technology proper: in the case of the Pennsylvania `K4s', for instance, the application after 1937 to several engines of poppet valves and redesigned steam passages that realized the full steam-generating potential of the tubby `K4' boiler. This enabled the

A sample of the US railroads' streamlined styling fad of the 1930s: Chesapeake & Ohio's New York-Cincinnati-Louisville `Fast Flying Virginian' makes speed between Ashland and Russell, Kentucky, behind a streamlined 4-6-4 rebuilt from a 4-6-2. (Cecil J. Allen Collection)

engines to run close to an illicit 100 mph (160 kmph) on the Fort Wayne-Chicago level with trains like the 'Broadway Limited', 'Manhattan Limited' and lightweight 'Detroit Arrow', and to sustain averages in excess of 80 mph (128.7 kmph) for 20-25 continuous miles (30-40 km).

The most exhilarating US inter-city race of the mid-1930s was fought out between Chicago and the Twin Cities of St Paul and Minneapolis, where three railroads were in contention with routes of roughly equal length and speed potential: the Chicago, Burlington & Quincy; the Chicago, Milwaukee, St Paul & Pacific; and the Chicago & North Western. The latter two had the commercial bonus of serving intermediately the sizeable city of Milwaukee. Until 1934 all three had been content to compete overnight for the approximately 400-mile (645 km) haul. But by then you could motor from Chicago to the Twin Cities in a little over 8 hours and the drift of passengers into buses as well as automobiles was beginning to hurt. On 20 July 1934 the Milwaukee fuelled up its Class 'F6' 4-6-4 No 6402, hooked it on to the morning train out of Chicago, a five-car train of 352 tonnes, and proved that the 85 miles (136.8 km) of the

route's well-aligned section from Chicago to Milwaukee could be rolled off in a fraction over 67^1/2 minutes. When Engineer William Dempsey opened up his 4-6-4 20 miles out of Chicago, they averaged 89.9 mph (114.6 kmph) for 68.9 miles (110.9 km) off the reel — whereat the Milwaukee insisted that the riband for sustained high speed claimed by Britain's Great Western with its 'Cheltenham Flyer' *tour de force* of 1932 was now theirs — and, so it was claimed, held a top speed of 103.5 mph (166.5 kmph) throughout the 5 miles (8.1 km) from Oakwood to Lake, Wisconsin.

Within a month all three railroads announced that at a stroke they would slash their Chicago-St Paul daylight transit times from around 10 to 6^1/2 hours. One of the trio, the Burlington, elected to go diesel straight away. The Chicago & North Western opted to run its new 'Twin Cities 400' with existing 'Pacifics', but rebuilt, and traditional coaching stock. The Milwaukee, however, went for brand new train-sets and a fresh breed of locomotive that evolved into one of the world's high-speed steam locomotive prodigies.

The reasons influencing the Milwaukee's decision to persist with steam are worth

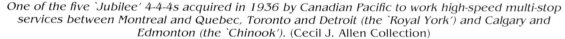

One of the five 'Jubilee' 4-4-4s acquired in 1936 by Canadian Pacific to work high-speed multi-stop services between Montreal and Quebec, Toronto and Detroit (the 'Royal York') and Calgary and Edmonton (the 'Chinook'). (Cecil J. Allen Collection)

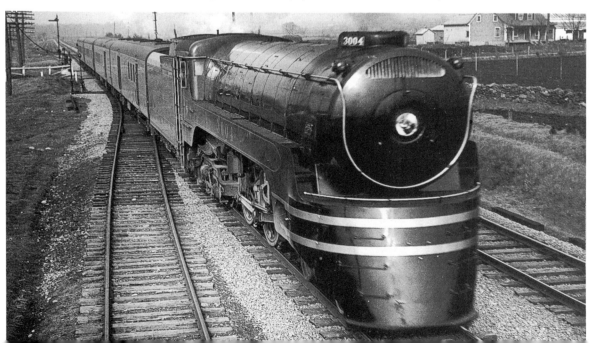

Milwaukee pioneer: Class `F6' 4-6-4 No 6402 draws a grandstand at Milwaukee on 20 July 1934 after topping 100 mph on the record run from Chicago that paved the way for the `Hiawatha'. (Cecil J. Allen Collection)

recall: they typified the considerations which railroad managements were having to weigh up now that diesel traction was showing such promise. First, said the Milwaukee, the new generation of streamlined diesel train-sets lacked the carbody space to create maximum travelling comfort. The fixed train-set was also inflexible, impossible to shorten or lengthen according to troughs and peaks of demand. With steam and individual cars there was no need to invest in new servicing plant. Given determination to employ full-size coaches, only steam, at that stage of diesel development, offered enough power to meet the schedules in mind, and particularly to put out sufficient horsepower at the top end of the speed bracket. There was also a minor but important consideration in the US environment: the ironclad front-end of a steam engine promised better protection for engine crew — and passengers too — than the more lightly armoured cab front of a diesel should the train come on a rogue driver at one of the many open road-rail grade or level crossings. Finally, and by no means least, at that time the capital cost of diesel traction was four times as much as

that of steam.

For the `Hiawatha', as the Milwaukee christened its new service, the road built America's first new 4-4-2s since 1914. These 131-tonne, oil-fired machines were the country's first steam engines to be streamlined from birth and the first to be designed expressly for high speed, with roller bearings on every axle, 300 lb per sq in boiler pressure and 7-foot (2.13 m) driving wheels. The colour scheme devised for the new engines and matched on the train was a delight: the traditional Milwaukee orange set off by horizontal maroon stripes, with huge stainless-steel wings draped around the front of the streamline cowling below the headlight.

On 8 May 1935 new `Atlantic' No 2, engine-man Ed Donahue at the throttle, was sent out from Milwaukee to New Lisbon for a spin with a full six-car set of the new `Hiawatha' stock. The trackside swarmed with bystanders — at least one school trooped out *en bloc* to line the local ballast — and the Milwaukee gave them full value. Their new `Atlantics', they had announced, were designed to cruise at 100 mph (160 kmph) and attain 120 mph (193.1 kmph). No 2 came pretty close to the prospectus that early in its career.

A battery of clicking chronometers in the train said she held 112.5 mph (181 kmph) for 14 miles (22.5 km) continuously. And the faster she went, the smoother she rode, crowed the enthusiastic Donahue. Back in the train, a few engineers kept an eye on a glass of water and proudly reported not a drop had splashed: the car riding was plu-perfect.

Commercially, the steam-hauled 'Hiaw-atha' never looked back. The public service schedule it took up at the end of May 1935 was well within the speed ceiling established by the test run, but even so the pace and creature comforts stimulated such demand that the 'Hiawatha' formation had to be steadily enlarged. The train had only been running for a year and a half before the Mil-waukee built a handsome new train-set for it. Such early updating was unprecedented anyway, but by the 'Hiawatha's' third anniversary, when its passenger count was near 900,000 since birth, a third renewal order, for 55 new cars, was on the produc-tion lines. Simultaneously ALCO was building six mighty new streamlined 4-6-4s to super-sede the 'Hiawatha' 'Atlantics'.

Arguably these Class 'F7' 4-6-4s were the finest high-speed passenger engines America ever saw, superbly handsome as well as almost legendary in their performance. Like the 'Atlantics' they had 7-foot driving wheels, but powered by bigger cylinders fed from a bigger though still 300 lb per sq in boiler. Unlike the oil-fuelled 4-4-2s, they were stoker-fired coal-burners, which postulated a big 12-wheel tender. The engine alone weighed 188 tonnes and the total weight, including a fully-loaded tender, ran out at 350 tonnes.

The so-called 'Hiawatha of 1939' entered public Chicago-Twin Cities service on 19 September 1938. By now the service each way had been doubled and there was a 'Morning Hi' and an 'Afternoon Hi'. Some curves had been realigned, too, so as to raise the degree of cant and make 100 mph per-fectly comfortable over more mileage. At the start the Milwaukee had applied a 90 mph limit to normal 'Hi' operation, but had given enginemen the nod for 100 mph in legiti-mate pursuit of lost time. Now there were no inhibitions about 100 mph at any time.

There couldn't be. To keep up with the diesel 'Zephyrs' on the rival Burlington route, the Milwaukee had by the start of 1940 trimmed the 'Hi' Chicago-St Paul timings to 6¼ hours for the 410 miles (659.7 km). Taking into account intermediate stops and

The first 'Hiawatha' train-set and streamlined 4-4-2 No 2 parade at Milwaukee. (Cecil J. Allen Collection)

The magnificent Milwaukee Class `F7' 4-6-4: No 102 heading out of Milwaukee with the `Afternoon Hiawatha' at the end of August 1941. (R.H. Kindig)

enforced slow running in the busy rail complexes of the route's big cities, the overall schedule could only be maintained by very tight timing over suitable open track — in fact, timing never before or after equalled in steam locomotive history. From Sparta to Portage, 78.3 miles (126 km), the `Morning Hi' eastbound was for a period allowed just 58 minutes start to stop, averaging 81 mph (130.3 kmph); on the Chicago-Milwaukee stretch, westbound `Hi' pass-to-pass allowances for the 57.6 miles (92.7 km) between Signal Tower A12 and Lake were no more than 38 minutes, demanding an average for the distance of 90.9 mph (146.3 kmph). Such scheduling didn't just encourage regular 100 mph running: it demanded it.

The magnificent `F7s' freely provided the speed, day in and day out, on the usual nine-car load of 388 tonnes (they were load-pullers too, mark you: one had once to tackle an emergency assignment of two night sleeper trains coupled as one and had the gargantuan 1,690-tonne load up to 70 mph (112.6 kmph) within 12 miles (19.3 km) of a standing start on level track). The most sparkling run to see printed detail, recorded by a meticulous North American train-timer, was made one snowy January day of 1941, when No 100 on the eastbound `Morning Hi' was making 100 mph (160 kmph) or more for 31 miles (49.9 km) consecutively from near Sturtevant to a slowing for level crossing removal works near Rondout. Speed peaked twice at 110 mph (177 kmph).

The Milwaukee was convinced that even

Despite its small-size drivers, a Norfolk & Western Class `J' 4-8-4 was timed at 110 mph (177 kmph).

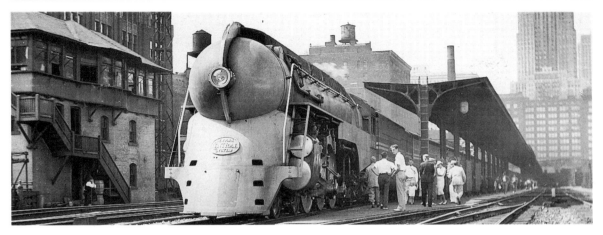

The streamlined version of the New York Central 4-6-4, ready to leave Chicago's La Salle Street station for New York. (Cecil J. Allen Collection)

this was well short of the optimum performance of the `F7s'. Experiment, they said, had shown that once it had accelerated 12 cars to 105 mph (169 kmph), an `F7' could maintain that speed comfortably on just 25 per cent cut-off with only 150 lb showing in the steam chest. On this trial, it was claimed, the 4-6-4 had needed little extra effort to climb to 125 mph (201.1 kmph) and hold 120 mph (193.1 kmph) on practically level track. In the light of this practical data the Milwaukee was minded to raise the line speed limit to 105 mph (168.9 kmph) and prune the Chicago-Milwaukee time to an even hour with a heavier train. But because its rivals were not equipped to follow suit and there was an unwritten pact between them to keep in schedule line, the plan had to be pigeonholed.

The Milwaukee's `Hiawatha' engines were to the rest of the world the best-known symbols of American high-speed steam power in the late 1930s. But fresh vitality was summoned from an extraordinary range of steam engines to fuel the brushfire of acceleration that suddenly, in 1936, had US railroads operating over 29,000 passenger train miles every day at schedules of a mile a minute or better. Never before or since, probably, has any industrialized country experienced such a rapid and widespread speed-up.

Two more US steam locomotive designs must be honoured with extended mention

before this chapter recrosses the Atlantic to complete the European high-speed steam story. The first is the Norfolk & Western Class `J' 4-8-4. The fully attested 110 mph (177 kmph) by one of these engines on an 830- tonne train was an astonishing feat for an eight-coupled engine in any event, but the more so because the `J's' driving wheels were only of 5 ft 10 in (1.78 m) diameter; on the particular engine being tested, moreover, tyre wear had reduced the measurement to 5 ft 8½ in (1.74 m). The `J's' maximum piston speed must therefore have been a staggering 2,878 feet (877 m) per minute.

US rail history records only one instance of higher steam locomotive piston speed. The New York Central was at the time studying the balancing of its magnificent Class `J3' 4-6-4s. On pre-greased rails one of them was deliberately slipped up to the equivalent of 164 mph (264 kmph) — very probably the fastest rate at which any locomotive was ever steamed. At that peak the `J3's' piston speed was 3,370 feet (1,026 m) per minute and its 6 ft 7 in (2.03 m) drivers were rotating at a dazzling 11.6 revolutions per second.

What has been termed the `Custer's Last Stand' of high-speed US steam was Baldwin's endeavour to obtain the punch of eight-coupled drive without the transmission snags of orthodox wheel coupling. Baldwin's solution: duplex drive — divide the coupled wheels

One of Pennsylvania's huge duplex-drive Class `T1' 4-4-4-4s, No 5527, leaves Fort Wayne with the Chicago-New York `Fast Mail'. (Cecil J. Allen Collection)

into two pairs, each with its own set of cylinders. Articulation was ruled out because of likely stability problems at high speed and the probability that a hinged connection between the two power units would demand over-costly maintenance. So a long, rigid-framed engine was conceived.

It was the Pennsylvania that took the Baldwin doctrine on board. Like the Norfolk & Western, it was one of the great coal-carrying railroads and thus both politically and economically motivated to persist with steam power so long as its technology could sustain the challenge to the insurgent diesels. But at the end of the 1930s the Pennsylvania had nothing newer than its basically First World War-designed `Pacifics' to power inter-city trains which were not merely faster but growing remorselessly heavier as air-conditioning became standard equipment. So in 1939, after exhaustive consultation with every major locomotive builder in the country, the Pennsylvania laid down at its Altoona Works

its own concept of a duplex-drive steam engine capable of exerting 6,500 ihp and keeping a 1,000-tonne train rolling along straight and level track at a steady 100 mph.

The outcome, Class `S1' No 6100, was a breathtaking creation. A 6-4-4-6 with 7-foot (2.14 m) driving wheels, 300 lb per sq in boiler pressure and 22 in by 26 in cylinders, the engine alone weighed 276 tonnes; throw in the 16-wheel tender and the scales were turned at a total of 481 tonnes. And the whole was flamboyantly streamlined by industrial designer Raymond Loewy. As for performance, No 6100's career has been crisply summed up thus by American writer David Morgan: `She was extremely fast, extraordinary powerful — but slippery as glass and simply too darned big'. She was scrapped in 1949.

In July 1940, however, the Pennsylvania decided to take the Baldwin duplex-drive design. Two poppet-valve 4-4-4-4s, again with distinctive Loewy sharknose styling, were ordered and delivered in the spring of 1942.

The newcomers, Class 'T1' Nos 6110 and 6111, were set to the 713-mile (1,147 km) run between Chicago and Harrisburg, which they had been designed to command with a single fuelling stop *en route*, since there were track troughs and the huge 16-wheel tender held 40 tonnes of coal. At once they showed that Baldwin had comfortably met the specification. On her very first through trip, No 6110 held a steady 100 mph most of the way from Crestline to Chicago with a 14-car, 900-tonne train, while sister engine No 6111 was timed to average 102 mph (164 kmph) throughout the 69 miles (111 km) of the route's Fort Wayne Division. Soon afterward, on Pennsylvania's stationary test plant rollers at Altoona, No 6110 chalked up power, steaming and calorific efficiency ratings that were a street and its sidewalks ahead of anything previously recorded. So, as late as 1945-6, the Pennsylvania had 50 more 'T1s' built.

At that eleventh hour, with the diesels' North American bridgehead expanded to near-occupation of many railroads, this was a startling investment decision. In the words of the US businessman's bible *Fortune*, it 'had the railroad industry by the ears'. For in the 'T1', proclaimed Baldwin, the Pennsylvania had a machine that could 'outperform a 5,400 hp diesel locomotive at all speeds above 26 mph'.

Yet little more than a year after the last of the 50 production series 'T1s' had taken the track, the Pennsylvania announced that it was immediately dieselizing its Harrisburg-Chicago main line.

Why the abrupt volte-face? First and most obviously, the plain facts of the diesel's availability for work, capability and economy were by now so patent that even the Pennsylvania, never a system to be led by the nose, could no longer ignore them — especially when, as happened in 1946, its accounts were sliding into the red. But in addition, the 'T1s' had an Achilles heel — or heels. Their unprecedented steaming efficiency, power and speed were unarguable: one was alleged to have whipped a 16-car train of nearly 1,000 tonnes up to 130 mph (209 kmph), though

the claim was never validated by acceptable evidence. Against its assets, though, had to be set the appalling costs in time and manpower of keeping the intricate poppet valve duplex-drive arrangements in good order. Moreover, notoriously prone to lose their feet in a frenzied slip, the 'T1s' were unkind to the track. Pennsylvania motive power men desperately experimented with other valve gears, but it was too late. Diesels had long since tolled the bell even for such impressive steam performers as the 'T1s'.

Steam technology was flowering in Western Europe too in the late 1930s, particularly in France under the hand of the Paris-Orleans company's brilliant locomotive engineer André Chapelon. Generally speaking, though, the effort on the mainland of Europe was directed to economical movement of increasingly heavy loads at standard speed, regardless of grade to the greatest extent possible, rather than (for the period) extraordinary end-to-end speed on specially selected services. Line speed limits well below 100 mph were rigorously applied.

A surprising exception was the Belgian State Railways. In 1933 this system at last completed its long-cherished project of a direct, finely graded and well-aligned route from Brussels through Ghent and Bruges to the port of Ostend. The general level of intercity service on the new line was promptly accelerated to a creditable enough standard for Europe in the late 1930s.

Then, in 1939, the Belgians indulged themselves in a *feu de joie*. A small stud of bulbously streamlined, two-cylinder 'Atlantics' with 6 ft 10$^{1}/_{2}$ in (2.1 m) driving wheels was built to shuttle a service of three-coach highspeed flyers over the 70.9 miles (114 km) between Brussels and Ostend Quay in the even hour, inclusive of a stop at Bruges. Between Ghent and Bruges the line speed limit was lifted to 90 mph (145 kmph) for these trains, so that they could be timed over the 57.8 miles (93 km) from Brussels Midi to Bruges in 46 minutes start to stop, which predicated an average speed of 75.4 mph (121.3 kmph); and that for a brief spell snatched the world's fastest daily steam train riband from the Milwaukee's 'Hiawatha'. The *rapides* were taken off in September 1939, but briefly reinstated in March 1940 when the Low Countries were deluding themselves that the Second World War was a non-event.

The only country in Europe to make new speed ceilings with steam power something of an objective in itself was Britain. Following its publicity success with the 1935 'Silver Jubilee', the London & North Eastern Railway had two years later unveiled companion streamliners, the King's Cross-Edinburgh 'Coronation' and the King's Cross-Leeds and Bradford 'West Riding Limited'. But its West Coast rival was stirring too. In 1936 the London Midland & Scottish Railway had revealed its ambitions by sending one of its comparatively new 'Pacifics', the unstreamlined No 6201 *Princess Elizabeth*, on a test run from London to Glasgow and back in which the $401^1/2$ miles (646 km) were despatched in 5 hours $53^1/2$ minutes northbound and 5 hours 44 minutes southbound, a shattering reduction of the everyday schedules then in force between the two cities. In 1937 the LMS therefore launched its own high-speed, lightweight streamliner, the Euston-Glasgow 'Coronation Scot'.

In August 1936 the LNER had inched the British speed record a fraction higher in a rather desperate effort on the southbound 'Silver Jubilee'. The LNER was out for marked advance on *Silver Link's* 112.5 mph of the previous year, but finesse was lacking on the footplate of sister engine *Silver Fox*. To get a run at the long descent from Stoke summit, she had been hammered so fiercely up the northern climb from Grantham that as she raced away downhill the big-end bearing metal of the middle of her three cylinders overheated to melting point. That allowed the big end itself so much play that it knocked out the cylinder end.

Everyone gritted their teeth as they heard the disintegrating metal strike showers of ballast against the floor of the leading coach, but they held on grimly until the graph of the dynamometer car specially inserted in the train registered — just — a new peak of 113 mph (181.8 kmph). At that the footplate crew were ordered to rein in fast. Live steam jetting from its gaping middle cylinder end, the streamlined 'Pacific' limped the rest of the way to London. This, incidentally, was

the only occasion in British history — and one of the few in all rail history — when management, not just a footloose engine-driver on his own initiative, deliberately set out for a speed record with a public service train carrying oblivious paying passengers.

The aura that now glowed publicly about the LNER and its 'Silver Jubilee' stung the LMS to attack the record on the pre-launch press demonstration trip of its 'Coronation Scot' on 29 June 1937. Unfortunately the LMS had nothing like the enticing LNER racetrack down from Stoke summit. Their nearest approach was $6^1/2$ miles (10.5 km) of steady downhill at the southern approach to Crewe. Streamlined 'Pacific' No 6220 *Coronation*, one of a quintet of new four-cylinder 6 ft 9 in (2.06 m) driving wheel engines created by William Stanier for the new service, was given the gun on the last few miles up to this stretch and they turned downhill with speed already on 93.5 mph (150.4 kmph). Her exhaust, in the words of one observer, 'humming with a continuous roar like that of an aeroplane engine', *Coronation* just made it to a new record of 114 mph (183.4 kmph) — or so it was claimed on the evidence of tape from the 'Pacific's' automatic speed recorder; three expert stopwatch timers on the train had recorded no better than a deadheat with *Silver Fox*.

At that critical moment Crewe and its maze of trackwork were already in sight. *Coronation's* regulator was shut fast, the brakes were slammed on and flames spurted from the 'Pacific's' flanges as the brake blocks fought for a hold. But speed was down only to 57 mph (92 kmph) as she hit the first of the crossovers leading to her platform berth in the station. The final 2.1 miles (3.4 km) to the grinding halt at the platform occupied just 1 minute 53 seconds. Bruises were the only physical marks of the experience the relieved passengers could discover as they picked themselves off compartment floors or disentangled unwonted embraces. Carnage, miraculously, was confined to cascading crockery and utensils in the restaurant-kitchen cars. The horrendous din from this quarter as the train keeled drunkenly through the crossovers had convinced many passengers within

Above: In 1939 a `Coronation Scot' train was shipped to the USA for display. `Pacific' No 6220 Coronation (in reality No 6229 in disguise) poses alongside the Baltimore & Ohio `Royal Blue' streamliner on Relay Viaduct, near Baltimore. (Cecil J. Allen Collection)

Below: The world's steam speed record-holder, Gresley Class `A4' `Pacific' No 4468 Mallard, lives on in the care of Britain's National Railway Museum: here it heads a Marylebone–Stratford-on-Avon special in November 1986. (John C. Baker)

earshot that the coaches were disintegrating.

The following year the LNER put the record firmly out of LMS reach. The pre-announced pretext for the events of Sunday 3 July 1938 was braking trials, but an invincible speed record was clearly the prime objective. By then four of the Gresley Class `A4' `Pacifics' had been fitted with one of the highly successful French devices to streamline internal steam flow, the Kylchap double blastpipe and chimney. Sensibly resisting friendly pressure from colleagues to turn out the `A4' which a grateful LNER had named *Sir Nigel Gresley* in his honour, Gresley mobilized one of the double-chimney engines, No 4468 *Mallard*, to head the 244-tonne test train of dynamometer car and three articulated twin-units from a `Coronation' train-set.

Starting southbound from Barkston, just north of Grantham, Driver Duddington gave *Mallard* full regulator up the northern slopes of Stoke. They entered the summit tunnel at 74.5 mph (119.9 kmph), then streamed away. Within 6 miles (9.7 km) she was making 116 mph (186.6 kmph), and for 3 miles (4.8 km) — now with steam shut off — she held 120 mph (193.1 kmph). The dynamometer car rolls registered an unarguable top speed of 126 mph (202.7 kmph). Short of the belated discovery of full supporting data for some of the superior claims mentioned in this chapter, that is the uncontestable world record for steam power.

3
Diesels and electrics show their paces

There were dreamers of 125 mph (200 kmph) electric locomotives even before the last century had turned. Stimulated by reports from America of a quest for speed on the New York-Philadelphia route, two engineers of the French PLM Railway set out determinedly to devise such a machine for the Chicago Exhibition of 1893. But the limitations of the electric traction art at that time defeated them.

They were not to defeat the Germans much longer. The German engineer Werner von Siemens had in the summer of 1879 achieved the world's first railed electric locomotive. Granted, it was only a 3 hp midget running on narrow-gauge track, drawing current from a centre third rail, which perambulated trainloads of 30 passengers on open `knifeboard' cars at 4 mph (6.4 kmph) round some 900 feet (275 m) of track in the Berlin Exhibition grounds. But it spurred some remarkably rapid development. Little more than two decades later German technology had proved electric traction was indeed capable of 125 mph on rails.

The practical outcome of the early German development was the spread of dc electric tramways, beginning at Lichterfelde in 1881. At the same time, there was eager pursuit of three-phase ac traction and a consortium for the study of high-speed electric railways (*Studiengesellschaft für Elektrische Schnellbahnen*) was formed. By the end of the 19th century it had its first prototype to test.

An appealing test track was the easily-graded 14.5 miles (23.3 km) of military railway between Marienfelde and Zossen, near Berlin. It was furnished with catenary supplying 15,000 volts ac, generated at the AEG power station at Oberschönweide, and here, in 1901, an experimental eight-wheeled centre-cab locomotive built by Siemens & Halske was run up to a world record of 101 mph (162.6 kmph). Later that same year two new vehicles were ready for testing.

Both were 50-passenger railcars, mounted on two six-wheel bodies, and each with a power output of 1,000 hp. The mechanical parts of both vehicles had been built by Van der Zypen und Charlier, but one had Siemens & Halske and the other AEG electrical equipment. The two cars were distinguishable by their quaint current collection arrangements. The line's three-phase current supply was arranged as three vertically spaced and parallel conductor wires strung up to masts at the trackside, so that the wires were to one side of the rail vehicle. The AEG had two sets of three pantographs, one set at each end of the car, the members of each set stepping up in size to align their sideways-facing contact pans to the supply wires. The Siemens & Halske car, on the other hand, had each set of three pantographs mounted one above the other on the same roof-mounted standard, looking like some esoteric radar device.

As soon as they had the two cars up above 75 mph (120 kmph) on the Marienfelde-Zossen line they were in trouble. Faces blenched as the ungainly vehicles pitched and yawed on the lightly-laid tracks and the sky erupted in vicious arcing as pans lost contact with the supply wires. At 160 kmph one car momentarily bounced a bogie clean off the rails, thumped it back and spread the track alarmingly. That was enough. The tests were suspended until the whole route had been comprehensively relaid with heavier rail and better foundations and the railcars had had their bogie wheelbases lengthened.

By 1903 the rebuilding was complete and on 6 October that year the Siemens & Halske car was hustled the length of the railway in just 8 minutes, reaching a peak of 126 mph (202.7 kmph). It did much the same on 23 October, except that it edged the record up to 128.5 mph (206.8 kmph). A few days later the AEG car snatched the laurels with a peak of 130.5 mph (210 kmph). Shortly afterwards a more significant achievement was recorded when the Siemens & Halske electric locomotive worked a train up to 130 kmph (81 mph).

These exploits sparked off a number of plans to electrify the Berlin-Hamburg main line for high-speed railcars, but the expense was too much of a deterrent. So the 1903 record remained unsurpassed for 30 years.

Quite soon after the Wright Brothers' first flight, an inventive German had visualized the speed potential of a prop-driven train. In 1917 the idea was put crudely to the test by mounting an aero engine on an orthodox railway van. The hybrid was run on the Berlin-Hamburg main line and is said to have shown a rare turn of speed, but there was no follow-through until 1931.

Eight years earlier there had been formed in Germany the *Gesellschaft für Verkehrstechnik* (GVT), or Association for the Advancement of the Science of Transport. For its first line of research it picked the monorail concept, with the idea of driving the suspended gondolas by airscrews, but in 1929 it switched to thoughts of powering an orthodox railcar in the same way. In conjunction with the country's Aeronautical

Research Association (DVL) in Berlin, the 1917 vehicle was dusted off, refitted with two BMW engines of 230 hp apiece and reputedly taken up to a speed of 109 mph (175 kmph).

A year later the partnership yielded a more refined version, Dr F. Kruckenburg's so-called *Schienenzeppelin*, or 'Zeppelin of the Rails'. This pencil-slim and aerodynamically streamlined railcar was aluminium-bodied, weighed a mere $17^1/_4$ tonnes and was mounted on just two axles at a lengthy wheelbase of 65 ft 7 in (20 m). Its propulsion was a rear-mounted four-bladed airscrew, driven by a 12-cylinder Otto petrol engine delivering 600 hp at 1,200 rpm.

After a preliminary 23 September 1930 jaunt between Hannover and Celle, when the car showed it could bolt from a standing start to 100 kmph (62.14 mph) in 66 seconds and 985 m (3,230 feet), and 113 mph (182 kmph) was reputedly attained, the *Schienenzeppelin* was let out on the German Reichsbahn's recognised racetrack, the Hamburg-Berlin main line, shortly before dawn on midsummer's day, 21 June 1931. Pressmen had chartered a plane to follow the *Schienenzeppelin's* progress. They had a job to hold the railcar in their sights, for she ate up the $159^3/_4$ miles (256 km) from Bergedorf to Spandau West in 98 minutes at an average of 95.7 mph (154 kmph), and held an average as high as 142.9 mph (230 kmph) for 6.25 miles (10 km) on end between Karstädt and Dergenthin.

History records little further track testing of the *Schienenzeppelin* in its original guise. For one thing, the slipstream as it hummed through stations was a menace to anyone or anything movable on the platform. More importantly, its characteristics precluded anything but single-unit operation; and to have kept the tracks adequately clear of conventional trains for such a low-capacity passenger vehicle would have been ludicrously uneconomic. Kruckenburg's name was to recur in rail speed history before the outbreak of the Second World War, but his *Schienenzeppelin*, after a period of trial as an orthodox axle-powered diesel-hydraulic railcar with a Maybach engine and the airscrew dismantled, faded from rail history in 1936.

Dr Kruckenburg's airscrew-driven Schienenzeppelin *of 1930, reputed to have averaged 142.9 mph (230 kmph) over 6.25 miles (10 km).*

To digress chronologically, some three decades later, an equally aimless stunt with aero engines was perpetrated in the USA by New York Central. In the mid-1960s, naturally, the power plant was jet engines — two General Electric J-47s, military surplus, which NYC mounted on the roof of a standard Budd RDC-3 diesel railcar built for branch-line baggage-passenger service in 1953. They gave the RDC new wheels, added shock absorbers to damp down vertical oscillation, grafted a streamlined prow on to the end beneath the jets, then at the end of July 1966 sent it careering down a piece of standard straight and level track between Butler, Indiana, and Stryker, Ohio. The car's normal diesel-hydraulic transmission had been disconnected and it was being driven solely by the jets.

Two minutes of full power from the screaming jets were enough to get the car up to 120 mph (193 kmph) from a standing start. Another four minutes and it had hit a maximum of 183.85 mph (295.8 kmph). At

that it was braked, having secured America a wheel-on-rail speed record still unbeaten by anything but electric traction.

To return to the early 1930s, a new age of sustained high speed was opened with the perfection of the compact, high rpm diesel engine. Dedicated research work by the US company Electromotive, which had been absorbed by General Motors in 1930, evolved the historic 201A engine that promptly quadrupled the contemporary diesel engine power/weight ratio, thanks chiefly to adoption of two-stroke instead of four-stroke design and welded construction with new alloy steels.

By then Henry Ford's Model T automobile had become the prized possession of countless American households and the railroads were being drained of passengers. One such was the Chicago, Burlington & Quincy, which had seen its passenger receipts quartered in a decade. The Burlington had already been intrigued by news that the Budd company of Philadelphia, a pioneer in several facets of

The three-car, Budd-built `Pioneer Zephyr'. (Burlington Northern)

automobile bodywork, was adapting what it had learned in that field to construction of a revolutionary lightweight stainless steel alloy rail coach body. This seemed a likely tool for greatly accelerated rail passenger service to recapture lost business, and Burlington had ordered a train-set of the new vehicles. Now the enterprising Burlington had that train equipped with Electromotive's new diesel engines.

Streamlining was in vogue and Burlington's Budd-built `Pioneer Zephyr' saw almost its first calculated application to an American train. The three-car articulated unit was not exactly a mass transportation unit, but the Burlington had only specified accommodation for 70 passengers (the service in mind was a daily out-and-home run between Kansas City and Lincoln, 250 miles (402.3 km) apart). The first vehicle of the 196-foot

(59.8 m) long, 88.5-tonne unit was entirely occupied by the 600 hp diesel-generator set, Railway Post Office and mail storage accommodation; there was more baggage and mail space in the second car, leaving room for just 20 passenger seats and a buffet-grill; and the third car had 40 more seats plus a 12-seat solarium observation lounge at the rear end.

Within two days of emergence from the Budd works in early April 1934 the `Zephyr' had glided up to 104 mph (167.3 kmph) on a 25-mile test run in the vicinity of Philadelphia. Then, in the course of a five-week promotion of the new Budd-Electromotive technology around the cities of the Eastern US, it zipped over the Pennsylvania racetrack between Ford Wayne, Indiana, and Englewood, on Chicago's outskirts, at an average of 80.2 mph (129 kmph) for the whole 140 miles (225.3 km). It was 26 May 1934, however, when railway history unmistakeably turned the page.

That day the Century of Progress exhibition in Chicago was to be reopened, and to publicize both the event and the new high-speed train concept Burlington agreed to stage an attempt on the transcontinental rail speed record. At the time the best regular schedule over the 1,015 miles (1,633 km) from Denver to Chicago was 26³/₄ hours, inclusive of 40 intermediate stops, but in 1897 a special had been hurried between the two cities in 7 minutes under 19 hours. Burlington set its `Zephyr' a target of 15 hours.

Extraordinary steps were taken to keep the 1,015-mile path of the `Zephyr' clear. In the preceding days track and track structures were meticulously examined; and as the `Zephyr' winged out into the early morning, nearly 1,700 railroad men were on special duty at open level or grade crossings. Excited by the radio publicity, too, grandstands were congregating from one end of the route to the other; around half a million people are said to have lined the track to watch the streamliner's astonishing progress.

They took it quietly at first, but crossing from Colorado into Nebraska the `Zephyr' was notched up to average 90 mph (114.8 kmph) for 129.5 miles (208.4 km) on end; it ran 19.1 miles (30.7 km) at 106.2 mph

(170.9 kmph); 6.4 miles (10.3 km) at 109 mph (175.4 kmph); and hit a peak of 112.5 mph (181 kmph). By Lincoln, Nebraska, 482.6 miles (776.5 km) from the Denver start, the clock showed an elapsed time of only 6 hours 7 minutes, so they had been averaging 78.9 mph (127 kmph) the whole way. And there was no sign of frailty in any `Zephyr' component, although one mischance could have rung down the curtain on the show but for the sort of knee-jerk reaction that subsequently earns a bravery medal. Severed by a slamming door, a faulty instrument cable set up a short circuit that burned out an engine starter cable and had the technicians scenting fire. The engine was promptly shut down while the technicians scrabbled madly for means to repair the split cable. The idling `Zephyr' had come down almost to walking pace before one technician decided enough was enough, seized the wire ends in his hands, and made contact between them in a searing flash that burned him quite severely — but restarted the engine.

When they cut the complementary timing tape at Halstead Street, Chicago, the `Zephyr' had reeled off 1,015.4 miles (nearly 1,634 km) in two seconds under 13 hours 5 minutes. The whole dawn-to-dusk hop had been wrapped up at an average speed of 77.6 mph (124.9 kmph) — a record for long-distance non-stop running which, in terms of mileage, has still to be surpassed. And they had done it on 418 gallons (1,900 litres) of diesel oil; at 1934 prices, would you believe, that represented a fuel cost for the journey of $16!

Burlington's `Pioneer Zephyr' was not the sole diesel streamliner on show at the 1934 Century of Progress show in Chicago. The Burlington had been just beaten to the post of displaying America's very first diesel streamliner by the unveiling in February 1934 of a train-set built by Pullman Standard for Union Pacific, another road to appreciate very early the potential of diesel traction. Unlike the `Zephyr', UP's oddly fish-headed and fin-tailed three-car articulated unit, the M-10000, was built of aluminium alloy and powered by an Electromotive 12-cylinder V-type distillate engine — that is, one fuelled

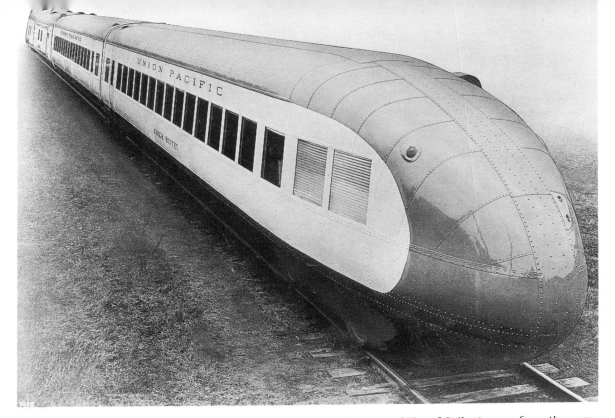

Union Pacific's first diesel streamliner, the three-car M-10000, later `City of Salina', seen from the rear.

with diesel oil but still using spark-plug ignition — as opposed to the `Zephyr's' eight-cylinder in-line diesel engine proper. The boldly yellow-styled M-10000 had seating for 116 and was designed to cruise at 90 mph (145 kmph).

In post-exhibition revenue-earning service as the `City of Salina' between Kansas City and Salina, the M-10000 immediately attracted and held a near 100 per cent loading of passengers day in and day out, so Union Pacific eagerly ordered a twin. This time a six-car unit was specified, with a 16-cylinder 1,200 hp engine and including Pullman sleepers, which were not only the first articulated Pullmans seen in the US but which also sported unique collapsible lavatories in each berth. On 22 October 1934 this second UP streamliner, M-10001, was sent out on the year's second record-shattering transcontinental run, this time from coast to coast.

At that date the best public service operative over the 3,259 miles (5,244 km) from Los Angeles to New York was 84 hours, inclusive of stops. M-10001 set out at 22.00, hummed easily up the severe grades through

the Rockies, and by the time it pulled into Chicago, 2,299 miles (3,699 km) from the California start, had already notched up a gain of 20 hours on that 84-hour timing. It had averaged 59 mph (95 kmph) start to stop over terrain where the long climbs had previously pegged averages at 35-40 mph. Over the plains between Cheyenne, Wyoming, and Omaha, Nebraska, 508 miles (817 km) had been reeled off at an average speed of 84 mph (135 kmph), and it was said that 120 mph (193 kmph) had been touched, but the only basis for this last claim seems to be one passenger's excited cry that he'd just seen 2 miles go by in a minute by his fob watch. Be that as it may, despite a 40 minutes' pause in Chicago and discreet forbearance to put `Twentieth Century Limited' timings to shame over the New York Central tracks onward to the East Coast, M-10001 glided to a stand in New York City in 56 hours 55 minutes overall from Los Angeles, a thumping $14^1/_2$ hours ahead of a long-standing 1906 coast-to-coast record time.

Trailing clouds of glory from this feat and graced with the title `Streamliner City of Portland', the six-car set was launched on regular

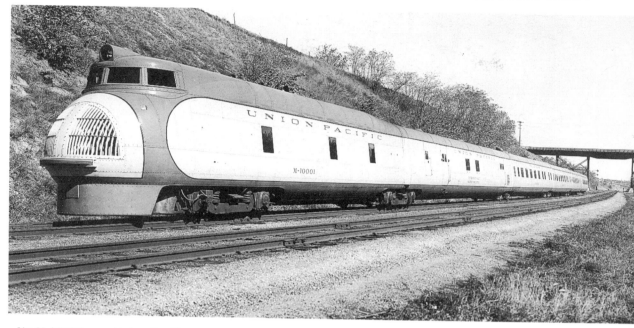

No M-10001 was Union Pacific's second diesel streamliner, star of a record-breaking transcontinental trip in October 1934. (Cecil J. Allen Collection)

public service between Chicago and Portland from 6 June 1935. It was set a 39³/₄-hour schedule for the 2,272 miles (3,656 km) that straight away lopped 18 hours off the previous steam timecard for the route. Scorning the slump that was impelling other railroads disconsolately to curtail their passenger services in the mid-1930s, the euphoric UP now laid orders with Pullman Standard for two eleven-car streamliners, with twin power units — a 900 or 1,200 hp booster articulated to the 1,200 hp cab unit by a span bolster — to encompass the added load. These, the original `City of Los Angeles' and `City of San Francisco', were inaugurated in the early summer of 1936. That year, confounding the trend on most other railroads, UP's passenger takings climbed by more than a third. Frequently, said UP in its annual report, business had to be turned away, so the road would now be stepping up to 17-car formations — which, following the debut later in 1936 of the 12-car `City of Denver' on a 16-hour end-to-end schedule for the 1,048 miles (1,686 km) between Chicago and Denver, inclusive of eight intermediate

stops, duly materialized in 1937-8.

Meanwhile, the other US diesel pioneer, the Burlington, hadn't been sitting on its hands. In the spring of 1935 came the first `Twin Cities Zephyrs', still three-car units but with reduced mail space to lift the seating space to 88. They went into immediate contention with the Milwaukee's new steam `Hiawatha' and the Chicago & North Western's brave `400', with its vamped-up conventional steam `Pacifics', on the thriving Chicago-Minneapolis and St Paul route. After only ten weeks of single out-and-home workings by each unit, the load factor was averaging 97.7 per cent. So at the start of June 1935 the Burlington rostered each unit to make two return trips daily totalling 882 miles (1,419 km) per set. Of course the diesel `Zephyrs' were now and then crippled by the usual ills to which all diesel hardware is prone, but that year their availability ran out at 97 per cent — an astonishingly high figure for units as yet so briefly service-hardened.

By early 1936 the Burlington, too, had decided diesel traction was handsomely

Union Pacific's `City of Denver' was the USA's fastest regularly scheduled train in the late 1930s. With a 3,600 hp cab-and-two-booster unit of Electromotive's 1936 build up front, the train cruises into Denver in September, 1940. (R.H. Kindig)

clear of its probation period. It could now be applied confidently to really long-distance service. Orders were handed to Budd for two 12-car `Denver Zephyrs' (also for two new seven-car `Twin Zephyr' sets). In the `Denver Zephyr' units the diesel streamliner for the first time took on the full interior trappings of the American rail transcontinental, with a cocktail as well as an observation lounge, and a wide range of sleeping accommodation plus a dormitory for train staff. And there was still more power up front — the `Denver

Zephyr's' cab unit mounted a pair of two-stroke 900 hp V-12 engines, its booster a single 1,200 hp V-16.

Ever since 1934 the Burlington had been miffed by repeated sniping that the original `Zephyr's' record run from Denver to Chicago had been done the easy way, because the west-to-east profile was effectively downhill all the way from a starting point some 5,000 feet above sea level at Denver to around sea level at Chicago. On 23 October 1936 the Burlington set out to silence the sceptics by

One of Burlington's 12-car `Denver Zephyr' sets of 1936, with 3,000 hp twin power unit. (Cecil J. Allen Collection)

pointing one of its new 'Denver Zephyr' 3,000 hp twin power units and six trailer cars from east to west. This time the route was slightly different and thus a trifle shorter, at 1,017 miles (1,636 km).

It was a cold, grey morning spattering snow as they left Chicago's Union Station, and for a long time the gods seemed to have thumbs down on the whole exercise. Some way out they discovered that, because of a maintenance man's negligence, they had been getting no power to the booster unit's traction motors. Not long after that there was a thunder-clap flashover in the lead unit. That repaired, an overspeed governor on one of the cab unit's engines tripped and shut it down temporarily to idling speed. After that, the breaking of an air line and the sudden jamming of the air horns must have seemed mere pinpricks.

Once the casualty ward had been cleared, though, there was no holding the 'Zephyr'. Over one 26.6-mile (42.8 km) stretch of Illinois level, average speed was held at 105.8 mph (170.2 kmph), and in Colorado they claimed the streamliner hit 116 mph (186.6 kmph). They touched down in Denver in 12 hours 12^1/$_2$ minutes from Chicago, which meant, despite the irritations along the way, a start-to-stop average speed of 83.3 mph (134 kmph). That still stands as a world record for sustained rail speed over a run of 1,000 miles or more.

The acceleration of American inter-city services spear-headed by the diesel streamliners and the last refinements of steam power like the Milwaukee 'Hiawatha' engines accumulated mileage with extraordinary rapidity in the second half of the 1930s. It got a fresh fillip in 1938 when Electromotive perfected its famous 567 range of diesel engines and launched the world's first range of successful production-line diesel-electric locomotives in the E6, fitted with a pair of the new 567 series 1,000 hp V-12 engines. From 29,301 miles daily in 1936, the runs covered at scheduled start-to-stop speeds of a mile a minute or more had jumped to 48,247 miles by the summer of 1938. Union Pacific led the field with an 81.4 mph (131 kmph) sprint over the 62.4 miles (100.4 km) from Grand Island to Columbus, and another at 80.3

mph (129.2 kmph) over the 95 miles (152.9 km) from North Platte to Kearney by its 'City of Denver'. But diesel locomotive-hauled trains were close on its heels. The Santa Fe's exclusive all-Pullman 'Super Chief' and supporting all-coach 'El Capitan' was timed over the 202.4 miles (325.7 km) from La Junta to Dodge City at a start-to-stop average of 78.3 mph (126 kmph).

Inexorably, wartime notwithstanding, the acceleration continued, until by the early 1950s the mileage scheduled for US trains at more than a mile a minute start to stop was over 150,000. By then, of course, over 80 per cent of it was behind diesel power, a mere 3-4 per cent with steam up front and the rest under live wires. There were to be no marked advances on the top average speeds already described in this book, not least because of the Interstate Commerce Commission's intervention with an edict that speed must be kept within 80 mph (128.7 kmph) on any line not equipped with both automatic cab-signalling and automatic train-stopping devices. Few roads were prepared to lay out the money on that just to benefit a handful of passenger trains over lengthy routes predominantly occupied by massive freight tonnage. That ICC ruling ended, for instance, the remarkable schedule applied for several years to the 'Denver Zephyr' between Denver and Omaha, on Union Pacific metals, which stipulated coverage of 560 miles (901 km) at an average of 73.9 mph (118.9 kmph) *inclusive of seven intermediate stops*. This was probably the world's most demanding timing for a considerable period of the 1940s.

Now steps must be retraced in time and space to recount the major European developments in diesel and electric speed up to the eve of the Second World War. Cynosure of interest on that side of the Atlantic was the other and parallel pioneer of diesel rail traction, Germany.

Another reason for German disinterest in Kruckenburg's *Schienenzeppelin*, despite its startling demonstration run in 1931, was Dr Rudolf Diesel's perfection of his art. Even as the Kruckenburg car was winging from Hamburg to Berlin, the Reichsbahn had a file of conclusive data to show that its long-cher-

Above: The Santa Fe 'Super Chief' rolls into Chicago in the late 1930s after a 41³/₄-hour transcontinental run from Los Angeles behind an ALCO 'DL-109' 4,000hp cab-and-booster unit. (Cecil J. Allen Collection)

Below: The 'Fliegende Hamburger' makes its debut at Hamburg. Note the packed grandstand on the footbridge in front of the train-shed.

ished ambition of an unassailable world speed crown was within the grasp of a diesel-powered twin-car set. So that same year the Görlitz works of Wagen und Maschinenbau AG, or WUMAG, was handed the order to build a diesel-electric prototype, its two cars articulated, and horsed with a pair of 12-cylinder high rpm 410 hp Maybach engines.

The prototype was finished in 1932 and put to exhaustive proving trials. Then, on 15 May 1933, it was committed to public service over the Berlin-Hamburg racetrack as the *Fliegende Hamburger*, or 'Flying Hamburger', and premiered a new epoch in European inter-city rail travel.

Comfort was not the outstanding characteristic of the 78-tonne articulated unit, of which the streamlined contour derived from extensive research at the Zeppelin works in Friedrichshafen. Into the two open saloons they crowded 102 seats, arranged in bays three-and-one athwart a central gangway, and catering service was limited to a four-seater Mitropa bar.

In speed, the *Fliegende Hamburger* immediately opened up a new European chapter. Its schedule of 138 minutes for the 178.1 miles (270 km) between Berlin and Hamburg demanded a start-to-stop average speed of 77.4 mph (124.6 kmph). Not only was that, in 1933, the quickest scheduled start-to-stop timing in the world: to observe it and take account of certain fixed speed limits *en route*, the new diesel train had to run regularly at 160 kmph (99.4 mph) over substantial stretches of the route — the first time such a pace had been accepted as day-to-day routine.

The German Reichsbahn was not indulging this new range of speed without additional safety precautions. The trains themselves had both Knorr air and electro-magnetic track brakes, capable of decelerating the unit from 160 kmph to a dead stand in 2,790 feet (851 m). And the Berlin-Hamburg route had been fitted throughout with the Indusi automatic train control system.

The *Fliengende Hamburger's* immediate commercial success and demonstrable economy in running costs compared with steam soon had the Reichsbahn scheming an inter-city network of similar units, but not without preliminary groundwork: a route had to be fettled up to a 'Special Class' category of track maintenance and be equipped throughout with the Indusi apparatus before the Reichsbahn would open it to the new diesel trains.

Orders for 17 more units were placed in 1935. Thirteen of them were diesel-electric twin-units basically similar to the prototype, which the Reichsbahn classified 'SVT877' (and which now reposes in the Nuremberg Transport Museum). But the production series Class 'SVT137' or 'Hamburg' sets embodied refinements of exterior styling and internal layout. In particular, seating was thinned out to a more relaxing 76 places in a two-and-one layout, and the outer ends were fitted with Scharfenburg automatic couplers so that the sets could be run in multiple. Set weight was increased to 91 tonnes.

Four of the 1935 order, the Class 'SVT137' 'Leipzig' series, were three-car units that took advantage of the newly-perfected Maybach 600 hp diesel engine. Two of these sets, moreover, had a new feature that was later to be the signal difference between German and American diesel rail traction practice: Voith hydraulic as opposed to electric transmission. The three-car sets, seating 139 each, had engine compartments at each end, unlike the two-car units. In the diesel-electric versions, the two inner articulation bogies were both motored (it was only the centre bogie of the two-car set that was powered), but in the diesel-hydraulic sets it was the two outer bogies that were motored. According to German sources, one of the diesel-electric 'Leipzig' units was tested up to a peak speed of 127.4 mph (205 kmph) on the Berlin-Hamburg route between Ludwigslust and Wittenberge shortly after delivery in February 1936, but I have never come across full supporting data; the three-car sets were, however, designed with a slightly higher service speed capability of 170 kmph (106 mph). A major change applicable to all the three-car sets, as compared with the two-car units, was that they were two-class and their 139 seats were laid out entirely in compartments; there was no seating in the buffet, from which passengers were served in their compartments. Weight per set was 117 tonnes.

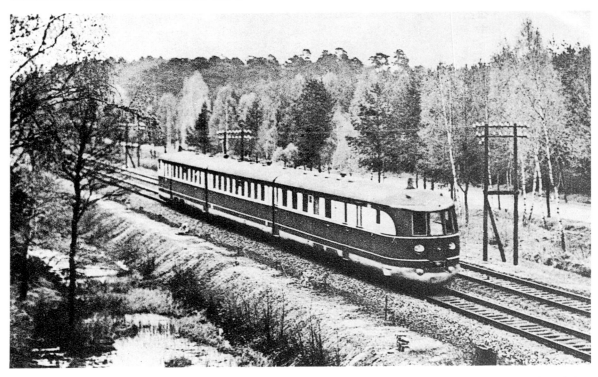

A three-car `Leipzig' near Berlin on the `Fliegende Schlesier' service from the capital to Frankfurt/Oder in 1936.

The diesel railcars stimulated as sensationally rapid an advance in German rail speed overall as the diesel streamliners had in the USA. In the mid-1930s the Reichsbahn gradually interlaced all he country's major population centres with each other and with the capital, Berlin, in a network of services. These services had the same cardinal commercial objective that informed much of Western European inter-city development after the Second World War — the establishment of primarily business services that would get executives to their destination by midday in time for a reasonable day's work, and have them comfortably home to bed the same evening. Most of the services were promoted under a common `Fliegende' brandname — `Fliegende Kölner', `Fliegende Münchener' — and so on.

By the summer of 1935 the Reichsbahn had not merely swept the European rail speed board comprehensively, but had grabbed the world lead in daily scheduled start-to-stop runs with not one but 13 services. Topping the table were the world's first timings in excess of 80 mph (128.7 kmph). There were four of them: Berlin (Zoo) to Hannover, 157.8 miles (254.1 km) by the evening train FDt16 in 115 minutes, average 82.3 mph (132.5 kmph); Leipzig to Berlin (Anhalt), 102.2 miles (164.4 km) by both the morning train from Frankfurt and the morning flyer from Stuttgart in 76 minutes, average 80.7 mph (129.8 kmph); and Sagan to Güben, 37.5 miles (60.3 km) in 28 minutes, average 80.4 mph (129.4 kmph). As outstanding as these tightly-timed sprints were the long distances covered by some of the railcars in a single high-speed day. The `Fliegende Kölner', for instance, had a daily itinerary of 719 miles (1,157 km) all run at an average of 71.2 mph (114.6 kmph). The Berlin-Munich train's daily stint was 851 miles (1,369 km), for which the overall average of 64.5 mph (103.8 kmph) may look superficially unremarkable, but was outstanding for the times considering the reduced speed enforced over the sinuous and sharply-graded stretch of its route through the hills between Leipzig and Nuremburg. Attention to the timekeeping of the railcars were punctilious; operating staff had strict instructions from Reichsbahn headquarters not to delay them for late-running connections.

In their final series of high-speed railcar units, the Reichsbahn abandoned articulation of coach bodies so as to increase coach length and augment seating space. These were the so-called 'Köln' series from Linke-Hoffman-Werke, of which 14 were ordered and of which deliveries began in 1938. In these three-car non-articulated units the centre car was a trailer and both outer vehicles power cars, each mounting a Maybach 12-cylinder high-speed turbocharged 600 hp engine with electric transmission. As a matter of policy the Reichsbahn had now made its diesel flyers exclusively one-class, which in the 'Köln' series was of compartment layout seating a total of 102 in one power car and the centre trailer combined. The other power car was a full-scale 30-seater kitchen restaurant.

It has been written that the Reichsbahn's diesel flyers were all withdrawn in the 1937-8 winter and never restored. This is a canard. A number of services were certainly suspended for a period at that time, partly because axle fatigue flaws had shown up and the whole fleet needed inspection; and partly because the Third Reich was exerting great strains on the whole national economy, particularly in its drive for self-sufficiency and hence reduced consumption of imported oil. The great majority of the railcar services were reinstated within a matter of weeks, however, and not finally killed off until the outbreak of war. Many of the units survived the Second World War and served either the West German or East German systems for a number of years: both 'Hamburg' and 'Köln' series units were active on the East German Deutsche Reichsbahn until 1959.

One last German pre-war high-speed diesel railcar exploit must be recorded. Here the redoubtable Dr Kruckenburg re-enters the stage. In 1937 the Cologne firm of Westwag-

gon was persuaded to build an aluminium-bodied and articulated three-car streamliner, with a protruding nose that looked like a cartoonist's grotesque distortion of the post-war German Trans-Europ-Express diesel multiple unit. After considerable problems in securing two 600 hp Maybach engines and Voith hydraulic transmissions to power the prodigy, Kruckenburg got his so-called 'Flying Silver Fish' on the track towards the close of 1937. Next year it was reported to have reached 121 mph (195 kmph) on test between Berlin and Cologne. Then, on 26 June 1939, it was set at the favourite Berlin-Hamburg course and reputedly held 200 kmph (125 mph) for a considerable distance, touching a maximum of 215 kmph (133.6 mph). Wherever the speedometer needle really fetched up, the exertion wrought such havoc with the outfit's power plant and running gear that it had not recuperated sufficiently for further operation until late in June 1938. It was consigned to limbo with the war's outbreak.

To overcome the then lack of continuous electrification in Northern Italy, and also with ambitions of bestowing a Rome-Berlin high-speed service on the dictators' Italo-German Axis, Fiat built nine unsightly diesel train-sets for Italian Railways (FS) in 1936-40. Classified 'ATR100', ATR standing for *Autotreno Rapido,* each was formed of three articulated and — for the period — luxuriously appointed cars. The inelegance lay in their frontal aspect, where an enormous radiator grille reaching from body-skirt almost to roof level gave the cab the look of a monkfish in the last throes of suffocation. Strengthening that impression were the extruding wheel splashers in the cars' deep body skirting, which hinted at retracted fins.

Only two of an 'ATR100's' eight axles were motored, the inner ones of each bogie, and in an odd fashion. A Fiat 12-cylinder 1,500 rpm engine of 750 hp was mounted on the bogie and drove through a multi-disc coupling and a four-speed mechanical gearbox.

On test in late 1936 the first 'ATR100' was said to have reached 106 mph (172 kmph), but the units' public service history was beset by flaws, and some nasty fires as well. They performed reasonably over the flat Po

One of the unprepossessing 'ATR100' diesel-mechanical train-sets built by Fiat in 1936-40 for an abortive Rome-Berlin high-speed service project.

plain between Milan and Venice, but gradients or snow found the adhesion of their two powered axles wanting. Fuel lines to the bogie-mounted engine were prone to fracture, too. The war put paid to the Berlin-Rome dream, had some of the sets robbed of their power plant for military use, and destroyed others in air raids. Five survived to be rebuilt for sporadic inter-city operation until 1962.

Deutsche Reichsbahn's crowning high-speed electric locomotive development, the Class 'E19' 1-Do-1; this one is seen in post-war Deutsche Bundesbahn employment as No 119,001-5. (Deutsche Bundesbahn)

Just before the onset of the Second World War, with electrification from Munich to Berlin programmed (because of the war, catenary got no further north of Munich than Dessau), the Germans at last set about high-speed electric locomotive development. Progenitor of the new range was the Reichsbahn's Class `E18' (later Deutsche Bundesbahn Class `118'), a 4,075 hp 1-Do-1 with a maximum speed of 93.2 mph (150 kmph) which AEG put on the drawing board in 1933; 55 were built, the last two after the war's end. Tests showed that the `E18', which won a grand prize at the Paris World Fair of 1937, could summon up a short-term output as high as 8,000 hp for pace in excess of 100 mph (160 kmph). By a clear margin it was the world's most powerful electric locomotive of the age. And that prompted a step up to a specifically high-speed design for express service over the Munich-Nuremburg-Leipzig-Berlin route when the latter's electrification was ready.

The first class `E19' (later DB Class `119') was delivered by AEG at the close of 1938. Again a 1-Do-1, it was visually almost a twin of the `E18'. But with a continuous power rating lifted to 5,360 hp it was designed for a maximum speed of no less than 140 mph (225 kmph) and its specification called for ability to accelerate an eight-car, 360-tonne train from rest to 112 mph (180 kmph) within $4^{1}/2$ minutes on straight and level track. The `E19's' maximum short-term output was well over 8,000 hp and on test one of the first pair was said to have bettered its specification to the extent of hustling 400 tonnes up to 125 mph (200 kmph) within 4 min 48 sec of a standing start.

The first two `E19s' were never run at their designed maximum speed, and in fact their permitted ceiling was eventually lowered to 112 mph (180 kmph). But German records hold that the final pair, built by Henschel and classified `E19.1', were definitely run up to the intended maximum of 140 mph (225 kmph) during their acceptance trials. The war rang down the curtain on further expansion of the class, but the original quartet survived to be taken into Deutsche Bundesbahn use between Munich and the East German border at Probstzella after the war. Through-

out their post-war service, however, the `E19s' were restricted to 87 mph (140 kmph). The last, No 119.12, was retired for preservation in 1977.

Electric traction generally scaled few new peaks of speed in the 1930s. But there were occasional *feux de joie*. One such was reported in 1938 from Switzerland, of all unlikely places. On the Simplon route through the Rhone Valley between Geneva and Brigue there are some temptingly straight and level tracts, and it was here that one of the Swiss Federal Railways' two three-car articulated `Red Arrow' electric multiple units, built in 1937-8 for day round-trip excursion work, was tested up to a peak of 180 kmph (111.9 mph). For years a jaunt on one of the `Red Arrows', whether one of the 1935-8 single units or the later triplets, could be fairly guaranteed to turn up higher speeds than the Swiss main-line norm; the triplets, in fact, were geared for a top service speed of 150 kmph (93.2 mph).

The most significant pre-war pointers to the electrified way ahead came from France and Italy. During 1938 French National Railways staged a high-speed test programme over the Paris-Bordeaux main line, which is admirably aligned for pace at its northern end. The test locomotive was No E704, one of a quartet of 4,950 hp 2-Do-2s (ie with idle front and rear bogies enclosing four independently motored driving wheels) which had been commissioned in 1934 to evaluate machines of considerably higher output than the standard traction units of the time. Foreshadowing what was to come in the 1960s, when this route was to become a shop window of French high-speed rail technology, No E704 crowned the tests by hustling a 176-tonne rake of four coaches up to 185 kmph (115 mph) and averaging 170 kmph (105.7 mph) over 20 km (12.4 miles) between Blois and St Pierre-des-Corps.

`First on land, on sea and in the air' was the Italian objective trumpeted by Mussolini's propaganda machine with tedious persistence in the 1930s. By the late 1930s no other European country's inter-city passenger service had been so transformed, speedwise, as Italy's. The 523 mile (841.5 km) trip from Naples to Milan, for instance,

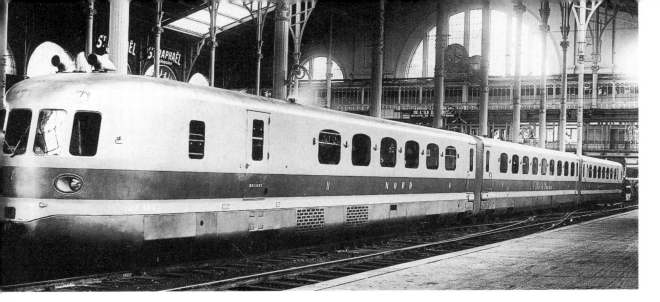

Above: One of the twin Maybach-engined 830 hp diesel-electric train-sets which the Northern Railway of France introduced between Paris, Lille and Tourcoing in 1934, seen at Paris Gare du Nord. On test one was worked up to 98.3 mph (158 kmph). French railways operated many inter-city services with various types of diesel train in the 1930s, but statutory limits on maximum speed denied them exciting end-to-end schedules.

Below: The PLM and State Railways of France were also extending the use of railcars for inter-city service in the mid-1930s. The best-known type was the 76-foot-long (23.2 m) Bugatti railcar adopted by the State Railway in 1933 and driven by four 200 hp petrol engines through mechanical transmission, two axles on each of the unusual four-wheel bogies being powered. During a pre-service trial of the prototype near Le Mans in May 1933, a top speed of 106.3 mph (171 kmph) was said to have been touched. This power car-and-trailer version was put on to Paris-Lyons 1st class only service in 1934 by the PLM and timed at start-to-stop average speeds as high as 72.8 mph (117 kmph) between Laroche and Dijon. (La Vie du Rail)

Above right: An Italian State Railways Type `ETR200' electric multiple unit of the type which made the remarkable 102 mph (164 kmph) average run from Florence to Milan in July 1939. (Italian State Railways)

which as recently as 1914 had sprawled over a wearisome 17 hours — and often more, because of chronically unpunctual working — was by the summer of 1938 down to eight hours by electric *rapido*. Compared with 1914 every trunk route timetable showed not merely cuts in average journey times ranging from 20 to 45 per cent (the crack trains were generally 100 per cent faster) but massive increases in service frequency, up to as much as 114 per cent between Rome and Naples.

The new flagships of this revolutionized Italian train service were a series of articulated three-car inter-city electric multiple units in Classes 'ETR201' and 'ETR221' that were introduced to the Italian State 3,000V dc system from 1936 onwards. These 110-tonne, 1,100kW train-sets were built with a 160 kmph (100 mph) maximum speed capability in regular service, but were tested at considerably greater pace. On the newly-completed Rome-Naples *direttissima* line via the coast, for instance, No ETR201 itself was taken up to a maximum of 125 mph (201.3 kmph) on 27 June 1938 in the course of eating up the 130.5 miles (210 km) in 83 minutes start to stop at an average of 94.3 mph (152 kmph).

That exploit was eclipsed by the extraordinary feat of ETR201 on 20 July 1939. The second of Italy's new rail *direttissima* lines, superseding some of the system's most tortuous or adversely graded routes with a more favourable alignment, had lately been opened through the mountains from Florence to Bologna via the impressive new 11¹/₂- mile (18.5 km) Appennine Tunnel. Chiefly for the greater glory of the regime rather than calculated railway purpose, one guesses, a special run was laid on over the new route that July day for the Minister of Communications and some hundred other invitees.

Now although the *direttissima* was a vast improvement on the old line in terms of curvature, it was still beset by a fair share of sharpish bends. So what was achieved on 20 July 1939 was astonishing. The traction current voltage had been specially boosted from 3kV to 4kV dc but so far as I know the track was not specially fettled up or any extraordinary precautions taken, yet they ran the whole 195.8 miles (315 km) from Florence to Milan in 115¹/₄ minutes at a start-to-stop average of 102 mph (164 kmph). Passage of those curves must have been trepidant. Even on the *direttissima* the climb up to the tunnel through the Apennines is 1 in 106, and there is nearly 11 miles (17.7 km) of it; yet the train strode up the hill at a steady 80-90 mph (130-145 kmph), then surged up to 109 mph (175.4 kmph) on the level deep under the mountains. Climax of the day was coverage of the entire 124 miles (199.5 km) from Lavino, north of Bologna, to Rovoredo, south of Milan, at a pass-to-pass average of 109.2 mph (175.8 kmph), with a top speed of 126 mph (203 kmph). It was the fastest long-distance journey on rails anywhere in the world until the post-war inauguration of a new rail speed era by the Japanese New Tokaido Line.

4

The French point the post-war way

efore the Second World War, as you will have inferred from their brief appearance in the preceding chapter, French Railways were not front runners in rail speed. The line speed limit of 120 kmph (74.5 mph) statutorily imposed on steam trains was still enforced by the discipline of self-recording speed indicators on the locomotives long after 90 mph (145 kmph) had become commonplace on some neighbouring British trunk routes, and 100 mph (160 kmph) was daily routine with US and German diesel trains — even with steam on the Milwaukee's `Hiawatha' in the US and the

From 1931 onwards a number of French railways used railcars with rubber-tyred wheels that had been developed by the Michelin company in pursuit of quieter, shock-free riding. One of the earliest post-war French Railways developments, in 1948, was the introduction of three streamlined locomotive-hauled train-sets employing lightweight coaches running on Michelin-designed chassis with novel bogies of ten wheels, all rubber-tyred. Hauled by streamlined 4-6-0s nicknamed the `Whales' by virtue of their appearance, the equipment operated between Paris and Strasbourg. (G.F. Fenino)

London & North Eastern streamliners in Britain. At the outbreak of the Second World War the fastest scheduled start-to-stop runs in French timetables represented averages of only 67.2 mph (108.2 kmph) with steam, 70.1 mph (112.9 kmph) with electric and 73.0 mph (117.6 kmph) with diesel traction.

High-speed inter-city passenger services were, however, a main plank in the SNCF's post-war reconstruction plan. Besides electrification, the other key tool for the objective's achievement was a thoroughgoing redraft of the timetable, so as to make the most of the prodigious reserve of power the French built into each successive breed of electric locomotive as a matter of policy. With this high power on tap for rapid acceleration from rest to full running speed, then to sustain maximum permissible track speed almost unvaryingly uphill or down, and by segregating the principal express trains in timetable groups or `flights' of equal schedule speed, the French built up on each main line a basic operating pattern that was commercially valid for a period of years. That done, the engineers could apply themselves uninterruptedly to an orderly exploration of new technological frontiers.

In 1954 French Railways' technicians set up a far-sighted high-speed research and development exercise. Principal objectives were to determine the practical performance limits of orthodox electric locomotives, to study the high-speed behaviour of rolling-stock, and to determine the resilience of the track, the efficiency of the current supply apparatus and the capability of the electrical equipment — fixed and mobile — to withstand the maximum loads exerted by the highest speed operation. A string of record-breaking performances ensued.

Track tests got off the mark in February 1954 on a 23-mile (37 km) stretch of track, almost dead straight and practically level south of Dijon, between that city and Beaune. Guinea-pig was one of SNCF's first dc electrics with all wheels motored, the 106-tonne, 4,740 hp No CC7121. These machines had already revolutionized day-to-day working on the newly-electrified Paris-Lyons line. Here they could sail up the route's only significant slope, the climb into

the Burgundy hills that culminates in 1 in 125 to Blaisy-Bas, with 700-tonne *rapides* at 80 mph (128.7 kmph). No CC7121, then just a few months old, was taken straight out of traffic and given no special preparation.

The tests lasted from 17 to 21 February 1954. While the three-coach, 109-tonne train of standard stainless steel coaches was on the move, the Dijon-Beaune section was closed to other trains and station platforms cleared of all but railwaymen. At that early stage of exploring high speed's side-effects, the French took the added precaution of tying down wagons in adjoining sidings in case they be set rolling by the test train's slip-stream.

On the first two days comparatively modest marks of 112 mph (180 kmph) and 121 mph (194.7 kmph) were set without extending the locomotive. The third day saw France's first 100 mph (160 kmph) start-to-stop sprint in the record books when the 22.9 miles (36.8 km) from Dijon to Beaune were gobbled up in 13^3/$_4$ minutes, and 143 mph (230 kmph) was touched. Sparkling acceleration distinguished the next run. Although curves restrained speed for the first 1^1/$_4$ miles (2 km) out of Dijon, No CC7121 reached 100 mph (160 kmph) within 3^1/$_4$ miles (5.2 km), and by 8^1/$_2$ miles (13.7 km) from the start had edged the maximum a little higher, to 145 mph (233.3 kmph). Then, on the final outing of 21 February, No CC7121 needed only 3 miles (4.8 km) from the start, inclusive of the speed-restricted exit from Dijon, to accelerate the train to 115 mph (185 kmph). Eight miles (12.9 km) out it registered the peak speed of these trials and a new world record, 151 mph (243 kmph) as the climax of an average of 145^1/$_2$ mph (234.1 kmph) over the preceding 5 miles (8 km).

The 1954 trials turned out to be just a curtain-raiser to the main event. French engineers now determined to leap clean out of the generally accepted limits of rail speed. The February trials had proved that modern locomotives could reach at least 150 mph without overtaxing their power or absorbing more current than their electrical equipment could tolerate. It was comparatively simple to regear the drive from traction motors to

The 'Mistral' with its stainless steel, air-conditioned coaching stock of the early 1960s, headed by one
of the 4,700hp 'CC7100' Class of 1952-4 which was to produce a world rail speed record-breaker.
(French Railways)

wheels for still greater speeds. The only essential was a different venue: the Dijon-Beaune section was not long enough for the target in mind.

The most likely alternative was the ex-Midi Railway route from Bordeaux to the Spanish frontier at Hendaye. For mile after mile across the flat Landes, the route is practically level; and in a 52³/₄-mile (85 km) stretch from Lamothe, south of Bordeaux, to Landes there is a solitary curve, and that a very gentle one, through Labouheyre station. It was the ideal race-track and would have been selected for the February 1954 trials except for one drawback.

The Midi had been electrified in 1927 and its catenary structure, suspended from quaint portal-shaped supports, was comparatively lightweight. In normal service the maximum permitted speed beneath it was 75 mph (120 kmph), despite the otherwise

speed-inviting characteristics of the route. Would it stand up to quite unprecedented stresses envisaged?

In June 1954 French Railways sent No CC7122, a sister of the February trial protagonist, to the Midi for reconnaissance. For the purpose No CC7122 was slightly modified with a new-model tubular pantograph, designed to reduce air resistance and also pressure on the catenary. The omens looked good. On 22 June No CC7122 took out a three-coach train and was held at 125 mph (200 kmph) or more for 12 miles (19.3 km) up to a peak of 140.5 mph (226 kmph). Next day a 10-coach, 430-tonne train was assembled to examine catenary and pantograph performance under heavier load conditions. The train was a *mélange* presumably improvized in the neighbourhood, since it included some vintage-looking coaches. Perhaps that was the reason why speed on the second sortie was not pushed much beyond 160 kmph (100 mph), though that pace or better was held for 15 miles (24 km).

The opening tests satisfied the engineers that the catenary could stand up to the purely mechanical stresses of moving pantograph contact at well over 100 mph (160 kmph) and for a considerable time. But the power transmitted had been some way off the strength needed to reach the speeds in mind. For the next series of tests in early December 1954, therefore, the engineers coupled a pair of Co-Cos, Nos CC7107 and 7113, but arranged them so that their combined current feed was taken through a single pantograph on the leading locomotive. To ensure adequate current strength throughout the test section, its five sub-stations were supplemented by the output of a mobile generating plant.

On 30 November the two Co-Cos were coupled to a 17-coach train of 715 tonnes. That day and the next they had three outings, attaining successively $102^1/2$, 115 and 121 mph (165, 185 and 195 kmph) with this heavy load. For the final essay on 2 December, two coaches were subtracted, slimming the formation to 620 tonnes, and with this the pair of Co-Cos maintained an average of $118^1/2$ mph (191 kmph) for $10^1/2$ miles (16.9 km), peaking at 131.3 mph (211.3 kmph). Throughout this high-speed stretch the single pantograph in use was taking current at 4,000 amps, so the engineers now had more of the data they needed.

Some of it was disconcerting. The engineers were particularly dismayed by the severe arcing between locomotive wheels and rails when current was flowing at maximum amperage. This was the current's normal return path, but ordinarily, of course, at a strength that gave no trouble. Fierce arcing in this area might dangerously deform either the locomotive wheels or the rail profile. Another problem was the serious wear of the current collector strips at the tip of the pantograph. That was bad enough to rule out reliance on a single pantograph at the speeds in mind; but on the other hand simultaneous use of both pantographs on a locomotive was equally a non-starter, as their random oscillations at 150 mph (240 kmph)

and more would be bound to snap the conductor wire.

The engineers now set themselves to intensive wind-tunnel study of new pantograph designs to meet the very exacting specification thrown up by the tests so far. The chosen model had to be capable of rapid and efficient raising and lowering against extreme wind pressures, since the plan was now to lower one pantograph of the test locomotive halfway through the speed trial, simultaneously raising the other to take over its function with split-second precision. The pantograph must also retain maximum stability once it was raised, despite the tremendous air resistance, to minimize the strain on the conductor wire. Eventually a new model, equipped with contactors of greater durability, was perfected, capable of elevation in 6 seconds and lowering in 1 second.

To mitigate arcing, the three-coach test train was wired up so that the return current would be dissipated through the wheels of the train as well as the locomotive. The three coaches, together weighing 100 tonnes, were specially prepared in other ways. All protruding fitments like door handles, ventilators and external steps were removed, and rubber fairings were stitched between the ends of each vehicle, including those of the locomotive and the leading coach; additionally, a streamlined tail nearly 8 feet (2.4 m) long was grafted on to the rear of the end coach.

Nos BB9004 and CC7107, the two locomotives picked for the ultimate trials, were given the new design of pantograph and had their gearing modified. As a safety precaution, protective resistances were inserted in series ahead of the ventilators and compressors and such unessential apparatus as the lighting and heating circuits were temporarily disconnected. Traction motors and every rotating part of each locomotive were submitted to ruthless workshop bench tests up to an equivalent 280 mph (450 kmph) before the road trials were started.

Out on the track the solitary bend at Labouheyre, superelevated for a comfortable 75 mph (120 kmph) in normal service, had its cant increased and its entrance and exit curves realigned to ease the radius to 4,370 yards (4,000 m), which was deemed fit for 137 mph (220 kmph). The curve was actually a long way — some 8$^1/_2$ miles (13.7 km) — beyond the anticipated peak-speed location at Ychoux, but the engineers were anxious to avoid sharp braking in the top speed range.

Elaborate photographic equipment was set up at the lineside to record speeds meticulously. At each kilometre post of the selected high-speed stretch they laid treadles which, when actuated by the locomotive's leading axle, would electronically fire off a camera and flashlight enclosed in a lightproof lineside box and focused on a brace of chronometers reading down to two-hundredths of a second. Finally, a second mobile power station was drafted to the area and linked to the catenary alongside the existing sub-station at Lamothe, where the train would be making its maximum accelerative effort.

On the morning of 26 March the Bo-Bo was let out of the slips. Minutes later No BB9004 had chalked up a new world rail speed record of 171$^1/_2$ mph (276 kmph) with so little concern to the engineers that they decided they were ready to go for the 300 — in kmph, that is — which had been their objective from the start.

The morning of 28 March looked good. Forecasters predicted a temperature not exceeding 15 degrees C (60 degrees F), which was important because an unseasonably high temperature had frustrated an earlier high-speed test — expanding in the heat, the conductor wire had undesirably lost tension. So, at 13.25 that afternoon, No CC7107 was signalled off the starting line at Facture.

All too soon nerves were jagged. The pantograph changeover was scheduled at the 70 mph (112.5 kmph) mark, but the test staff had not foreseen that the critical point would be reached near a sectioning point in the conductor wire. At that crucial spot the rising rear pantograph kissed the wire. Immediately there was violent arcing from which the pantograph collector strips emerged decidedly the worse for wear. That upset the current feed, so that from 100 mph (160 kmph) onwards the locomotive did not accelerate as smoothly and rapidly as expected.

The first coach of the train had been fitted up with periscopes so that the testing staff

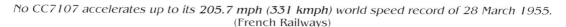

No CC7107 accelerates up to its 205.7 mph (331 kmph) world speed record of 28 March 1955. (French Railways)

could keep eyes glued to the all-important behaviour of the pantograph. It was a painful job now: vicious arcing marked the passage of every catenary support and it was almost blinding the periscope watchers. But in the ever briefer interludes between the arcing, as speed surged up to 150 mph (240 kmph), they could see enough to set them nervously debating whether to call off the attempt. Anxious calls went out over the direct-wire telephone to the locomotive cab and the radio-telephone link with the test directors at the trackside headquarters.

Then suddenly the current flow became less erratic. Gradually, with speed climbing to around 185 mph (300 kmph), it stabilized. The news was passed excitedly to the command post and back came the order: take the risk — so long as performance remains normal, carry on so long as the pantograph will stand it.

The pantograph stood it — but only by threads of metal. At 190 mph (305 kmph) or thereabouts the periscope watchers were appalled to see the collector strips burn red hot and then deform so grotesquely that they threatened to foul parts of the catenary. Barely had the locomotive crew been warned to prepare for instant lowering of the pantograph — they were now hurtling at 199 mph (320 kmph) — than one disintegrating strip did brush a catenary fitting and get partly shorn off. That actually eased the risks momentarily. But it wasn't long before the remnants of the collector strips began to melt; soon it was the pantograph frame itself that was rubbing the conductor wire.

That was the danger point. The periscope watchers jabbed a button, a red light flared on the locomotive's driving desk and at this prearranged signal the driver instantaneously lowered the wrecked pantograph. At that moment speed was 205.7 mph (331 kmph). For nearly 7 miles (some 11 km) the train had been careering at over 185 mph (300 kmph) and for nearly 4 miles (all but 6.5 km) at over 199 mph (320 kmph), whipping up ballast to carriage-window height with the force of its slipstream. Despite its realignment, the Labouheyre curve imparted some fairly sick-making lurches to the train during the careful deceleration, but otherwise the

A remarkable photograph that catches No BB9004 at its 205.6 mph (331 kmph) peak on 29 March 1955. The forward pantograph has just been raised and its collector strips are already red-hot from the clearly visible arcing.
(French Railways)

riding at least had added nothing to the day's alarms.

Despite its erratic acceleration rate after the pantograph change, No CC7107 attained the top speed some 2^1/$_2$ miles (4 km) ahead of the expected location. In the ensuing weeks, after precisely the same speed had been claimed for No BB9004, and some British and American commentators were openly sceptical that two runs at such hurricane pace could have been so nicely judged, one journal alleged a secret confidence from one of the trial's participants that the six-axle locomotive had been reined in at 197 mph (317 kmph). French Railways officially rebutted the report. Even if it were true, a discrepancy of 8-9 mph in this speed range is no speck, let alone a blot, on a stupendous technical achievement. Anyway, no one has ever contested that on 29 March 1955 No BB9004 certainly achieved 205.6 mph (331 kmph), this time a whole 4^1/$_2$ miles (7.2 km) ahead of the predicted location.

For this second trip new precautions had been taken to ease the strains on the pantograph. Copper collector strips had been replaced by ones of harder-wearing steel, and the conductor wire had been thoroughly greased to reduce the friction-generated heat. This time the pantograph exchange was to be deferred until speed was around 110 mph (175 kmph), to shorten the time during which the rear pantograph would be subjected to the really severe high-speed stresses. That set up a new hazard, of course. At the higher speed the driver would need to deploy still greater dexterity, to make sure both pantographs were not in simultaneous contact with the conductor wire; or conversely that no more than a fraction of a second elapsed with neither pantograph in contact, which would interrupt acceleration. Finally, the second run was timed to start much earlier in the day, at 7.35, to avoid any risk of rising ambient temperatures slackening the catenary's tension.

This time the early stages of the run had no one nailbiting. The change of pantographs was deftly executed at the planned higher speed, and at first all that bothered the train party was billowing smoke from burning grease on the conductor wire. But then, steel strips or no, pantograph troubles recurred.

As on the first trip, a deformed and disintegrating strip was partly hacked off when it caught a catenary support. Peering through a periscope increasingly fouled by a spatter of burning grease and liquescent red-hot metal, the train staff's anxiety mounted by the second as they were dazzled by fiercer and fiercer arcing. At around 180 mph (290 kmph) the driver was warned by telephone to get ready for disengagement of the pantograph — and almost at once the collector strips melted completely away.

But in the cab of No BB9004 they had decided on a desperate gamble. Once more — but this time with speed mounting towards 200 mph (320 kmph) — they changed pantographs. And once more it was done with supreme dexterity. Despite its earlier

stint in maximum acceleration from rest, there was enough resilience left in the forward pantograph to withstand the final stages of the climb to 205.7 mph (331 kmph). But then its collector strips too were glowing red. The peak reached, it was hauled down and the controlled deceleration began.

For several years after the 1955 record runs, SNCF concentrated on acceleration by sustained speed rather than sensational maxima. Not until 1965, in fact, was the ceiling raised from 150 kmph (93 mph) to 100 mph (160 kmph) on favourable stretches of the Paris-Lyons main line following the development of new braking systems on *rapide* stock. Long before then, however, French Railways had in 1957 bestowed on Europe its first regular post-war start-to-stop 80 mph (128.7 kmph) schedule by running the 'Mistral' from Paris to Dijon, 195.3 miles (314.2 km), in 146 minutes. And in 1959 the French had wrested the 'world's fastest' title from the fading American inter-city service by covering the 41.1 miles (66 km) between Arras and Longueau in 29 minutes, average 84.9 mph (137 kmph), with one of the *rapides* introduced between Paris and Lille following 25kV ac electrification of the former Nord main line. These star performances, though, were merely the frills tipping a fan of inter-city services radiating from Paris to every major French population centre that was unequalled for average speed in Europe.

By the early 1960s French Railways were calculatedly preparing to step up top speeds, and from 1961 to 1964 they conducted several series of lengthy tests to evaluate the costs that would be incurred in such areas as additional signalling and safety devices, tracklaying with heavier rail, easing of curves and strengthening of bridges. The theme of this research programme was consistent high speed with substantial trainloads rather than exceptional maxima.

French Railways began their first 125 mph (200 kmph) operation in daily service in 1967. The selected stretch of track, the 31.1 miles (50.1 km) of the Paris-Limoges-Toulouse main line between Les Aubrais and Vierzon, on the Orleans cut-off, was actually equipped with signalling and safety devices sophisticated enough to permit 250 kmph

(155 mph), and four standard 'BB9200' Class 1.5kV dc electric locomotives were modified to operate at that pace. But like their colleagues in other major railway managements, the French recoiled from the high cost of superimposing the special-purpose signalling for such speed on the existing system to benefit a comparative handful of trains; and also from the economic consequences of trying to operate traffic of very widely contrasted maximum speeds over one route. Instead, French sights were already focused on the construction of brand-new passenger-only railways where present and prospective traffic flows would justify the investment in a really glittering transformation of end-to-end speeds.

The first regular 125 mph (250 kmph) train over the Les Aubrais-Vierzon stretch was the 'Capitôle', introduced at the end of May 1967 on a 6-hour evening schedule over the 443 miles (713 km) between Paris Austerlitz and Toulouse in each direction. At the start it was worked exclusively by six specially-modified Class 'BB9200' locomotives and two distinctive air-conditioned train-sets,

basically of the then standard UIC (International Union of Railways) pattern but with several refinements, such as electro-magnetic track brakes as well as normal electro-pneumatic braking. Electro-magnetic track brakes, incidentally, are spring skids suspended just above the rails from the equalizing beams of coach bogies. Their retarding effect is derived not from friction, but from magnetic strength when they are energized by windings connected to the vehicle's electrical system. A braking force of some 30 tonnes can be exerted when all four electro-magnetic brakes on a coach are applied simultaneously; consequently they are cut out to leave control entirely to the vehicle's conventional braking in final deceleration to a stand from about 30 mph (50 kmph).

With evening working each way, the service initially made decidedly extravagant use of the two complete train-sets, each with its own restaurant car crew serving only dinner as a day's work. But from September 1968 the operation was doubled to a 'Capitôle du Matin' and 'Capitôle du Soir' in each direction, giving each train-set a much healthier

French Railways began to gear their electric locomotives for a 100 mph (160 kmph) maximum with their 5,160 hp, 82-tonne Class 'BB9200' B-Bs for the 1.5kV dc system introduced in 1957. One is in charge of the 'Mistral' in this 1969 photo, taken after the train's re-equipment with new air-conditioned stock. (Y.Broncard)

roster of an 886-mile (1,426 km) round trip daily — and, moreover, one at consistent high speed.

With the aid of 125 mph between Les Aubrais and Vierzon, the `Capitôles' were timed as tightly as an allowance of 2 hours 54 minutes for the 248.5 miles (400 km) from Paris Austerlitz to the first stop at Limoges, for an average of 85.7 mph (138 kmph). But at the same time the spread of 100 mph (160 kmph) authorizations to considerable lengths of other French main lines — Paris-Lille, Paris-Aulnoye (on the way to Brussels), Paris-Le Havre and Paris-Bordeaux — was already allowing the power of French electric traction to attain still faster end-to-end speeds elsewhere. By the end of 1967 the record Arras-Longeau time of the Nord Region's Paris-Lille service had been screwed up to a start-to-stop average of 88.1 mph (141.8 kmph), and two trains were covering the 135.1 miles (217.4 km) from Paris to Douai at a booked start-to-stop average of 86.2 mph (138.7 kmph).

By 1970 the SNCF had a dossier of evidence that higher speed pays dividends. The `Capitôles', despite 1st class exclusivity and supplementary fares, had more than doubled peak-hour travel on the Paris-Toulouse route and attracted fresh passenger revenue 70 per cent in excess of the extra direct costs debitable to provision for 125 mph (200 kmph) operation. Their publicity side-effect was substantial, too. Concurrently passenger carryings as a whole on the route from Paris to the South-West increased nearly 9 per cent and the rate of growth on parallel domestic air routes was trimmed by two-thirds. Nor had running costs been startlingly inflated.

So, in the later 1960s, French Railways prepared for 125 mph (200 kmph) running over a much greater distance than the characteristics of the Paris-Toulouse line allowed. The focus was now on the Paris-Bordeaux line, probably the best aligned in all Western Europe for sustained high speed. Its original builders kept it so free of curvature and junctions that nearly two-thirds of the 359.8 miles (579 km) from Paris to Bordeaux in the flat farmlands of Central France were practical 125 mph (200 kmph) territory, before the route strikes harder going across the foothills and beautifully wooded valleys sweeping

Proof that high speed pays off: the four trains on the right of this view of Paris Austerlitz on Friday 28 May 1971 are all labelled `Capitôle du Soir', for demand required the train to be run in four parts on that day, all headed by 8,000 hp `CC6500s'. The three parts in the centre platforms are formed of `Grand Confort' stock, the one on the extreme right of original `Capitôle' equipment. Another `CC6500' heads the `Aquitaine', and to the left of that is the overnight train to Madrid, the `Puerta del Sol'. (Y.Broncard)

The ten four-voltage 4,480kW `CC40100' locomotives introduced on Paris-Brussels services by the SNCF were designed for a 240 kmph (149.2 mph) maximum speed, but have never regularly operated at that pace. (G. Freeman Allen)

westwards to the Atlantic from the Massif Central. In May 1971 the French were ready on this line to amaze Europe yet again with the fastest really long-distance train the continent had yet seen, the `Aquitaine'.

The `Aquitaine' brought a new look to French traction. Up front was the latest expression of French high-power policy, one of the new range of double-six-wheeled-bogie electric locomotives built to a taxing performance specification. The 1.5kV dc `CC6500s' were required to hold 100 mph (160 kmph) up a 1 in 200 gradient with an 800-850-tonne train, not drop below 93 mph (150 kmph) with the same tonnage in tow on a 1 in 125 slope, and be able to sustain

The Paris-Bordeaux `Aquitaine' at speed near Ste Genevieve des Bois, between Paris and Orleans, headed by a `CC6500'. (Y.Broncard)

125 mph (200 kmph) on the level with 550-600 tonnes.

In another of the long French catalogue of sustained speed trials since 1950, the then almost new No CC6509 set up in March 1970 a target schedule for the new Paris-Bordeaux *rapide* following the line's readiness for 125 mph (200 kmph) operation. With a 10-coach train grossing some 500 tonnes it had tossed off the 359.8 miles (579 km) in 3 hours 33 minutes at a start-to-stop average of 101.4 mph (163 kmph) without exceeding 133.6 mph (215 kmph). The inaugural schedule of the `Aquitaine' nevertheless was set at a prudent 4 hours, but this was subsequently trimmed to 3 hours 50 minutes.

Little more of French Railways' historic infrastructure was fettled up and equipped for 125 mph. There were several reasons. The high short-term power built into French electric locomotives made them capable of such sustained speed, even with heavy loads, that despite maximum pace limited to 160 kmph (100 mph), and in a few areas

170 kmph (105.7 mph), they could still put up end-to-end speeds that were competitive in early 1970s market conditions, even over lengthy routes. The exclusive and weighty `Mistral', for instance, could be timed over the 675 miles (1,086 km) from Nice to Paris in just over 9 hours, representing a throughout average of 74.8 mph (120.4 kmph), despite nine intermediate stops.

The costs of higher maximum speed substantially outweighed the benefits. The existing traction current supply system was not designed to absorb the demands within the same feeder section of a couple of 8,000 hp locomotives working flat out to hold 200 kmph (125 mph) on 600-700-tonne trains. On the other hand, to elect just a few trains to higher speed would not adequately remunerate the outlay on special signalling and other measures deemed essential for 200 kmph operation. Furthermore, such selective widening of the speed band of traffic using a route would also reduce the line's operating capacity.

For its 100 mph and 100 mph-plus services on historic infrastructure, SNCF in the 1980s had a large fleet of 4,360kW Bo-Bos in dc, ac and dual-voltage versions. This 25kV ac `BB15000' is leaving Basel for Paris. (G.Freeman Allen)

The final Bertin Aérotrain research and development vehicle, with rubber-tyred wheels driven by diesel engines and a pusher airscrew for high speed travel.

Finally, the French were by 1970 already deep into the planning for their busiest trunk route of a new railway, and the trains to go with it. Both would be purpose-built for a speed far beyond any imaginable capability of their historic infrastructure. Of that, much more in later chapters.

One should mention that in the late 1960s steel wheel-on-rail was under threat from another aspiring French high-speed technology. This was Bertin's *Aérotrain,* a hybrid of monorail and hovercraft systems, in which the vehicle straddled, catamaran-like, a guidance rail of low wall dimensions on an elevated trackbed. Since the mid-1960s the Bertin company had enjoyed generous government finance to set up a 6 km (3.73-mile) test track south-west of Paris and accumulate over 18,600 km (11,560 miles) of test running with a small four-seater vehicle.

At first the car's drive was by piston engine and airscrew, but in the ultimate phase of the test programme it was fitted not only with a turbojet engine, but two booster rocket motors to boot. The total thrust of this armoury was equivalent to 2,700 hp — and all to shift a car weighing a mere 2.5 tons! Small wonder that on 4 December 1967 its intrepid driver finally managed to belt the vehicle up to 378 kmph (235 mph) within 4 km (2.49 miles) of the test track's start. At that point a very smart switch of the jet engine to reverse thrust and release of two tail-end parachutes was needed to halt the car within the residual 2 km of the track.

Persuaded that the *Aérotrain* had realistic potential, the government then doled out many more francs for the construction of an 18 km (11.2-mile) test track north of Orleans, sited so that it could be incorporated in a putative Paris-Orleans route, and for development of a bigger car with up to 40 seats. This second test vehicle was even more of a cross-breed, allying a diesel-mechanical drive of rubber-tyred wheels with a rear-end pusher airscrew for extra punch in acceleration to high speed. The Bertin company was also toying with linear motor propulsion technology.

However, by the end of the 1960s the prospect of roaring aero engines blasting ears close to ground level was raising public hackles. High-speed inter-city *Aérotrain* schemes were ditched, and Bertin's men were left only with a project for a commuter link between the burgeoning La Défense commercial area of Paris and the city's new Cergy-Pontoise dormitory town. But in 1974 a French government desperate for economies in the aftermath of the Arab-Israeli war oil crisis recoiled at escalating *Aérotrain* costs. The plug was pulled not only on the La Défense-Cergy proposal, but on the whole *Aérotrain* programme.

5
Japan's `Bullet Trains'— The Shinkansen

On 1 October 1964, a few days before the Olympic Games opened in Tokyo, Japan ceremonially inaugurated a new vision of inter-city railroading — a brand-new, 320-mile (515 km) railway dedicated exclusively to passenger trains, able to move over 6,000 passengers an hour at standard inter-city average speeds of 100 mph (160 kmph), almost like a long-haul Metro. It was a mass transit development then without parallel anywhere in the world.

This, the New Tokaido Line, the first of Japan's Shinkansen, or `new high-speed railways', was born of Japan's phenomenal economic boom following the Second World War. The country's geophysical character compresses its constantly swelling population into narrow belts, chiefly along the islands' coastlines. Little more than 15 per cent of the country's land surface is flat enough to encourage industrial and population development and as a result 40 per cent of the people were crammed into 1 per cent of Japan's total area. That elongated antheap was the Tokaido belt of Honshu island, from Tokyo to Osaka, where in the 1960s nearly three-quarters of the country's industry was concentrated.

The original Tokaido railway was Japan's first long-distance line. Laid to the 3 ft 6 in (1.067 m) gauge that is standard throughout the traditional Japanese National Railway system, the post-war industrial resurgence was soon taxing it to the limit. Though it represented only about 3 per cent of JNR's total route mileage, it was being loaded with nearly a quarter of the system's total passenger and freight volume. That had to be operated over a route of around 100 intermediate stations, no fewer than 1,060 level crossings, by no means easy grades and curvature, and with all the capacity limitations of narrow gauge. With road and motor transport development yet to take wing, and rail fares politically pegged at absurdly uneconomic levels as a social measure, the railway was clearly facing strangulation. Electrification and resignalling, completed in 1956, only deferred the crisis.

Japanese National Railways had sensed possible trends during the latter stages of the war and reconnoitred the outline of a new 3 ft 6 in railway in the Tokaido belt. The bold Shinkansen concept of an entirely new railway divorced from the existing JNR system, however, stemmed from the report of a study group set up by the Japanese Government in 1957. It rejected any solution based on expansion of narrow-gauge capacity because of the route's heavy weight of passenger traffic: enlargement of the existing railway's traffic capacity could not eliminate its inherent speed limitations. The recommendation was smartly accepted by the Government and JNR immediately set up a massive research and development apparatus to define and perfect a technology for which it had no prototypes.

Four important principles were established from the start. First, new and old lines should each operate within the narrowest possible speed bands, to maximize use of their respective operating capacities. That dictated concentration on the old line of intermediate passenger business and practically all freight traffic, and dedication of the new railway to inter-city passenger traffic between a strictly limited number of conurbation railheads.

Next, it was agreed that the new railway must be of wider gauge than 3 ft 6 in (1.067 m) to allow a substantial lift of the speed ceiling with comfort and safety. Despite the resultant incompatibility with the rest of the system, the standard 4 ft $8^1/2$ in (1.435 m) gauge was eventually selected. Third, in the light of French developments in high-voltage electrification at the industrial frequency, it was decided to adopt the 25kV ac system, but at 60Hz, instead of the 1.5kV dc previously standard on the JNR. Finally, a self-powered train-set format was adopted, both to spread traction gear weight and reduce maximum axle-loadings, and to quicken terminal turnrounds.

For the next six years nine design teams applied themselves unremittingly to evolving the detail technology of the new railway. The first earth was turned to build the New Tokaido Line in April 1959 before the research work was complete. Incredibly, considering the massive civil engineering work involved, the new railway was complete and operational within five years.

Intermediate stations on the new line were restricted to ten, all but those at Yokohama, Hajima and Shin-Osaka ('Shin' simply means 'new') alongside the platforms of the old 3 ft 6 in line to facilitate passenger interchange. For the same reason the new tracks' two island platforms at Tokyo were made an annexe to the existing main station rather than segregated in a new edifice. Gradients were allowed to run as steep as 1 in 65 in places, given the mighty traction power to be built into the train-sets. Minimum curve radius for the intended maximum speed of 130 mph (210 kmph) was fixed at 2,735 yds

(2,500 m), a slightly more generous figure than the minimum that research had established for passenger comfort and safety.

The New Tokaido was the first trunk railway in the world to dispense with lineside signals, and to rely entirely on continuous cab signalling associated with a sophisticated system of continuous automatic train control and protection. The signalling commands, automatically transmitted to driving cabs via coded track circuit frequencies that were picked by trainborne induction coils, provided for four restrictive limits of speed — 100, 68, 44 and 18 mph (160, 110, 70 and 30 kmph) — below the line maximum. The whole route was overseen from a combined traffic and electric power control centre at Tokyo.

At the intermediate stations trains set up their own routes. This was only a matter of fitting up each train to signal to lineside receivers an electronic code that identified it as stopping or non-stopping at a station ahead. None of the stations had idiosyncratic layouts, just the standard loop off each running line, so there was only one possible routing for each type of train to be activated according to which of the two descriptive codes it was beaming. That usefully reduced the routine workload of the Tokyo controllers.

Every axle of each first Shinkansen Series 0 train-set was motored, giving the ultimately standard 16-car formation (initially trains were operated in 12-car format) a stunning installed power of 11,040kW (15,875 hp) for a total train weight of 967 tonnes. Coaches were arranged in pairs to form a complete traction unit, with or without driving cab. All the equipment was mounted underfloor and distributed so as to equalize axle loadings as nearly as possible. As for external appearance, it didn't take long for the projectile styling of the driving cars to inspire the 'Bullet Train' alias by which most of the world now knows them.

In its evaluation of six prototype cars delivered before the New Tokaido Line's opening, JNR was worried by an effect that still bothers high-speed practitioners: the sharp increases of air pressure inside vehicles that are set up when they pass each other at top

speed in tunnel, which sensitive ears find extremely uncomfortable. The Shinkansen design team's answer was compressed-air devices, automatically activated at the approach to a tunnel, which force entrance and vestibule doors hard against their frames to seal the train as near hermetically as possible. At the same time the track circuiting automatically closes shutters over the tunnel's ventilating shafts until the train is back in the open.

The New Tokaido Line was an instantaneous — in fact, phenomenal — commercial success in its first few years of operation. A year of relaxed schedules was sensibly programmed for the new roadbed to settle and teething troubles to be overcome. But in November 1965 the minimum Tokyo-Osaka time for the limited-stop 'Hikari' trains, calling *en route* only at Nagoya and Kyoto, was trimmed to 3 hours 10 minutes, representing an end-to-end average of 101.1 mph (162.8 kmph) for the 320-mile journey.

Within a few years the New Tokaido Line timetable was offering over 80 high-speed trains each way daily. The fastest point-to-point bookings demanded a start-to-stop average of 106.5 mph (171.5 kmph) between Nagoya and Kyoto, 83.4 miles (134.3 km), from a number of the 'Hikari' services, which made only two stops between Tokyo and Osaka (the all-stations trains were branded 'Kodama'). Fractionally

Above: An original Series 0 Shinkansen train-set on the Tokaido line soon after the latter's opening.

Left: New Tokaido Line trains pass at the approach to Tokyo Central station in the early years of Shinkansen operation. These are the original Series 0 design of train-set, designed for the originally envisaged maximum operating speed of 161.5 mph (260 kmph).

slower were the 'Hikari' non-stop timings of only 120-123 minutes for the 212.4 miles (342 km) between Tokyo and Nagoya, the tightest of which represented a start-to-stop average of 106.2 mph (171 kmph). By the end of the 1960s the New Tokaido Line timetable yielded the staggering total of 444 daily point-to-point runs scheduled at average speeds in excess of 90 mph (145 kmph).

Just as electrifying as the trains themselves was the popular response to the new service. From around 60,000 a day at the start, the New Tokaido Line's carryings surged up through 200,000 in 1967 to a peak on 5 May 1969, when holiday crowds aggregating 520,000 were moved in a single day on this one route. Came the big international 'Expo 70' show at Osaka in 1970 and the New Tokaido Line's passenger count was averaging 254,000 a day for six months as packed 'Hikaris' and 'Kodamas' swarmed out of Tokyo at 5- and 10-minute headways in the peak travel hours.

The classic simplicity of the railway operationally and its high quota of automation made it a model of cost-effective investment. By 1969 JNR deduced that its New Tokaido staff were on average four times as productive and were earning per man nine times the revenue of their colleagues on the 3 ft 6 in network. Whereas the narrow-gauge system was sliding deeper year by year into a mammoth accumulated deficit, the NTL's consistently high passenger load factors were generating revenue that cleared direct operating costs by over 40 per cent.

The moment the New Tokaido Line had shown its mettle, JNR planners were at work on its first extension, and the first 103-mile (165 km) stretch of the New Sanyo Shinkansen, from Osaka to Okayama, was opened to traffic in March 1972. Major civil engineering works were entailed — nearly 60 miles (97 km) of bridgework and 35 miles (56 km) of tunnel, including the 10.2-mile (16.4 km) Rokko Tunnel at Kobe, which took $4^1/2$ years to bore through solid granite.

Even before the first 'Bullet Trains' hummed into Okayama, the Japanese Government had proclaimed widespread Shinkansen extension to be an essential ingredient of the country's economic growth

and the only way to encourage population dispersal from the teeming industrial complexes of the coastal belts. In May 1970 it promulgated a Law for the Construction of Nationwide High-Speed Railways which ordered further extension of the New Sanyo Line to Hakata, on Honshu island, and three entirely new Shinkansen: the Tohoku, from Tokyo northwards to Morioka; the Joetsu, from Tokyo north-westwards to Niigata, on the Sea of Japan coast; and the Narita, from Tokyo to its new airport at Narita, then expected to pursue an untroubled course to full commercial operation in 1977.

Three years later the prospectus was euphorically lengthened to include projection of the Tohoku line to the northern tip of Honshu island at Aomori and then to Sapporo, on the northernmost of Japan's three main islands, Hokkaido, by a Hokkaido Shinkansen burrowing under the Tsuguru Strait in a new Seikan Tunnel 33.5 miles (53.9 km) long, no less; extension of the New Sanyo Line beyond Hakata to Nagasaki and Kagoshima by the Kyushu Shinkansen; and another Tokyo-Osaka Shinkansen, the Hokuriku. This last was advocated partly because traffic strangulation of the original New Tokaido Line was a credible threat, and partly to open up another area of the country economically; the Hokuriku would trace an inverted-'U'-shaped route between Tokyo and Osaka so as to touch the western Sea of Japan coastline at Toyama. That added up to another 1,480 route miles (2,381 km) of Shinkansen. But a further 12 Shinkansen routes were also endorsed in principle, so that the ultimate network then envisaged would total about 4,350 route miles (7,000 km).

The New Sanyo Line extension to Hakata was opened throughout from Tokyo in March 1975. Yet again the engineering task was awesome — more so, probably, than in any previous Shinkansen project. Not only was there the 11.6-mile (18.6 km) tunnel, the second longest in the world after Switzerland's Simplon, to be sunk under the Kammon Strait between Honshu and Kyushu islands, but on land the railway was cutting through mountainous regions of very different character from the heavily-populated

Tokaido coastal belt. In the 247 miles (398 km) from Okayama to Hakata, 111 tunnels aggregating 138 miles (222 km) had to be bored.

New Tokaido Line experience dictated a number of changes in design parameters for the New Sanyo Line. Above all they concerned the track. Despite the care lavished on weight economy and load distribution in the train-sets, track wear had become a mounting worry on the New Tokaido Line, becoming more expensive in cash and in time than JNR had estimated. The track engineers were all too often stretched to cram their work into the night-time lull in service. For the New Sanyo Line, therefore, a more solid track foundation was ordered with heavier 60.8 kg/m rail (which was also applied to the New Tokaido Line whenever and wherever relaying was due).

Over two-thirds of the New Sanyo Line was laid with concrete slab track. This would have been adopted throughout but for susceptibilities to subsidence, which might have fractured the formation. In the JNR version the rails were attached directly to fastenings cast into 5-metre-long concrete slabs, which were then fixed by a mix of cement and bitumen into a cast-in-situ concrete roadbed. Several major railways had made scattered, short-stretch installation of concrete slab track, but none had laid it so extensively as the Japanese on their Shinkansen. There is no doubt that its semi-permanent solidity cuts maintenance under intensive traffic to an extent that should offset its high initial cost within a year or two. But not only does it cost at least twice as much to make and install as orthodox sleeper-and-ballast track; the laying operation shuts the track under renewal for much longer and as yet the specialized laying machines are scarce.

The original maximum speed target for the New Tokaido Line was 155 mph (250 kmph), but in the event the operational ceiling was lowered to 130 mph (210 kmph). That was initially the limit on the first route extensions, though the New Sanyo Line and its train-sets were specifically designed for regular operation at 162 mph (260 kmph). Amongst other things, this stipulated an easing out of the minimum curve radius from the New

Tokaido Line's 2,500 m to the New Sanyo's 4,000 m (4,280 yds).

Apart from building extra train-sets to cover the extended service to Hakata, JNR had to continue production to renew the entire Shinkansen fleet during the 1970s; for another mark of the intensive train service was that after only a decade of sustained high-speed pounding the original units were exhausted. During the 1974 summer, in fact, the New Tokaido Line suffered a traumatic four months' concatenation of track, rolling-stock and signalling failures that made a fiction of its timetable for over six weeks. Thoroughly alarmed, JNR quickly decided to relay the whole route throughout with heavier rail at a cost of nearly £300 million and to renew the entire catenary by 1984.

With the New Sanyo Line fully open, passenger business soared again and within two months, on 5 May 1975, the Shinkansen lines topped the million-passengers-in-a-day mark for the first time. From the start of the Shinkansen's public service day at 06.00 to its shutdown for nocturnal maintenance as midnight approached, over 100 trains each way were now scheduled over all or part of the combined New Tokaido and New Sanyo Lines — on public holidays significantly more.

Despite the triumphs of Shinkansen technology, and despite the new railways' enviable profitability and productivity, the Shinkansen network builders were not working overtime in the later 1970s and early 1980s. One contretemps after another had cooled Japanese ardour for the concept.

First there was the energy crisis set off by the Arab-Israeli war of 1973. This had no severer impact than on Japan, a country dependent on imported fuel to generate 86 per cent of its energy, and drawing as much as 99.7 per cent of its oil from overseas. The outcome was raging inflation and a sharp setback in Japan's economic growth. Even before the oil price explosion JNR had been facing serious cost escalation in Shinkansen construction. Back in the 1960s it had built the New Tokaido Line at an average of just over £1.75 million a mile, but as early as 1972 that figure had doubled for the initial stage of the New Sanyo Line. By 1977 the average was reckoned to be over £5.5 million a mile. Within metropolitan areas the cost was soaring far higher because of a stratospheric climb of land prices.

But overriding national economic considerations apart, the 3 ft 6 in gauge bulk of JNR was sliding helplessly into the financial mire, downtrodden by a combination of overmanning, a market share of both passengers and freight that was being sharply eroded by competition, maintenance of totally uneconomic rural services at political insistence, and absurdly uneconomic fare scales, again the result of political fiat. Was this the time to throw a mint of good money after a heap of bad?

Nor was the case for Shinkansen as a means to encourage population and industrial mobility quite so strong as in the early 1960s. Road transport was much more highly developed, as JNR's balance-sheet testified all too starkly. And wide-bodied jets, with the benefit of considerably improved airports and city-centre-to-airport access, had greatly strengthened air travel's competitiveness in time, convenience and cost. That was put to unhappy practical proof early in 1977, after the Government had at last grasped the uneconomic rail fare nettle and ordered a 50 per cent price rise at a stroke. Thereupon Shinkansen carryings slumped by a drastic 15 per cent almost overnight and the airlines took most of the pickings.

Least expected, perhaps, was the disenchantment with Shinkansen that soured public opinion. It was sparked off by growing complaints of noise from people living near the new railways. In designing the New Tokaido Line, JNR engineers had taken some care to limit noise and vibration to levels no worse than those experienced in the proximity of the 3 ft 6 in gauge system, but they had not foreseen the effects of the intensive service which rising traffic demands quickly generated. By now Japan, which had previously tolerated the foulest industrial pollution, was on a highly emotive ecological kick. Self-seeking politicos pounced on the alleged environmental disturbance of the Shinkansen as a symbolic issue, public opinion was roused and controversy erupted over much of the projected new Shinkansen

routes. Late in 1972 the Government's Environment Agency stepped in with a diktat on maximum permissible decibel level in the vicinity of Shinkansen routes. This forced JNR to spend over 70 billion yen — no less than £200 million at 1990 exchange rates — on noise-abatement measures throughout the New Tokaido and Sanyo lines.

In the cold light of the inflationary and recessionary late 1970s, expert Japanese opinion became more and more convinced that many of the routes projected in the vast Shinkansen network outline of 1973, directed to far less populous regions than the Tokaido and Sanyo, would never cover even their direct operating costs. Some JNR executives had bluntly said as much at the time.

The Tohoku and Joetsu Shinkansen schemes, nevertheless, did laboriously hack through the undergrowth of economic stringency and local environmental protest. Once forecast to open its metals to traffic by 1977, the Tohoku project finally took on its first tracklayers early that year.

Not until mid-1977 were years of niggling argument over the two lines' course into Tokyo resolved. Ever since 1971 the people of Omiya, a satellite town about 20 miles from Tokyo's centre, had striven to drive the Tohoku beneath ground in their neighbourhood. It took five years to win their grudging consent to elevated tracks, but that cost the Shinkansen operators the inconvenience of yielding Omiya its own Shinkansen station and an agreement to stop all trains there. In Tokyo itself the JNR was pig-in-the-middle of local trench warfare. The old 3 ft 6 in gauge main line from northern Japan has its separate Tokyo terminal at Ueno, and when JNR promulgated a logical plan to concentrate all Shinkansen routes converging on the capital in one station elsewhere, shopkeepers in the vicinity of Ueno terminus raised Cain at their threatened loss of casual trade. But just as strident were Ueno's ordinary residents, who refused to be disturbed by an above-ground Shinkansen. The outcome? As you might expect, face-saving but costly Oriental compromise: JNR reluctantly mollified both factions by undertaking to run the Tohoku Shinkansen into an underground terminal at Ueno.

Until March 1985, when the extension to Ueno was at last completed, Tohoku and Joetsu trains terminated at Omiya, a 20-mile (32.2 km) traipse by narrow-gauge train from downtown Tokyo. The Ueno extension still left the two new lines divorced from the Tokaido/Sanyo Shinkansen. Not until 1989 did work begin to thrust a 3.5 km (2.1-mile) connection from Ueno to the Tokyo Central station start of the Tokaido line. That link-up was achieved in June 1991.

Both the third and fourth Shinkansen were completed and opened to business in 1982: the 289-mile (465 km) Tohoku to Morioka, northern Honshu, in June; and the 167.8-mile (270 km) Joetsu to Niigata in the following November (the distances quoted in both cases are from Omiya). Penetration of trains' vital underfloor apparatus by snow had been a sporadic nuisance on the first two Shinkansen, but the two new lines crossed territory inured to very heavy winter falls. That was above all a concern on the Joetsu, which cut through the country's dorsal mountain chain where snow can lie at least 12 feet deep.

At its highest level, therefore, the Joetsu was dipped below ground for no less than 65.9 miles (106 km) of the 85.1 miles (137 km) between Takasaki and Nagaoka. Within that distance the Joetsu threaded what is presently the world's longest land-surface rail tunnel, the 13.8-mile (22.23 km) Daishimizu. Open stretches between the tunnels were protected by shelters. Exposed line in the foothills was equipped with devices that sensed the onset of snow and automatically sprayed the tracks with warm water to stop the fall accumulating or freezing. Other distinctive equipment included earthquake sensors that had traffic automatically signalled to a halt the moment they detected a threatening tremor.

The combined impact on construction costs, on the one hand of environmental constraints that compelled resort to elevated infrastructure in open country, and on the other of daunting terrain, can be gauged from these few figures. Of the Tohoku line's total route mileage, 56 per cent is elevated, 16 per cent is over bridges and 23 per cent in tunnel. For the Joetsu the respective ratios are 49, 11 and 39 per cent — which leaves just 1 per cent innocent of extraordinary civil engineering!

A Series 200 train-set on the Joetsu line. Note the slab track, the flanking noise-baffling walls and the length of the viaduct.

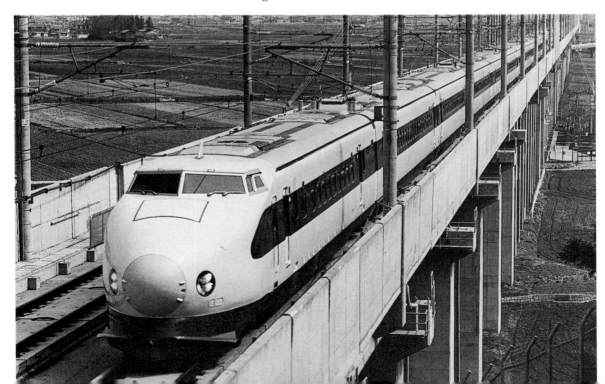

The shorter distance between stations of the Tohoku and Joetsu lines and their lengthier gradients demanded a new train-set design, the Series 200. Series 0 had been steel-bodied, but Series 200 adopted welded aluminium alloy for bodies that had deep below-floor skirts to exclude snow. Train-set length was cut to 12 cars (as it was in 1985 for the Series 0 sets on Tokaido line 'Kodama' services) and motor rating was hoisted to 230kW per axle. On the Tohoku line the fast and semi-fast categories of train service were exotically designated 'Yamabiko' (Echo) and 'Aoba' (Green Foliage) respectively, and on the Joetsu 'Asahi' (Rising Sun) and 'Toki' (Crested Ibis) respectively.

The Tohoku opened its account with 60 trains daily, the Joetsu with 42. But though both lines pulled in slightly more initial business than expected, they were just as unprofitable as had been forecast. Four years after inauguration, the Tohoku's operating ratio — costs as a percentage of revenue — had dropped from an initial 254 no further than to 177, that of the Joetsu from an opening 263 to just 195. In contrast, the Tokaido ratio by that time was a very buoyant 51.

Both Tohoku and Joetsu started with the Tokaido/Sanyo speed limit of 210 kmph (130.5 mph). In 1985 the first uplift of Shinkansen top speed came with approval of 240 kmph (149.2 mph) on the Tohoku. That was almost exclusively the product of moves that held lineside noise to the same decibel level at 240 as at 210 kmph. Suppressive action centred chiefly on toning down the whine of current collection, and stabilizing contact between pantograph and traction current wire to reduce the arcing that nettled the Shinkansen's neighbours. The solutions were primarily redesign of pantographs, surrounding them with shields, and running a rooftop 25kV power line the length of a train-set, so that a 12-car formation could run with only three pantos operative instead of six, one on each pair of cars. Rail noise was cut by intensifying the frequency of surface grinding.

It was 1988 before the Joetsu maximum was raised to 240 kmph. By then the train service on both this and the Tohoku had been strengthened by 50-60 per cent. That accompanied the completion of the lines' access to a Ueno terminus in Tokyo, which stimulated an immediate upsurge in their

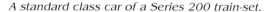

A standard class car of a Series 200 train-set.

carryings — of as much as 45 per cent in the case of the Tohoku.

As the decade closed, the 240 kmph Tohoku was pressing France's 300 kmph TGV-Atlantique hard in terms of average start-to-stop speed. Every day six Tohoku trains were booked to dismiss the 171.1 km (106.3 miles) between Morioka and Sendai in just 48 minutes. That represented a mean of 213.9 kmph (132.9 mph), not far short of the peak 224 kmph (139.2 mph) average asked of two TGV-A trains daily between Paris and Le Mans, 201.6 km (125.3 miles) apart. And the timetables displayed 41 more daily start-to-stop runs at an average of better than 200 kmph (124.3 mph).

In March 1990, moreover, permissible speed was lifted to 275 kmph (170.9 mph) on a stretch of the Joetsu that was largely in tunnel: and where, consequently, the extra decibels generated through increased pace could be muffled. To exploit that licence some of the line's existing Series 200 train-sets were modified with reinforced braking (to preserve compatibility with the sig-nalling's deceleration distances), boosted power output, additional devices to moder-ate pantograph noise, and means to limit current pick-up to two of the 12-car train-set's pantographs. Results proved that though the Joetsu line had been engineered for a maximum of 260 kmph (161.6 mph), the solidity built into the infrastructure as an earthquake safeguard had made track and catenary impervious to the higher speed. Management was confident that by the mid-1990s the Joetsu would be operating almost throughout at a standard 275 kmph (170.9 mph); and by the end of the 1990s at 300 kmph (186.5 mph) with a new breed of train-set. At the same time the Tohoku manage-ment was aiming to clear part of that Shinkansen for 300 kmph as early as 1993, and practically the whole of it for that speed two or three years later. Clearly the French were in for a tougher race yet.

The Tokaido and Sanyo Shinkansen were together scheduling just over 300 trains daily in the second half of the 1980s. Service fre-quency over the Tokaido's 320 miles (515.4 km) between Tokyo and Shin-Osaka was unparalleled over such a distance. Every day,

from 07.00 to 10.59, 23 limited-stop 'Hikari' trains swarmed out of Tokyo; from 11.00 to 14.59 there were four or five 'Hikari' depar-tures in each hour; and then, from 15.00 to 18.59, 24 more, seven of them in a single hour from 18.00 to 18.59. These 'Hikari', moreover, were complemented by two all-stations 'Kodama' services in each hour. At least two 'Hikari' per hour travelled beyond Osaka on to the Sanyo line. The fastest of these services wrapped up the 664.4 miles (1,069 km) from Tokyo to Fukuoka in 5 hrs 47 min, inclusive of six intermediate stops, thus notching an average end-to-end speed of 114.9 mph (184.9 kmph). In 1989 the Tokaido line alone registered 112 million passenger journeys.

By the start of the 1990s the high-speed lines' traffic was being boosted by a new class of user — 'Shinkansen Tsukin-sha', or long-distance commuters. Driven to emigrate from metropolitan Tokyo by the capital's extortionate housing costs, the staff of major companies found their employers so keen to retain skilled labour that they were prepared to subsidize Shinkansen commuting. For the employee, furthermore, the benefit was untaxed unless its value exceeded about £2,300 a year. By mid-1990 more than 50,000 Shinkansen season tickets, known as FLEX passes, were in circulation.

The Tokaido's tighter curves and their degree of superelevation parameters ruled out speed much higher than 230 kmph (142.9 mph) with existing rolling-stock if pas-senger sensitivity to lateral g was respected. In 1986 the limit on the Tokaido and Sanyo was inched up to 220 kmph (136.7 mph) for the Series 0 train-sets. However, slightly higher, 230 kmph (142.9 mph), could be conceded to a new Series 100 design, a pro-totype of which had emerged in 1985. Fol-lowing evaluation of a pre-production series of six train-sets, Series 100 proliferated into a substantial fleet in the later 1980s.

The Series 100 combined pursuit of sleeker aerodynamics, more economical use of energy and still more effective stifling of noise with marked advances in passenger accommodation and amenities. Wide-body jet flying time between Tokyo and Osaka air-ports had come down to a flat hour, so that even with realistic allowance for downtown-airport travel, centre-to-centre journeys by Shinkansen now took half an hour more than by plane. With no means immediately available for a further lift of Tokaido speed, more had to be made of the train's scope to offer a superior travel environment.

Under that head the conspicuous innovation was the 12-car Series 100 set's inclusion of bi-level cars. One type had an upper-level restaurant served by a lower-level kitchen. The other combined an upper-level `green' — the Japanese equivalent of 1st class — saloon with lower-level compartments of varying sizes, starting with a two-seater, that were ranged athwart a central corridor. Generally speaking, the Series 100 sets each include a bi-level of each type, but some plying the lengthy Tokyo-Hakata route embody four bi-levels.

Technologically, the Series 100's plus was its 17 per cent more thrifty use of traction current on a standard Tokyo-Osaka timing

than a Series 0. Adoption of a technically refined, more compact 230kW motor, various weight-saving constructional ploys, detail smoothing of exterior surfaces, and nose ends remoulded into even more aggressive projectile shape — the benefit of these changes in sum enabled the designers to dispense with motored axles on four of a Series 100's 12 cars. Even so, output of the eight motored cars in a set still grossed a hefty 11,040kW for a total train weight of 922 tonnes.

The Series 100 is this book's first encounter with the so-called `intelligent train' — that is, one in which performance of vital apparatus is continuously monitored by advanced electronics. The diagnostic faculties of the system not only warn the train crew instantly of any actual or incipient malfunction, but also advise on its rectification and store the facts electronically.

A fibre-optics transmission system links all cars of a Series 100 with microprocessor-

A Series 100 train-set including four bi-level cars on the Tokaido/Sanyo Shinkansen. (JR West)

Close-up of a Series 100 train-set's bi-level cars.

based control units, video screens and recording units in each driving cab. The facts and location of any malfunction are promptly flashed on the driver's screen, and then the effectiveness of such counter-measures as he takes. A driver can also call up real-time data on a range of performance-related items, such as traction motor current, air pressure, overhead current line voltage, rectifier and auxiliary power voltage. In many cases the cab screen will identify by colour or other schematics the facts for each pair of cars in the train-set. All this data is automatically recorded and can be radio-transmitted from the speeding train to ground controllers or maintenance staff.

Series 100's debut coincided with the death throes of Japanese National Railways,

Dining salon on the upper level of a Series 100 bi-level car.

A two-seater 'green' (1st) class compartment on the lower floor of a Series 100 bi-level car.

which by the mid-1980s was in such horrendously deep financial water that draconian action was unavoidable. At last a government had the stamina to force through a drastic reorganization and contraction that took effect in April 1987. JNR was geographically dismantled into a Japan Rail Group of six passenger railways, which also played host to a national rail freight company. Initially the new companies were kept in the public domain and were in varying degrees propped up by public money. But the objective was that all should set out their stalls for early privatization. And by 1990 the dramatic improvements in human and asset productivity swiftly effected by the new managements had some of them much closer to market than originally anticipated.

There was special treatment for the Shinkansen lines. Initially their existing infrastructure was vested in a Shinkansen Property Corporation. But the routes' upkeep, their rolling-stock and its expansion, and operation of Shinkansen services, were parcelled out amongst the new passenger companies through whose territory the high-speed lines ran. These companies would pay track rental to the Shinkansen Property Corporation.

As a result, the Tokaido line from Tokyo to Osaka became a fief of the new JR-Central Railway. The JR-West Railway took over the Sanyo line from Osaka to Hakata; and the JR-East Railway both the Tohoku and the Joetsu Shinkansen.

A single-minded approach to Shinkansen technological development by the railways, the Japanese railway supply industry and the country's Railway Technical Research Institute persists under the new order. The first new-era product of that alliance is a third-generation Series 300 Shinkansen train-set with which, in 1993, JR-Central aimed to premiere a quicker 'Super Hikari' peak-hour service and protect Tokaido traffic from the publicity attending that year's opening of Osaka's new airport. (JR-West was working up a different design of its own, tagged Series 500, of which little was known at the end of 1990.)

Series 300 is much lower-slung, slightly narrower in body and considerably lighter than its predecessors. Aerodynamically a set's outline is made the more arresting by fully-faired, Concorde-like cab ends, and there are no bi-level cars to break the roof line.

Traction is new-generation, supplied by three-phase ac 300kW motors under GTO (Gate Turn Off) thyristor-inverter control.

The driving desk of a Series 100 train-set. Note, at the extreme right of the desk, the video screen on which the data from the train's microprocessor-driven diagnostics systems are reproduced.

Their enhanced power combined with yet more intensive weight reduction in the aluminium alloy-bodied cars requires only 10 of a Series 300's 16 cars to be motored on all axles. So total weight of a Series 300 tumbles to 691 tonnes, compared with a Series 100's 922 tonnes.

Series 300's characteristics permit it a 270 kmph (167.8 mph) top speed on the Tokaido with no more track modification than adjustment of superelevation on curves. As for the noise problem, only two of a set's five pantographs will be active at a time; and new designs and mountings have been devised to contain contact whine.

There is a signalling snag in raising top speed on a line equipped, like the Tokaido, with a highly sophisticated automatic train control system. If the rise is considerable it will make a nonsense of the speed bands and braking distances that set the parame-

ters for the cab-display commands to the driver and automatic braking in the event of non-compliance. Adding stations is just as troublesome. Five new ones were opened on the Tokaido and Sanyo combined in 1987, but as the original 1964 apparatus was by then comprehensively outdated by subsequent progress in electronics, the opportunity was seized to couple the essential revision of the automatic train control with renewal and redesign of the Tokyo control centre.

The Series 100 was made able to decelerate from 230 kmph within the same distances as the 220 kmph Series 0 by adding eddy current brakes to its other braking resources. As a supplementary for deceleration from top pace, European railways have so far preferred the electro-magnetic track brake for their high-speed rolling-stock. That presses bar magnets into contact with the rail to generate braking force by frictional resistance. The linear eddy current brake makes no contact and so is immune to wear and tear; other advantages are that its force is precisely controllable and, at its peak, more powerful. But there are debits. It demands a much higher current supply, and thus sets up electro-magnetic fields of a strength that may interfere with signalling circuitry. And in action it may heat up rails to a degree that risks their deformation. On this latter ground the French rejected it for their TGVs; and the Germans are applying eddy current brakes experimentally to just a handful of their high-speed IC-Express train-sets.

The Series 300 have eddy current brakes on their trailers. But this does not compensate adequately for a leap from a 230 to a 270 kmph top speed. The Japanese have for the present avoided another complete and costly rejig of the whole Tokaido automatic train control by superimposing on the existing system a network of active track-mounted transponders that provide the required commands related to the 270-230 kmph speed band. (The same expedient was adopted to cover the Joetsu line's partial operation of selected trains at 275 kmph, described earlier.)

The 'Super Hikari' Tokyo-Osaka journey time with Series 300 was to be $2^1/2$ hours for the 515 km (320 miles), average speed 206 kmph (128 mph), a saving of 22 minutes on the best schedule of 1990. Meanwhile, in March 1991 JR-Central tested the Series 300 prototype at up to 325.7 kmph (202.4 mph). That eclipsed the previous Tokaido Shinkansen record — 319 kmph, set by a one-off Series 961 unit in 1979.

Whether added noise and vibration at 300 kmph would infringe the statutory limits set for Shinkansen and rule out subsequent commercial operation at such pace remained to be seen. But JR-Central management was certain that those constraints would never allow Tokaido speed to exceed 350 kmph (217.5 mph).

Stuttering moves to renew Shinkansen network extension in the mid-1980s did not get very far, as much because of national economic uncertainties as of Japanese National Railways' desperate financial state. But coincidentally with JNR's dissolution in 1987 the government was being badgered by the West to reduce its massive export payments surplus by stimulating domestic consumption. One of its reactions was to reactivate Shinkansen construction.

It took two years to hammer out an infrastructure plan and financial arrangements that were even marginally tolerable to the railway companies who would operate the lines. The latter were invited to shoulder half the construction costs. For the first time local prefectures to be served by the extensions were asked to stump up 10 per cent, leaving the Government to bear 40 per cent of the bill.

The frugal infrastructure scheme strictly limited the spread of full-blooded high-speed routes. New construction would be of three kinds:

Type 1. Engineered for 300 kmph by Series 300 train-sets

Type 2. Mixing of existing 3 ft 6 in (1.067 m) gauge route with 1.435 m gauge, possibly with some realignments, for use by new reduced-profile Shinkansen train-sets, but at no greater pace than 130 kmph (80.8 mph)

Type 3. Infrastructure built to Shinkansen 1.435 m gauge parameters, but initially laid with 1,067 m gauge track fit for 160-200 kmph (100-125 mph)

Of the new Hokuriku line, branching from the Joetsu at Takasaki and running for 205 km (127.4 miles) to Honshu island's north coast, only the first 116 km (72 miles) to Nagano, site of the 1998 Winter Olympics, would adhere to the full Type 1 standard. The final 89 km along the north coastline from Nagano to Kanazawa would be of Type 3 character. The original notion of continuing this Shinkansen in a semi-circle back to reunion with the Tokaido at Osaka was shelved. In August 1991 the Transport Minister approved construction as far as Nagano, for completion by the Olympics' inauguration.

The prospectus for extension of the Tohoku Shinkansen to the north-eastern tip of Honshu at Aomori was curious. A central 64 km (40 miles) would be Type 1, though dual-gauged for use also by 3 ft 6 in gauge freight traffic, but new stretches aggregating 125 km (77.7 miles) north and south of that would be Type 2. The 1973 intention to project the Tohoku line beyond Aomori via the now-operational 53.9 km (33.5-mile) under-sea Seikan Tunnel to an end-on junction with a new Hokkaido island Shinkansen was left on the back-burner. The tunnel was bored to 1.435 m gauge Shinkansen dimensions, but seems likely to carry only a 1.067 m gauge railway for a good many years to come.

Finally, a Kyushu Shinkansen was approved to run from the Sanyo Shinkansen's limit at Hakata to the other end of Kyushu island at Kagoshima. This would be built to Type 3 parameters. Both Tohoku and Kyushu extensions were given the ministerial go-ahead in August 1991.

The financial effect of adulterating the original Shinkansen concept would be to halve the total capital cost of the three projects just described, were all to be constructed to Type 1 standards throughout. But at first the Government had been slow to disgorge finance and the railway companies insisted that they themselves could not afford to meet the bills for an attack on the construction work proper.

Eventually, at the end of 1990, a new *modus vivendi* was agreed. The Shinkansen Property Corporation would be wound up and the Shinkansen network sold to the three railways running trains over it, at prices approximating the values on which they had been paying track rental. Thus JR-Central would pay 60 per cent of the assets' worth, JR-East 30 per cent and JR-West 10 per cent. Relieved of their rental outgoings, the railways would draw on their increased Shinkansen operating surplus to fund their share of new construction costs. The Government provided for its slice of the investment in its 1991-92 budget.

Obviously none of the existing Shinkansen train-set types will be compatible with 1.067 m gauge clearances. The kind of small-profile unit required for Type 2 extensions that graft 1.435 m gauge rail on to 1.067 m gauge infrastructure was unveiled by the JR-East Railway in 1990. That company did not wait for endorsement of a national expansion plan, but enlisted local support for mixing to 1.435 m gauge its 88 km (55-mile) line from Fukushima, on the Tohoku Shinkansen, to Yamagata.

JR-East's small-profile Series 400 is a six-car unit with all axles powered by thyristor-controlled 220kW motors. The cars are of the same height as the Tohoku's Series 200, but bodies are significantly narrower, so that by comparison each Series 400 saloon's seating bay has one less seat per lateral row. Between Tokyo and Fukushima on the Tohoku Shinkansen proper, a Yamagata-bound Series 400 runs coupled to a Morioka-bound Series 400 at the full 240 kmph (150 mph) line speed. A prototype Series 400 unit was run up to a new Shinkansen speed record of 336 kmph (208.8 mph) on the Joetsu line in March 1991.

One final tribute to the Shinkansen deserves payment. Many subsequent high-speed inter-city rail developments might never have been born — certainly would not have been so confidently conceived — had it not been for the gleaming model of the New Tokaido Line.

*Prototypes for speed, 1975–1992. In **Britain** (above), the prototype turbine-powered APT-E and the prototype diesel-electric High Speed Train meet at Swindon during the former's high-speed trials on the Western Region's Paddington-Swindon main line, August 1975. (British Rail) (Below) **Japan**, and the prototype Series 300 Shinkansen electric train-set of the 1990s.*

*Above left: **Germany**. A locomotive-hauled Inter-City train headed by a DB Class `120' Bo-Bo on the Hannover-Würzburg new 'NBS' line near Burgsinn. (Deutsche Bundesbahn)*

Left: DB's 'InterCity Experimental' unit wings over the Main Valley viaduct near Gemünden, on the Hannover-Würzburg new line, at 300 kmph (187.5 mph) on a day of press demonstrations in November 1986. (G.Freeman Allen)

Below left: An IC-Express train-set, which began public service in June 1991. (Deutsche Bundesbahn)

*Above: **Italy**. Nose-ends of the prototype FS Class `ETR401' Pendolino of the late 1970s (nearest the camera) and the Rome-Milan `ETR450' of the late 1980s compared. (FS)*

Below: FS's 300 kmph prototype ETRX500 power car and two trailers under test in 1990, having reached a new Italian speed record of 316 kmph the previous year. (FS)

*Left: **France**. The first TGV scheme, TGV-Paris Sudest, proposed in 1969, near St Laurent d'Andenay, demonstrating the switchback character of the route, which kept earthworks to a minimum and obviated the need for tunnels altogether. (SNCF.CAV)*

Below: One of the world's first high-speed mail trains on the TGV-PSE. Introduced in 1984, the near-windowless cars carry the French Post Office's (PTT) brilliant yellow livery. (SNCF.CAV)

Above: A TGV-Atlantique (TGV-A) train-set crosses the Loire at Montlouis. (SNCF.CAV)

Right: The supreme moment of speed: TGV-A unit 325 frozen by the camera as it hits 515.3 kmph (320.26 mph) on 18 May 1990. (SNCF.CAV)

United States. Amtrak's Swedish-designed but US-built `AEM-7' electric locomotive introduced specifically for high-speed passenger haulage of 'Metroliners' between New York and Washington. (Amtrak)

Canada. VIA Rail's disappointing LRC high-speed tilt-body train, which has never regularly operated at its full design speed of 125 mph.

Spain. *RENFE's Class `269-200' Bo-Bo rebuilt for high-speed research.*

Switzerland. *SBB's new 1990s breed of rolling-stock is designed for 200 kmph-plus; this is one of the new Class `460' Bo-Bos.*

*Above: **Australia**. A New South Wales XPT train-set, to a design derived from British Rail's HST, one of which set a new Australian rail speed record in 1981, albeit only 183 kmph (113.7 mph).*

*Below: **Korea**. One of Korean National Railroad's diesel-hydraulic train-sets that advanced Seoul-Pusan speed to 150 kmph over existing tracks in the late 1980s. But, as in Australia, new electrified railway schemes are planned for much higher speeds in the 1990s. . .*

*Bottom: The way ahead? MLU 002, the full-size single-car vehicle engaged in **Japan**'s MagLev research in the late 1980s, which has reached 250 mph.*

6
Britain's InterCity model for Europe

The Second World War left Britain's railways in a deplorably run-down condition. Fixed structures had had no more than the minimum maintenance essential to keep them usable. Replacements were limited to renewal of equipment crucial to the war effort. But came peace and the railways were still workable. Successive Governments, Conservative as well as Labour, therefore decided that they had very low priority in the industrial queue for scarce raw materials and capital investment.

So, by 1951 only two of the 50 most important inter-city rail routes in Britain had had their services restored even to 1939 speed levels, let alone improved. Worse still, only seven major towns and cities — Bradford, York, Newcastle, Edinburgh, Glasgow (by the East Coast Route from London King's Cross, not the primary West Coast Route from London Euston), Portsmouth and Cardiff — had faster trains from London than before the First World War. Two of the country's most important cities, Birmingham and Sheffield, had not merely no faster trains from the capital than in 1939, but a markedly slower service overall than just before the First World War.

Mind you, one must not overestimate the difference an earlier opportunity for British Railways to modernize might have made to this stark picture. Up to 1955 such money and resources as the railways had been permitted to spend on replacing their most antiquated steam engines had gone on yet more steam power, and the pilot main-line dieselization scheme drafted by at least two of the pre-nationalization 'Big Four' was discarded by the new management of the nationalized British Railways. Sir Nigel Gresley's triumph over the German diesel competition before the war was not all gain. Without it, British Railways might have built up a methodical step-by-step experience of diesel traction which would have greatly accelerated their post-war recovery.

Hope of an ultimate speed revival in Britain was fortified by the 1955 Modernisation Plan's espousal of electrification for both East and West Coast main lines out of London, the former as far as the West Riding of Yorkshire and York itself, the latter as far as Birmingham, Liverpool and Manchester. It was soon obvious, though, that industrial resources would only run to one scheme at a time. Choice fell on the Euston-Birmingham/Liverpool and Manchester — and also on the 25kV 50Hz ac method, in a reversal of previous British policy motivated by the now patent success of French pioneering in high-voltage ac traction. But the costs of the electrification were soon vastly outrunning estimates. The then Minister of Transport, no champion of railways at any time, halted the scheme after its first provincial stages had been completed, and the future of inter-city rail services in Britain looked bleak.

On other trunk routes British Railways' first main-line diesels, lumbering machines with a very unimpressive power/weight ratio, were incapable of much improvement on steam's end-to-end schedules. Consequently the railways were steadily losing traffic to the roads. There were those in British Railways who counselled that this be accepted gracefully as the inevitable beginning of the end of the inter-city passenger train. In the late 1950s the rot had set in across the Atlantic; by 1970, it was confidently predicted, the North American passenger train would be a dodo — and nothing, some said, would stop the British inter-city train going the same way within a decade.

Not so, insisted the management of one sector of British Railways in particular. Even with steam, the Eastern Region had proved the commercial potential of a daylong regular-interval service of comparatively lightweight trains, timed as nearly as possible

to a standard schedule and accelerated to the limit of the locomotives' endurance and economy. Now the Eastern Region was determined to lay its hands on power that would make this sort of inter-city service practicable at the 75 mph (120 kmph) end-to-end averages research showed would keep it fully competitive with road travel over the country's new motorways. If the Eastern couldn't have electrification, then British industry had just unveiled a diesel prototype which looked the next best thing.

That was the English Electric 3,300 hp 'Deltic' diesel-electric. The locomotive was so called because it was built around two of the opposed-piston engines of triangular cross-section, resembling an inverted Greek letter *delta*, which English Electric's subsidiary Napier had developed to meet a British Admiralty specification for a high-powered diesel engine to drive fast naval patrol boats. A prototype 'Deltic', the most powerful single-unit diesel on the world's railways

English Electric's 3,300hp 'Deltic' diesel-electric Co-Co prototype, vividly liveried in light blue with yellow patterning, pulls into Preston during its early trials on BR's Euston-Carlisle main line in the late 1950s.

Deltic' in a hurry: one of the production series of 22 3,300hp units for BR's East Coast main line, No 55 009 Alycidon, *speeds from Edinburgh to London King's Cross.* (Peter J. Robinson)

at the time, had demonstrated some phe-nomenal tractive powers on test with British Railways in the summer of 1956; and it could be happily geared for a maximum speed of

105 mph (169 kmph). The Eastern pressed for and in 1958 won a production series of 22 to take over the principal inter-city ser-vices between London King's Cross and the

Another East Coast route `Deltic', No 55 006* The Fife and Forfar Yeomanry, *hums along the North Sea coastline north of Berwick with the down `Flying Scotsman' in 1977. (J.H. Cooper-Smith)

West Riding, the North-East and Edinburgh.

The inauguration of the first fully-'Deltic'-powered East Coast Route timetable in the summer of 1962 was the post-war turning point in British Railways' inter-city passenger services. It wasn't just the startling acceleration, with the 'Flying Scotsman's' London-Edinburgh journey time slashed overnight by an hour, to come down to 6 hours for the 392.7 miles (631.9 km), and the opening up of stretches of the route to regular 100 mph (160 kmph) maximum speeds. Equally significant was the dexterous timetabling and rostering of both 'Deltic' locomotives and train-sets, to extract the maximum possible daily mileage from the equipment and offer with strictly limited resources an intensive and fast regular-interval service from London to all the major industrial centres on the East Coast Route.

Even so, the potential of the 'Deltics' was not fully realized. In tightly-knit Britain, sizeable towns and cities almost jostle each other by comparison with the distances that separate them in, say, central France. Many of them in Britain are the site of railway junctions, which generally were not laid out with a far-seeing eye to the speed of through traffic. Furthermore, no British main line was built free of speed-restraining curvature in its open stretches to anything like the extent, for example, of France's main line from Paris to the south-west. Consequently the 'Deltics' were wasting far too much of their considerable energy working up to top speed for short spells, then having to slow to 20 mph (32 kmph) to negotiate the serpentine layout at Peterborough or to 30 mph (48 kmph) for the sharp bend at Durham (to quote two notorious examples); after which they would be expensively opened up to regain 100 mph (160 kmph) as quickly as possible, only to be slowed yet again perhaps 20 miles further on: and so on.

Again the Eastern Region went to bat. At comparatively modest cost compared with electrification, an extensive programme of track and signalling improvements costing over £60 million was put in hand on the East Coast Route. Tracks were relaid; junction layouts simplified; two-track bottlenecks widened; some of the worst curves ironed out (two of the most awkward, at Peterborough, were treated by rebuilding the whole station); level crossings eliminated; and multiple-aspect colour light signalling controlled from a few strategic centres installed in place of outdated, manually-operated semaphores, to establish much better traffic control and extend braking distances. At the end of the day the route had been made fit for 100 mph (161 kmph) the whole way from London King's Cross to Doncaster, 156 miles (251 km), and for 85 (136.8) of the 112 miles (180 km) on to Newcastle. A good deal of the track was in fact fettled up for 125 mph (201 kmph), with an eye to the coming High Speed Train era to be described later in this chapter.

So by 1976 the East Coast Route timetable could show a fastest London-Edinburgh time of 5 hours 27 minutes by the 'Flying Scotsman', representing an end-to-end average speed of 72.1 mph (116 kmph) for the 392.7 miles (631.9 km), inclusive of an intermediate stop at Newcastle. Over shorter distances there were many timings at 75 mph (120 kmph) or better start to stop, up to a best of 80.8 mph (130 kmph) for the 204.7 miles (329.4 km) between Darlington and the outer London railhead at Stevenage.

The travails of the West Coast Main Line electrification ended eventually. A full electric service was opened from Liverpool and Manchester to Euston in the spring of 1966, and Birmingham and the West Midlands were brought into the network a year later. Timetables were transformed, not only in terms of pace, but also by their remoulding on a basis or intensive fixed-interval frequency. The new service was launched under the brand-name of InterCity, which would soon become the European trademark for rail service of the same pattern. Electric traction's superior accelerative power, of course, allowed considerably more West Coast mileage to be run at the permitted maximum of 100 mph (160 kmph) than on the East Coast Route, so that the newly electrified railway became immediately the fastest in the country.

The commercial impact of that mid-1960s inauguration of revolutionized East Coast and West Coast Main Line timetables con-

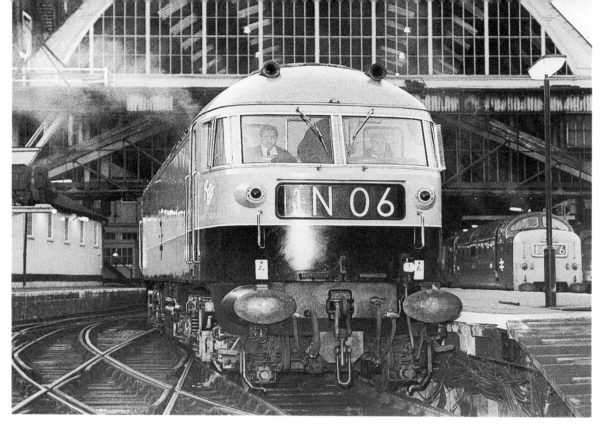

The 4,000hp Hawker Siddeley 'Kestrel' prototype powered by a single Sulzer V16 engine, was designed in the late 1960s for 125 mph (200 kmph) operation, but British Rail found it too heavy on the axles for such pace. It was never run in Britain at that speed and was eventually sold to Russia. Here it heads the 7.55 Newcastle train out of London King's Cross in October 1969.

founded the sceptics in the corridors of British power as well as within British Railways management. In 1965 British Railways, then under its Beeching regime, had issued a policy document which accepted the eventual eclipse of the inter-city passenger train. But freight tonnage drained steadily away, whereas passengers flocked on to the speeded-up and intensified inter-city services. By the end of the 1960s the West Coast electric services had doubled passenger carryings between London and the North-West. Between London and Birmingham public response was such that service frequency was soon stepped up to half-hourly each way throughout the day.

The Government as well as British Railways chiefs turned about, the latter smartly, the former with rather less alacrity. First fruit of the changed attitudes was authorization to extend the electrification beyond Weaver Junction (diverging point of the Liverpool route north of Crewe) to Glasgow, a project over which the Government had dismally dragged its feet for years.

British Railways' passenger management now badgered the mechanical and civil engineers to deliver still higher speed. The latter had no ready-wrapped answer.

It was not the traditional railway engineers who came up with a seemingly triumphant solution to the problems of lifting pace over BR's historic infrastructure without punishing track or discomforting passengers, but the covey of brains British Railways had recruited from a contracting aerospace industry to found its Derby research and development centre in 1962. This centre was established at a time when British Railways' coach riding was under withering fire for its proneness to 'hunting', or vicious lateral oscillation, at speed, often when vehicles were almost fresh from overhaul. One of the new team's first remits, therefore, was to study the behaviour of flanged wheel on steel rail.

After 18 months of exhaustive research

the Derby team evolved a concept which, it was claimed, would achieve the commercial speed targets without sacrifice of travellers' comfort or extravagant energy consumption on existing track. The outline was unveiled in 1967 as Britain's 155 mph (250 kmph) Advanced Passenger Train, or APT. The APT, they said, would be no more expensive to run than an orthodox locomotive-hauled train: but it would be capable of a 50 per cent higher speed, would be able to take curvature 4 per cent faster, and all without alteration of existing track or modification of the existing signalling system's braking distances. Far from just avoiding any aggravation of speed wear and tear on track and vehicles, it would actually reduce the problems.

The heart of the Derby concept was a suspension system that positively 'steered' the wheels into and through curves, eliminating any juddering contact between flanges and railhead. At the same time an electro-hydraulic servo system on each vehicle would counteract the centrifugal force effect on passengers by a smoothly graduated inward tilt of the coach body. The tilt movement would be automatic, initiated and controlled by sensors continuously measuring the lateral accelerations experienced in the passenger area; and each vehicle would tilt independently of its neighbours, so that throughout the train there would be ideal reaction to a curve's configuration from its start to its finish.

It is not so much safety as passenger comfort which demands this extra artificially-stimulated lean into a curve. For a conventional train the derailment speed on a curve is normally well above the ordained limit, which is set at the mark beyond which the centrifugal force effect on passengers will be uncomfortable — or, in railway jargon, there is 'cant deficiency'. This latter limit can always be raised by canting the track more sharply inward. But that is only sensible if at the same time you can raise the minimum speed of any trains using the route. Too high a degree of cant in relation to the slowest-moving trains will result in excessive wear on the inner rail of the curve. Thus the degree of a curve's cant, or superelevation, is always a compromise between the ideals for the fastest and slowest trains on the route. Needless to say, if you build new railways for exclusive use by standard high-speed passenger train-sets, as the French and Japanese have done, higher curving speed becomes possible without resort to body-tilting. The cant degree can then be ideally

A model of one of the first APT concepts. (British Rail)

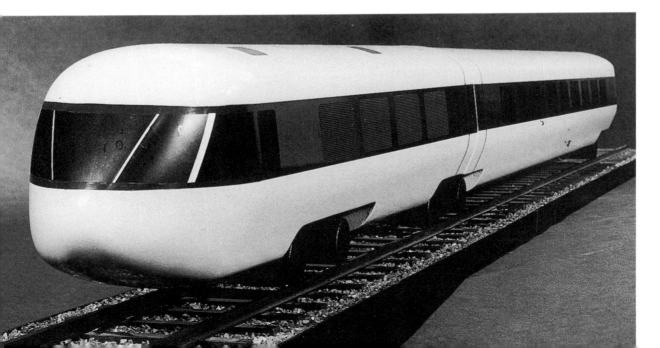

related to the characteristics of one type of train-set and one only.

Naturally, the greater the degree of artificial tilt that the actuating mechanism can apply to a coach body, the higher the amount of cant deficiency that can be offset and the faster a tilt-body vehicle can take a curve than one without. But several other factors restrict permissible tilt. For example, a body cannot tilt so far that it will infringe clearances with fixed structures or non-tilting vehicles on an adjoining track (even a modest degree of tilt dictates that carbody sides be tapered inward from their waist upward to reduce overhang when curving). Another constraint is the sick-making effect on passengers of over-generous body rolling, particularly through a reverse curve.

At the time that the wraps were taken off the original APT designs, gas turbine traction using aerospace's new compact, low fuel-cost engines looked the white hope of economical high-speed trains. The APT was to be powered by a single Rolls-Royce Dart turbine of 1,500 hp. As for the promise that it could be braked from its intended top speed of 155 mph (250 kmph) within existing signalling distances, that would be ensured by a multiple-disc system of aircraft type.

Give us the money and the tools and APTs can be in squadron high-speed service by the end of 1972, promised a confident British Railways Board. That, alas, was just the first of many pious hopes to be set at naught by a combination of divided opinion within both Government and British Railways (sharply at odds in the latter case); technical second and countless subsequent thoughts; pinched funding; flawed project management; and plain over-optimism. The contrast between the coherent, step-by-step advance to higher speed just across the English Channel and the collapse of BR's attempted 'great leap ahead' into one pitfall after another was painful.

For a start, the Government was not anxious to provide a cash-hungry British Railways with the research and development funds. It was uncertain at that stage whether tracked hovercraft, or hovertrains, were not a better investment, particularly since perfection of the British-developed linear electric motor as potential tractive power. Not until 1973 did the Government finally acknowledge the nonsense of investing vast sums in a totally new and far from proven inter-city passenger system.

Within British Railways the born-and-bred railway engineers scorned the APT as near science-fiction fantasy. They had little time

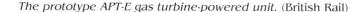

The prototype APT-E gas turbine-powered unit. (British Rail)

for the young upstarts from aerospace who had not come up the hard way of coaxing dirty steam-age machinery into good running order. To stake the inter-city train's future on cramming so much practically untried and innovative technology into one package was madness. British Railways, they urged, must first allow conventional engineering another chance.

But now Derby's parvenus found kindred spirits among newly-appointed scientific advisers in Government. The latter were persuaded that APT technology was not merely the sole hope of salvation for British Railways' inter-city traffic, but also an export world-beater. So, in 1968, the Government stumped up half the projected research and development cost. Not only that, it actively discouraged any further investment in conventional inter-city passenger equipment, such was its new-found faith in APT. At last, in the summer of 1969, the first orders were placed for prototype APT hardware.

By then, more than a year had already been spent waiting for Government endorsement. Just as well, perhaps, for the APT designers were still changing their minds. They had veered from two-axle to bogie running gear and back again; become disaffected with the Dart and attracted to a new range of inexpensive 350-500 hp turbines which motor manufacturers Leyland were developing for heavy road freight vehicles; and adopted a hydrokinetic device as the main braking system. Briefly, a hydrokinetic brake achieves its effect by opposing to movement the pressure of a water-glycol fluid; the energy thus created is converted into heat that is dissipated to the atmosphere.

Meanwhile, a team of BR's traditional engineers were beavering away at a step-up of conventional technology. As the 1960s closed they hoisted disconsolate passenger managers' spirits with the offer of an ability to produce within two years a prototype train capable of sustained 125 mph (200 kmph) on existing trunk routes. So in August 1970, with three years gone by and still no trace of APT hardware, the BR Board endorsed a High Speed Diesel Train (HST) programme. This was to prove the most commercially reward-

ing investment taken on BR since nationalization.

The HST would be a double-ended diesel train-set in which seven or eight air-conditioned cars of a new 75-foot-long (23 m) design would be enclosed by two power cars each equipped with a 12-cylinder Paxman Valenta 2,250 hp engine driving through an electric alternator transmission. Two years later, as promised, a prototype was ready for track testing, in the course of which it was propelled up to a new world speed record for diesel traction of 143 mph (230 kmph) over near-level track between Darlington and York on 11 June 1973.

The first routes to be allocated production HSTs were those of the Western Region between London's Paddington and Bristol/South Wales. For a number of reasons, mainly beyond the control of British Railways management, the production programme lagged well behind schedule and it was not until the spring of 1977 that the full planned service could be launched, under the brandname of 'InterCity 125'. That full service took British Railways at a bound up to second place in the world rail speed table, yielding best only to the Japanese Shinkansen for combined speed and frequency. And the overall coast of designing and building all the train-sets, and of the track and signalling work necessary to maximize their speed potential, had been slightly less than the final APT research and development bill was to total.

As on the East Coast Route of British Railways, a great deal of the extra speed was won by ironing out curves and relaying junctions in the course of a thoroughgoing reconstruction of the track from the foundations up to ensure durable quality under intensive 125 mph (200 kmph) running. The outcome was that HSTs humming out of Paddington could make almost immediate use of their ability to reach 125 mph within $5^1/2$ minutes of a standing start on level track. They could hold that speed for 72 miles (116 km) continuously to Swindon, except for an 80 mph (129 kmph) check through Reading. On the Bristol route, curvature ruled out further top speed, but South Wales-bound HSTs had about 25 more miles (40 km) in which they

British Rail's prototype HST diesel train, No 252 001, approaches Hatfield on the East Coast main line.

could make 125 mph before diving into the Severn Tunnel. Little modification of the route's multiple-aspect colour light signalling was required, since it was a cardinal point of the HST specification that deceleration from 125 mph to a dead stand must be unfailingly possible within the existing minimum braking distance of 6,600 feet (2,164 m).

An HST on the Western Region main line from Paddington to Devon and Cornwall in May 1977.
(Stephen Miles)

In its initial two-power-car, seven-trailer version (an eighth trailer was subsequently added to most sets) the HST had a power/weight ratio of 11.8 hp/tonne. Advanced lightweight construction technology, including use of aluminium alloy for components like the fuel tanks, trimmed the weight of each power car to 70 tonnes. Thus HST axle-loading, a crucial consideration in limiting high-speed wear and tear on track and train, was little more than 17 tonnes — a commendable achievement in a diesel power unit.

The HSTs proved fully capable of 100 mph (160 kmph) start-to-stop timings on the Western Region. The official working timetables in the 1970s required several trains to eat up the 41.3 miles (66.5 km) from Swindon to Reading at a start-to-stop average of 103.3 mph (166 kmph), though the public timetables showed a slightly easier allowance. Every day over 70 trains were timed start-to-stop at an average of 90 mph (145 kmph) or more.

A second squadron of HSTs was assigned to the East Coast main line and its King's Cross-Newcastle-Edinburgh and King's Cross-West Riding services in 1978. Initially the HSTs accelerated the `Flying Scotsman' to a non-stop timing of $3^{1}/_{2}$ minutes over 3 hours between London and the train's first stop at Newcastle, representing a start-to-stop average of 87.7 mph (141 kmph). Even this first-stage HST timetable, in which the inaugural batch of East Coast train-sets had to be found paths amongst a preponderance of slower, locomotive-hauled services, showed a start-to-stop timing as fast as 100.9 mph (162.3 kmph) over the 48.75 miles (78.4 km) from Stevenage to Peterborough by the 08.00 King's Cross-Edinburgh.

So what, meantime, of the Advanced Passenger Train?

Eventually a turbine-powered prototype emerged simultaneously with the prototype HST. In outline the articulated four-car unit was a vastly different animal from the models and sketches published at the announcement of the project (and which had subsequently changed shape almost from year to year). Practically all its evaluation was done in private, the road tests on a specially

In 1978 the HSTs made their regular service debut on the London King's Cross-Newcastle-Edinburgh service. This shot is of a set storming through Hitchin in July 1980 and forming the `Flying Scotsman'.
(J.G. Glover)

prepared stretch of otherwise disused track in the Midlands. Whereas the French were proudly broadcasting the latest speed exploits of their TGV Paris-Sudest prototype train, TGV001, and buttonholing every visiting VIP for a high-speed jaunt in the unit, British Railways treated their prototype, known as APT-E, like a secret weapon. Not until 1975 were its doings declassified.

In August that year APT-E was suddenly brought front of stage for a series of Sunday speed tests on the Western Region's Paddington-Bristol main line, and whipped up to 151 mph (243 kmph) over a 5-mile stretch between Reading and Swindon. Two months later APT-E's competence over typically unregenerated British main line was proved by setting it at the Midland route from London's St Pancras to Leicester. Here conventional trains were at the time limited to 90 mph (145 kmph) throughout. Held at 125 mph (200 kmph) most of the way, but unleashed to 135 mph (217 kmph) between Luton and Bedford, APT-E sailed through the 99 miles (159 km) in 58 minutes at a start-to-stop average of 102.4 mph (165 kmph). People on the train were particularly impressed with the barely perceptible 75 mph (120 kmph) negotiation of a curve at Market Harborough which enforced 50 mph (80 kmph) on all conventional trains.

Towards the end of 1974 the Government authorised construction of three more APTs, termed pre-production prototypes and designated APT-P. Unlike the APT-E, they were to be 25kV ac electric. For one thing, there was no longer any practical power plant in view for a non-electric APT. The Leyland gas turbine's early promise had faded even before the 1973 oil crisis wiped out turbine traction's economic advantage, and no high-power diesel engine on the market looked readily adaptable to the APT's configuration. But in addition, British Railways was beginning to appreciate the speed gains attainable on a number of key inter-city routes by the partnership of HSTs and not impossibly expensive track works. The sensible route on which to blood the APT was therefore the electrified West Coast main line between London's Euston and Scotland. And there the APT-Ps were to take on their first passengers. However, though they had been tested up to their design speed of 150 mph (241.4 kmph) on the open line, in public service they were to be limited to 125 mph (200 kmph).

Why the caution? First, while you can design a train to work at up to 150 mph (241.4 kmph) within the limits and distances of existing lineside signalling — and APT-E's hydrokinetic brake fulfilled that specification during its Western Region road tests — you can't bulldoze reluctant railwaymen into driving it without the benefit of more sophisticated aids to judgement. British Railways came to realize that they could not introduce regular operation at speeds in excess of 125 mph without some form of continuous cab signalling. British Railways could not then cope financially with the costs of such a system's widespread application.

The APT-P format comprised two articulated sets of six trailers, each with a driving cab at one end, enclosing two cabless power cars in the centre of the unit. This esoteric arrangement avoided adding the weight of orthodox buffers and drawgear to the axle loading of the power car and allowed both of them to take current from one pantograph: test running at high speed proved the superior efficiency of current collection through the one pantograph. But the reverse of the coin was lack of room alongside the power plant for more than a pencil-slim emergency walkway to connect the two articulated trailer units on either side of the power cars. Passengers could not roam freely between the two sets of passenger accommodation; and that meant each must have its own catering. Before commitment to fleet production, the intention was to execute a major redesign of the APT as an end-cabbed-power and ten-trailer unit.

The aircraft-style, semi-monocoque constructional techniques applied to APT-E were discarded as too expensive for mass production, and each trailer car body was now welded up from aluminium extrusions running the full vehicle length. Combined with weight-saving through articulation and in many components, notably a special low-energy air-conditioning plant, this brought the APT-P trailer out at only 23 tonnes, less than three-quarters of the weight of a Mk III coach, but with near-identical seating capacity.

Although steel-built, a 4,000 hp APT-P power car turned the scales at only 69 tonnes. Like the rest of the set, it had an automatically tilting body, but the pantograph had to be mounted on an anti-tilt device that stabilized it under the overhead current wire whatever the posture of the power car body. The layout of the drive from the power plant to the road wheels was novel at that period of time. The higher the speed in mind, the lower the unsprung mass of a vehicle needs to be to contain track wear and tear, above all the impact on rail joints and crossing components. On APT-P the unsprung mass had to be reduced well below that of an HST, which debarred the hitherto customary bogie-mounting of the traction motors. The motors were therefore in the car body in a mounting that incorporated the hydrokinetic brake; from the brake a transfer gearbox took the drive to a cardan

shaft that led to a final drive gearbox mounted on the bogie frame, whence there was quill drive to the road wheels. The thyristor-controlled traction motors, incidentally, were Swedish-built by ASEA, the firm that first perfected the thyristor control system; nevertheless, the decision to import traction gear for such a front-runner in the British rail industry's export effort raised many a pained eyebrow.

After about a year's bedding down in existing timetable paths, the prototype APT-Ps were advertised to start public service in 1980 and open up 100 mph (160 kmph) average journeying between London and Glasgow on a 4 hours 10 minutes timing for the 401.5 miles (646 km), inclusive of a single intermediate stop at Preston. That would represent an end-to-end average of 96.4 mph (155 kmph).

By the end of 1979 exhaustive work by a commissioning team seemed to have mastered all the APT-P's early frailties on the track. Not only were all the innovative systems

A full APT-P set of two central power cars and 12 trailers leans to the curves of Beattock bank, north of Carlisle. (British Rail)

Close-up of an APT-P trailer articulating bogie. (British Rail)

enthusiastically reported 'go' by their minders, but in December the set under supervision was spurred up to a new British speed record. On 13 December, returning to its Glasgow depot base, the unit hit 156.6 mph (252 kmph) six miles south of Beattock.

A 2nd class saloon interior of the APT-P. (G.Freeman Allen)

Exactly a week later, in the same area, the rate was edged up to a peak reported officially at the time as 160 mph, though men on board subsequently insisted that their instruments had clocked 162.2 mph (261 kmph).

However, 1980 soon found the trio of APT-Ps plagued by more malfunctions and inadequate component performance that demanded redesign. It was December 1981 before BR had the confidence to commit any of them to public service. And then the debut was a fiasco, exultantly publicized by the TV newsreels with footage of stricken APT-Ps in tow from Class '47' diesels. Only partly culpable was the unlucky coincidence of a savagely Arctic spell of weather, to which the trains' more sensitive apparatus was especially vulnerable. Within weeks the exercise was abandoned and the APT-Ps were sidetracked for another period of redesign.

Three more years elapsed during which the temperamental body-tilting system in particular was substantially modified. At last, in August 1984, all APT-P systems were proven reliable enough for the units to be applied to West Coast main line relief services. And in December of that year the potential of the technology was triumphantly shown off when

one APT-P hurried a press party from Euston to Glasgow in flawless comfort in 7 minutes under 4 hours at an end-to-end average speed of 105 mph (168.9 kmph), but nowhere exceeding 130 mph (209.2 kmph). By then, though, BR's InterCity management, under mounting pressure to become financially self-supporting, had decided that its next generation of rolling-stock should eschew the costs and complexities of lightweight, body-tilting vehicles. Early in 1985 the curtain was rung down on the APT project.

The subsequent conception by Fiat in Italy and ABB in Sweden of active body-tilting systems that are successful not only on their home railways but in export applications, makes the APT story still more dispiriting. Root cause of the humiliation was the project's lack of fully committed hands-on management at the higher levels. That was the conclusion of consultants called in by a red-faced BR Board after the ignominious attempt at revenue-earning service in the 1981 winter. Their recommendations led to radical changes in the management system applied to design and construction of Inter-City's ensuing development, the Class '91' and Mk IV coach sets for an electrified East

The APT-P unit of a single power car and six trailers which reached 162.2 mph (261 kmph) in December 1979. (British Rail)

Coast main line.

The effort to make APT-P operationally fool-proof was frustratingly slow and faltering because the small team entrusted with the project was embedded in the old-school Mechanical & Electrical Engineering organization. There it was hemmed in by sceptics at best, but as the lowest of their priorities. Only in the topmost M&EE echelon did the APT have credibility — but until near the death, not even there a desk-thumping champion.

The many unprecedented features of the concept, particularly the small-wheel articulating bogies and the hydrokinetic brake, demanded not only more dedicated development work but also meticulous attention in manufacture and maintenance. That way the embarrassments of chronically dragging tread brakes, of gearbox lubrication traumas, of hydrokinetic brake bearing failures that were potentially hazardous, and not least of a misassembly that led to a wheelset collapsing and derailing an APT-P at 125 mph (200 km/h) near Oxenholme in April 1980, would likely have been avoided. Finally, there was the inadequate funding that had the APT-Ps essay public service without the duplicated means of conveying activation signals from curve sensors on one coach to the body-tilting mechanism on the next vehicle in rear. For lack of that standby feature tilt failures became depressingly frequent.

The collapse of the APT project left the electrified West Coast main line pace stagnant until the 1990s. Throughout the 1970s and for most of the 1980s the standard-bearers of BR InterCity speed had to be the diesel-powered HSTs of the East Coast and Western Region. Without them, and the resilience with which they met the demands of an InterCity service without European superior for its combination of speed, frequency and distance over historic infrastructure, BR's InterCity would never have secured its future by meeting a Government target of full financial self-sufficiency in 1988-89.

No diesel-powered equipment anywhere in the world has been submitted to such punishing duty as the HSTs. The traffic growth they stimulated (with a backing of adept mar-keting) drove InterCity to contrive ever more intensive and ingeniously woven HST work diagrams.

Pressures were aggravated by the Department of Transport, which refused to sanction construction of the full number of HST units that the East Coast Route felt essential to meet demand. Charge more, the civil servants countered, and that would end the overcrowding.

It is not just that HSTs have been taxed with rosters that spanned over 1,000 miles per 24 hours and kept them at work for 15 and more hours of the 24. Even on limited-stop services, HSTs were forced by the characteristics and mixed traffic of BR trunk routes into frequent cycles of deceleration and full-power acceleration that subjected their engines to exceptional stress. By the early 1980s BR's timetables required HSTs to average 90 mph (144.8 kmph) start to stop, day in and day out, over a total 14,633 miles (23,644 km). But this aggregate was derived from 210 station-to-station timings. Thus the mean distance of each sprint was only 69.7 miles (112.1 km).

The strains became fiercer, on the Western in particular, because HST speed encouraged an outward drift of the London dormitory belt. In conjunction with a management wish to standardize main-line passenger service on the HSTs, this required that in the peak hours particularly the HSTs cover more stops. By the 1980s London office-workers from Reading, Didcot and Swindon had the world's fastest commuter train service, though as the decade closed they were losing that distinction to the Japanese Tokaido Shinkansen, as described in the preceding chapter.

There is no room here to detail the evolution of HST 'InterCity 125' services on the East Coast and Western, and the later introduction of the units to the Midland line out of London St Pancras and the North-East/South-West cross-country route. It must suffice to record that in the fading 1980s, on the eve of the route's electrification, East Coast HSTs were providing half-hourly service almost daylong between London and Edinburgh, as well as to and from some cities further south; and that the fastest schedule between

London and the Scottish capital had been brought down to 4 hours 23 minutes, including stops at York and Newcastle, which represented an end-to-end average of a whisker under 90 mph (144.8 kmph) for the 392.8 miles (632 km). The Western's intensive `InterCity 125' operation showed 15 trains daily scheduled to average over 100 mph (160 kmph) start to stop over parts of their itinerary, in 13 instances over just 41.3 miles (66.5 km) of Brunel's superb infrastructure between calls at Swindon and Reading.

The world record for average journey speed with diesel traction was progressively raised in staged HST runs during the 1970s and 1980s. With France's TGV not yet operational and only Japan's first Shinkansen to beat, the Western briefly held the world title for any form of power unit with an exploit of 10 April 1979. That day, with the line uncharacteristically innocent of any temporary speed restriction, an ordinary service HST was spurred from Paddington to Chippenham, 93.9 miles (151.2 km), in 50 min 32 sec at a start-to-stop average of 111.5 mph (179.6 kmph), but without exceeding 126 mph. This was bettered on 30 August 1984

when an HST reduced to five trailers reeled in the 117.5 miles (189.2 km) from Paddington to Bristol via Badminton in 62 min 33 sec, averaging 112.7 mph (181.5 kmph). That nudged up the world record for diesel traction. But by 1984 France's electric TGVs were setting still higher marks.

The climactic HST performance was put on by the East Coast, on 27 September 1985, in a stunt to publicize the following week's launch of the `Tees-Tyne Pullman' service on the route's prime Newcastle-London HST working. For this epic, not only were the selected HST's trailers reduced to five, but the power cars had their speed governors cut out so that they could attain the 140 mph (226 kmph) for which there was special dispensation over parts of the route.

The HST actually hit 144 mph (232 kmph) on the descent of Stoke bank as it belted from Newcastle to King's Cross, 268.6 miles (432.5 km), in just under 2 hours 20 minutes. That rewrote the end-to-end journey speed record with diesel traction at 115.4 mph (185.8 kmph). On its return to Newcastle the HST added a postscript by equalling Gresley `Pacific' *Mallard's* world steam record

An HST on a Midland route Nottingham-London St Pancras service calls at Luton in 1988.
(John C. Baker)

of 126 mph (202.7 kmph) on Stoke bank — but this time going *up* the hill.

It remains to add that the peak speed recorded by an HST is 148 mph (238.1 kmph). That was notched up on the flat between Darlington and York on 1 November 1987, during Sunday tests of a Mk III trailer mounted on a Swiss SIG-built bogie of the type in mind for the next breed of InterCity car, the Mk IV.

A joint BR-Department of Transport study completed in 1982 made an irrefutable economic argument for rapid pursuit of further main-line electrification. The Thatcher Government accepted this conclusion in principle. But when it came down to hard cases, the bureaucrats played for time by tinkering with the financial criteria. Not until July 1984 did the BR Board winkle out of the Department of Transport approval to wire the entire East Coast main line from King's Cross to Leeds, and to Newcastle and Edinburgh. Target date for completion in full was the spring of 1991, with a flat 4-hour King's Cross-Edinburgh schedule one of the commercial objectives.

Just what the electrified East Coast Route's

traction would be was not clarified until 1985. The successful submission to the Department of Transport had been based on fleet use of the 125 mph Class '89' Co-Co prototype which Brush was then gestating. At the same time some opinion inclined to an electric version of the HST. So at the start of 1984 BR was minded to buy five electric HST-Es and evaluate them against the then forthcoming Class '89' heading a rake of Mk III cars.

The HST-E scheme was soon dropped. Not only would the cost of two HST power cars substantially exceed that of a locomotive per kW of power, but other locomotives would be needed for overnight sleeper and parcels trains, because the HST power cars would be effectively inseparable from their train-sets.

What became the Class '89's' powerful challenger as 1984 unfolded was the concept of an APT-P Bo-Bo car without tilt. This had been salvaged from the ashes of the APT project and nurtured under a brandname of 'InterCity 225' for resonance with the HSTs' 'InterCity 125' — a crafty switch from mph to kmph accounted for the stunning numerical difference. However, a target speed of

The Brush prototype Class '89' 4,350kW Co-Co heads an East Coast main line train near Abbots Ripton in 1988. (John C. Baker)

225 kmph, or 140 mph, would be unattainable in everyday public service until a route was equipped with an Automatic Train Protection (ATP) system providing a continuous in-cab signalling display and automatic control of deceleration in the face of adverse signals. This was a stipulation of the Department of Transport's Railway Inspectorate.

By the end of 1984 InterCity management had plumped for an `InterCity 225' Bo-Bo locomotive. But it took assiduous lobbying to convince the Department of Transport that state-of-the art technology had by now made a four-axle locomotive equally competent on high-speed and heavy-haul work — as the French, the Germans and others were proving beyond a peradventure — and thus a more economical choice than a Co-Co.

The case won, `InterCity 225' became the tag for East Coast electric train-set development in its entirety. The exercise was to be marked by some new departures for BR.

For the first time final design was left to the selected builders. BR would simply provide a detailed performance specification which the builders' own ideas must precisely fulfil. Next, BR's own manufacturing subsidiary, BREL, soon to be sold off to the private sector, was no longer automatic choice as contractor. The `InterCity 225' orders had to be open to international bidding.

In two respects, `InterCity 225' was to be a world front-runner. First, the electrified East Coast Route would run the fastest service anywhere operated push-pull, with the traction concentrated in a single vehicle at one end of the train-set and just a driving-cab-fitted trailer at the other. InterCity was now intent on applying this format to all its electrified routes. It would accelerate terminal turnrounds, thereby permitting the same intensity of train-set use as with a double-ended HST, but with the flexibility of independent locomotives; it would consequently reduce the number of locomotives needed.

Second, when the conditions for day-to-day running at 140 mph (225 kmph) had been met, and short of some as yet undisclosed development abroad, the East Coast route would operate the world's fastest train

`InterCity 225': a Class `91' Bo-Bo forges north from Peterborough with a King's Cross-Leeds train of Mk IV cars. (John C. Baker)

service on historic infrastructure — in other words, without benefit of a new route purpose-built for high speed. This would be achieved without recourse to body-tilting, partly by progressive realignment of the BR route's most speed-handicapping curves and junctions; and partly by the contribution of APT research and experience to the design of the new locomotives and coaches, so that they could curve at relatively high cant deficiencies without detriment either to track or to passenger comfort.

A pre-qualification process whittled the final bidders for the locomotive contract down to Brush, ASEA of Sweden, soon to merge with Brown Boveri as ABB, and GEC, likewise close to marriage of its rail activity with Alsthom's. The winner, early in 1986, was GEC, which rejected derivation from the APT-P power car design and worked up a new Class '91' Bo-Bo design from scratch.

Metro-Cammell, subsequently absorbed by the GEC-Alsthom alliance, secured the order for a new Mk IV breed of InterCity coach. This was to have a tapering body cross-section

suitable for automatic tilting should that technology one day be resurrected.

Both GEC and Metro-Cammell farmed out parts of their contracts. BREL was commissioned to assemble the Class '91'. Breda of Italy was employed by Metro-Cammell to manufacture some of the Mk IV bodyshells. And a controversial last-minute decision deprived an enraged BREL of a seemingly cut-and-dried order to supply Mk IV bogies in favour of the Swiss company, SIG. BREL, it was said, could not unequivocally guarantee that its proffered model would meet InterCity's ride performance specification within the deadline for vehicle delivery, whereas SIG could.

The first Class '91' was rolled out spot on contracted time in mid-February 1988. The comparatively short period allowed for completion of a new design and translation to hardware had counselled against adoption of the three-phase ac motor technology by now standardized in the latest French and German traction. But the '91's' new GEC separately-excited dc motors under thyristor

The other end of 'InterCity 225': a Leeds-London train of Mk IV cars fronted by a Driving Van Trailer (DVT), with a Class '91' Bo-Bo propelling. Photographed at Sandy. (John C. Baker)

converter control represented a major updating of dc practice. As to power, the Class '91's' continuous rating was 4,530kW, its peak output 4,700kW.

Delivery of new Mk IV cars with their purpose-built driving van trailers (DVT) was not concurrent with completion of the acceptance routines of the first Class '91s'. So the new electric traction's public service initiation in May 1989 was briefly as substitute for one power car of a diesel HST set, with the latter's other power car modified for control from the '91'. Discounting for the diesel engine's surrender of some power to the train's air-conditioning and to losses in transmission, such a hybrid train-set could call up at least 7,600 hp to shift a gross weight of around 430 tonnes, traction included.

That showed. The relatively high gearing of both the '91' and the HST power car restrained their initial acceleration from rest. Even so, the pair could whip their load from rest to 125 mph (200 kmph) within a fraction over 2.4 miles (3.9 km) of 1 in 200 downgrade on a restart from the outer London railhead of Stevenage.

Later that year, on 17 September, a Class '91' on its own was let off the leash on a Sunday programme of complete 'InterCity 225' equipment evaluation between Grantham and Peterborough. On the final run south down Stoke bank with a rake of five Mk IV cars and DVT, the '91' scythed through a deluge of rain to a peak of 161.7 mph (260.2 kmph). Returning from Peterborough it surged up to 145 mph (223.3 kmph) on the climb of Stoke bank. Needless to say, there was special dispensation for the day's substantial excess of the line's everyday speed limit. But InterCity was sanguinely forecasting that by 1993 all would be in place, including ATP, for the electrified East Coast to live up to its 'InterCity 225' branding.

With BR still to evaluate and make a choice of competing ATP systems in 1991, it became improbable that 'InterCity 225' would justify its title before 1994/95. But even within the East Coast Route's continuing ceiling of 200 kmph, the electric Class '91' would sharply accelerate schedules. After a preliminary speed-up in July 1991,

the following October saw London–Edinburgh journey times for two trains each way cut to a minute less than 4 hours. That represented an end-to-end average of 98.7 mph (158.8 kmph) for the whole distance of 393 miles (632.6 km), inclusive of two intermediate stops. A new record British start-to-stop average speed of 111.4 mph (179.3 kmph) was demanded of two trains from London to York.

Here and there on the West Coast Route maximum permissible pace had been inched up from 100 to 110 mph (160 to 177 kmph), and journey times had had a further modest shaving through improvements in track configuration and track maintenance. But West Coast Route speed had not significantly advanced since the 1970s. As a result, to cite two centres practically equidistant from London, York's fastest East Coast train from King's Cross was in 1990 taking 32 minutes less than Manchester's quickest West Coast train from Euston.

Abruptly, in June 1990, BR InterCity unwrapped proposals to invest £750 million to achieve 'InterCity 250' on the existing West Coast Route. A key objective was to slice off about a third of the 1990 rail journey time between Manchester and London, bringing it down to 2 hours, or even 1 hr 50 min, which would predicate an end-to-end average of 105 mph (168.9 kmph). At that speed — substantially faster, incidentally, than the London-Manchester timing proposed for the aborted APT — InterCity would again contend forcefully with air as well as motorway in the lucrative London/North-West England market.

Just how 'InterCity 250' was to be realized — and not least realized within the investment ceiling quoted — was unclear at the time of writing. Plausibility was first of all undermined by an admission that '250' was a promotional tag, a more felicitous step-up from 225 than, say, 240 or 245; a maximum speed of 250 kmph (155.4 mph) was not in itself an overriding objective. The top speed target would be determined economically, by what was required to secure, for an optimal return on investment, the journey times that would attract the most additional passengers. However, a route-long increase of line

BR West Coast main line InterCity in 1990: a 3,730kW Class `90' Bo-Bo in Scotland, heading a London Euston-Glasgow train of Mk III cars near Lamington. (John C. Baker)

speed beyond 125 mph at most would almost certainly postdate the introduction of `InterCity 250' rolling-stock, because it was inseparable from a 10-year programme of West Coast Route resignalling and Automatic Train Protection installation.

The shape of an `InterCity 250' train-set as envisaged when this was written, at the close of 1990, was a push-pull unit of a Class `93' locomotive and ten Mk V trailers, one of the latter a kitchen driving trailer (the Department of Transport barred conveyance of passengers in the lead vehicle of a propelled high-speed train). The `93' was seen as a development of the Class `91', but with a higher output — perhaps 5,500kW — because of the West Coast Route's gradients. The Mk V car would be longer than the Mk IV, 26 m as against 23 m. Provision of automatic body-tilting was thought unlikely, but not ruled out.

The original `InterCity 250' schedule set 1994 as delivery date for the first of the new

trains and 1995 as the target for the start of an accelerated West Coast service. But in late 1990 BR was forced to defer these deadlines by at least a year because its finances were eroded by the impact of rising inflation, punishing interest rates and deepening recession on its passenger businesses.

Were further postponement necessary, political events might require a redraft of the `InterCity 250' synopsis. Before formulating `InterCity 250', BR had studied but rejected as unremunerative the case for reactivating the trackbed of the abandoned Great Central main line as the core of a new 300 kmph (186.5 mph) West Coast exit from London as far as Nuneaton. But the platform on which the Labour Party would fight the country's next General Election, due by 1992, included a pledge to do just that, plus new infrastructure from Birmingham to Manchester, under a scheme to create a high-speed route reaching from the Channel Tunnel to Scotland.

7

From IC to ICE in Germany

Reparation of appalling damage was not the only Herculean task confronting the new West German railway system, Deutsche Bundesbahn, after the Second World War. Another was geographical reorientation. The pre-war Deutsche Reichsbahn had been rebuilt up to serve the mainly lateral traffic flows of a united Germany, but the post-war partition turned the natural commercial axis of West Germany north-to-south. That thrust the main weight of passenger and freight traffic on to lines which for much of their distance either lacked track capacity to handle it or were physically unsuited to high speed. In some cases the handicaps were combined.

Until the early 1960s the maximum speed limit anywhere on the Deutsche Bundesbahn (DB), or German Federal Railway, was 87.5 mph (140 kmph). Electrification had been pushed ahead rapidly after the war, however, and by 1960 many trains were being timed to the minimum that speed ceilings conceded. Over the speed-conductive Mannheim-Karlsruhe-Freiburg stretch of the trunk route to the Swiss border at Basle, for example, the timetable showed several start-to-stop bookings demanding averages of around 75 mph (120 kmph) by trains like the `Rheingold', `Helvetia', and the Hamburg-Basle `Komet'. This last was an improbable eight-car articulated diesel multiple unit composed entirely of sleeping accommodation

that was built in 1953 but did not survive long into the 1960s.

Whatever its place in the world inter-city speed table at this juncture, DB was unarguably ahead of all comers on comfort. In the late 1950s its new standard 86 ft 7 in (26.4 m) coach body on heavy Minden-Deutz bogies, very efficiently soundproofed though as yet not fully air-conditioned, set parameters of size and ride quality that were to be adopted by every major railway on the mainland of Europe.

Coupled with its advance in this area, DB was extending continuous welded rail more rapidly than any other European system at the time. Coaching technology and cwr in conjunction set a German Federal inter-city trip of the 1950s apart from any other European rail experience for serenity and silence of ride.

German Federal stepped up its first post-war 100 mph (160 kmph) running in May 1962. The standard-bearer was one of the most charismatic of the pre-war international luxury trains, the `Rheingold' from Holland through Germany to Switzerland and Italy, now reborn with the new coaching stock that was to become the standard pattern for all DB inter-city services until the early 1990s. Amongst its standard seating cars the `Rheingold' and its companion, the Dortmund-Munich `Rheinpfeil', each conveyed a pair of eye-catching special vehicles: a kitchen-diner

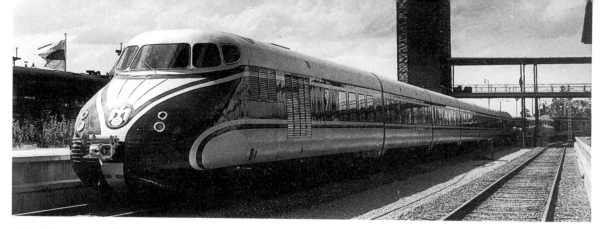

West Germany's first post-Second World War train-sets built new with 100 mph (160 kmph) capability were a pair of one-off streamlined diesel multiple units that attracted a lot of attention when they were exhibited at the Munich Transport Exhibition of 1953. One was a seven-car, 135-seater day-train unit articulated throughout over a single axle between cars, the other an eight-car all-sleeper unit — uniquely in diesel multiple unit history — with berths for just 40 in its 29 sleeping compartments; this set was also articulated, but on two-axle bogies. Both sets made extensive use of light alloy in their construction to achieve very light weight. After lengthy testing to eliminate teething problems, the day-train saw several years' service as the `Senator' between Frankfurt and Hamburg from 1954. The night train, which was owned by the West German sleeping and restaurant car company, DSG, and wore the DSG emblem on its nose (illustrated), operated as the `Komet' between Basle, Switzerland, and Hamburg. Each unit was eventually fitted with four 210 hp engines and transmissions were hydro-mechanical. The German Federal Railway's classification was `VT10.5'.

German Federal's first contribution to Western Europe's `Trans-Europ Express' rolling-stock pool was the Class `VT11.5', later `601', seven-car diesel-hydraulic multiple unit introduced in 1957. Speed did not quite match up to the impression enforced by the aggressive streamlining, for the units were limited to the then all-line maximum of 87.5 mph (140 kmph). (Deutsche Bundesbahn)

The southbound 'Rheingold' of the 1960s streams away from Cologne up the Rhine valley. Up front is 8,100 hp Co-Co electric No 103.126. (Deutsche Bundesbahn)

buffet, with a double-deck service area, kitchen upstairs and scullery below; and an observation car, bar at one end, train secretary's and train telephone room at the other, and in the centre a raised vista-dome saloon above a mails/baggage room. The vista-dome had been carefully shaped to shoe-horn through all the bridges and tunnels of the 'Rheingold's' normal route, but clearance problems could arise if emergency forced a

On the upper floor of the 'Rheingold' observation car. (Deutsche Bundesbahn)

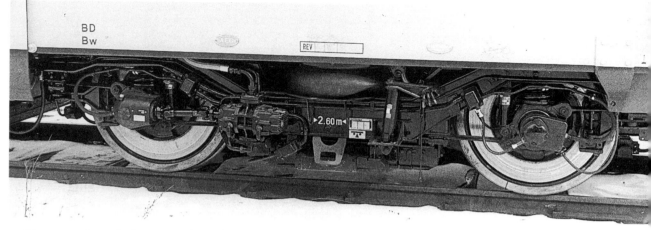

Close-up of an electromagnetic track brake, in this application on a German Federal Class 'ET403' electric multiple unit. The flat shoe can be seen, raised out of use, below the centre of the bogie frame. (Deutsche Bundesbahn)

detour. So in 1977 DB sold off the vista-dome cars to a German travel agency, which trimmed their contours slightly to fit the vehicles for wide-ranging use in the agency's holiday special trains. In 1990 the cars, now owned by a Swiss travel company, were still operational.

The equipment which allowed German Federal to push the 'Rheingold' up to 100 mph (160 kmph) over suitable track was the supplementary electromagnetic track brakes fitted to every vehicle. These safeguarded braking within existing signalling distances. As a result, the train could be given a timing as fast as 62 minutes for the 83.1 miles (127 km) from Freiburg to Karlsruhe, averaging 80.4 mph (129.4 kmph), and one almost as tight in the southbound direction.

Even before the new 'Rheingold' took the tracks, German Federal was set on speeds higher than 100 mph (160 kmph). At the start of the 1960s it had invited the major West German traction builders to submit their designs for a 125 mph (200 kmph) locomotive, on six axles all motored to keep the axle loadings in check. The chosen design, a joint project by Henschel and Siemens, materialized in early 1965 as the first four prototypes of Class 'E03', later designated Class '103'. After four years of evaluation, this handsome and extremely powerful 108-tonne design, continuously

rated at 5,950 kW but boasting a one-hour rating of 6,420 kW at its 125 mph (200 kmph) top speed, was adopted as standard. Deliveries of a production series began in 1970 and the fleet, eventually numbering 149, became the staple power of German Federal's inter-city expresses until the late 1980s. On 13 September 1973 No 103 118 of the class, hauling three research department vehicles, was tested with power advanced to 7,440 kW and with specially-modified gearing up to a new German electric locomotive speed peak of 157.2 mph (252.9 kmph).

The first four 'E03s' emerged in time for DB to lay on a public demonstration of 125 mph (200 kmph) operation concurrently with a big international exhibition that was staged at Munich in the summer of 1965. The 38.5 miles (62 km) of track between Munich and Augsburg were fettled up and throughout the exhibition period a special train of 'Rheingold' stock shuttled between the two cities in 26 minutes start to stop, average 88 mph (140.8 kmph). This was inclusive of a crawl over the long curving exit from the Munich exhibition station, a 50 mph (80 kmph) slowing for a curve *en route* and a final decorous entry to Augsburg.

The combination of the Class '103's' rheostatic braking and the 'Rheingold' stock's electromagnetic track brakes were, however, not deemed adequate for deceleration from 125 mph (200 kmph) within existing signalling distances. The new locomotives were therefore fitted up to work with a new inductive loop system of continuous cab signalling, which would give advance information on signal aspects and provide automatic speed control. This was the birth of LZB, the Automatic Train Protection (ATP) system which is now standardized on all DB inter-city track run at over 100 mph.

The inductive cable loop, laid on the sleepers, is crossed over every 100 m (328 feet), which changes the magnetic field. Train-borne processors work out the train's position on the route by keeping count of the magnetic field changes from the start of a loop, which can be as long as a mile. Apparatus at each signalling interlocking continuously addresses every train within a loop at split-second intervals in electronically-coded messages, requesting automatic return of data on each train's speed and position from the trainborne data-processing devices. These outgoing signals are introduced to the loop at a higher frequency than the incoming commands, to segregate the two coded streams.

The basic *modus operandi* of LZB is to monitor continuously that a train making top speed is never less than a specified minimum distance from a signal or other situation demanding a full stop, or the appropriately reduced distance from a graded speed restriction. Continuously scrutinizing the state of the line in its controlled area, the lineside apparatus is transmitting its commands to a train as 'target speed', to which the driver must adjust his automatic speed regulator upward or downward. The lineside control's data-processor also advises the distance ahead over which the 'target speed' should be maintained. The data-processor on the locomotive reproduces this data visually on a driving desk dial. At the same time it is comparing actual with dictated speed and will activate emergency braking if it detects serious wrong-side discrepancy.

When I rode the demonstration Munich-Augsburg train at the end of June 1965 there was one ominous moment. Rounding a long curve between Nannhofen and Haspelmoor at 127 mph (204 kmph), our coach wheel flanges bit really hard into the outer rail and centrifugal force imparted some pretty violent lateral judders to the usually battleship-steady 'Rheingold' coach bodies. We weren't at safety risk, of course, but the cant deficiency through the bend was plainly excessive for reasonable passenger comfort at that speed — or, one was certain, for the track's health under continuous pounding at 125 mph. And so it was to prove.

From May 1966 German Federal substantially accelerated its Munich-Hamburg 'Blauer Enzian' and allowed the train up to 125 mph (200 kmph) over the Munich-Augsburg stretch. This was Europe's first public service operation at that speed, the Munich-Augsburg demonstrations apart. But within a couple of years or so a limit of 100 mph (160 kmph) was reimposed.

A German Federal civil engineer had complained to me at the 1965 Munich exhibition that even 100 mph running was punishing track upkeep costs with an extra 20 per cent. Still higher speed was now threatening to load the usual bill with an extra 50 or 60 per cent. The continuous signalling system was pretty costly too, but it was the wear and tear on track that chiefly decided German Federal to cry halt while it re-examined its track and vehicle technology.

Weight of engineering opinion on German Federal now was that the only economical tool for higher speed was a multiple unit which spread the weight of traction gear throughout the train and reduced axle-loadings. The double-ended format also looked to have some operational point, considering the number of major stations that were termini involving reversal in inter-city itineraries — Frankfurt, Stuttgart and Munich, for example.

So in 1973 there appeared the three sleek Class 'ET403' electric multiple units, smoothly streamlined four-car articulated units with every axle motored so that maximum axle-loading was only 14.7 tonnes, but with installed power of 5,150 hp. They were built by Linke-Hoffmann-Busch and Messerschmitt-Bölkow-Blohm, with electrical equipment by AEG, Brown Boveri and Siemens,

The striking outline of a Class 'ET403' electric multiple unit is emphasized in this action shot.
(Deutsche Bundesbahn)

and air-suspension bogies by MAN. The four cars seated 183 (and incorporated a restaurant and a train secretarial room) in a setting as elegant as that of the railway's locomotive-hauled inter-city stock, but a trifle less roomily, for the units' bodies were contoured for automatic body-tilting and hence were of more constricted cross-section.

The 'ET403s' were based at Munich and went into regular inter-city service over the main line thence to North Germany. But even they were kept to the 100 mph (160 kmph)

Interior of the Class 'ET403' unit.

limit until the spring of 1977, when German Federal once again cleared the Munich-Augsburg route for 125 mph (200 kmph). The following spring the speed ceiling was raised to 125 mph over four main stretches — Munich-Augsburg, 38.5 miles (62 km); Augsburg-Donauwörth, 26 miles (42 km); Hannover-Uelzen, 58 miles (93 km); and parts of Hamburg-Bremen, 76 miles (122 km). By then, though, the multiple-unit format had been discarded as too inflexible operationally. The trio of `ET403s' were dismissed to occasional special train work until the 1980s, when Lufthansa took them on charter to furnish a daily `Airport Express' connecting service between Düsseldorf and Frankfurt Airports. The trains retimed at 125 mph in 1977 were locomotive-hauled by Class `103' electrics.

Choice of high-speed equipment, however, was very much a secondary consideration compared with finding the scope to exploit its potential over a considerable distance. Only in the plains of North Germany and in the Upper Rhine Valley were DB main lines reasonably aligned for speed. Here and over

isolated stretches elsewhere German Federal was in the 1970s carrying out track and signalling improvements to enlarge significantly the route mileage passed for 125 mph (200 kmph) when it launched in the spring of 1978 the first phase of its present-day Inter-City (IC) system.

Outside the topographically speed-suited areas, German Federal confronted another limitation. Some of its most curve-harassed routes were so heavily occupied by freight, the average speed of which could not be raised without massive expenditure on more sophisticated freight vehicle braking, that tinkering with curve superelevation would be counter-productive. Extra speed without detriment to passenger comfort would only be bought at the cost of aggravated track wear by the freight traffic.

The only practical course was to move for brand-new, well-aligned bypasses of the most constricting trunk route sections. So, in 1970, German Federal presented to its Government a plan for seven new railways, totalling 590 route miles (950 km), which would be laid out for an ultimate top speed

In 1990 the three `ET403' units were in Lufthansa livery, operating a charter service for the airline between Frankfurt and Dusseldorf airports. One is seen here on the Rhine valley at Boppard.
(John C. Baker)

Scenically a delight, but a severe handicap to economical rail operation — the winding Rhine Valley, one of the speed-restricted trunk route sections to be bypassed in the German Federal's plan for new railways. A northbound inter-city train has a Class `103' electric in charge. (Deutsche Bundesbahn)

of 186 mph (300 kmph). Additionally, the railway wanted to upgrade and resignal a further 775 miles (1,250 km) or so of main line for operation at 125 mph (200 kmph). The Government accepted the plan as part of its developing national transport strategy and the railway was then optimistic of opening by 1985 the first four of the new lines — from Hannover over the Mittelgebirge ranges to Gemünden; from Cologne through the hills east of the Rhine Valley to the outskirts of Frankfurt; from Würzburg to Aschaffenburg, opening up a new approach to Frankfurt from the north-south route; and from Mannheim to Stuttgart. The anticipated time-scale proved, however, to be hopelessly optimistic.

The Hannover-Würzburg line was started in the summer of 1973, but only for a few tentative miles to the south. The project was not finally endorsed throughout until 1977, when the Mannheim-Stuttgart line at last got the green light.

The complex, two-tiered procedures of the country's land planning and use statutes gave individuals as well as communities extraordinary latitude to pursue objections to new railway construction. Many of the complaints were pettifogging. There was, for instance, the case of smallholders whose demand that their potato fields be tunnelled under, not bisected, by a new railway, had to be accorded the same generous hearings as more serious communal concerns.

DB took five years to get the Hannover-Würzburg project through just the first phase of planning approval, which established a line of route in principle. Then came the second phase in which the precise alignment of each route section had to be argued out, in some places literally metre by metre. The uneven pace at which these second-phase negotiations were concluded meant that construction work forged ahead on some parts of a new line before the detailed course of other sections could be finalized. At the start of the 1980s the frustrating delays had DB in the rare state, for a European railway, of inability to spend more than half the investment money its Government had made available for route upgrading.

The consequences did not stop at laborious protraction of agreement to alignments, or, so far as the Cologne-Frankfurt line was concerned, the shelving of the whole project for more than a decade largely because its projected course was so environmentally sensitive. With Germany's 1980s upsurge of Green politics adding weight to local demand for protection, DB was eventually compelled to load the topographically-driven civil engineering expense of the new lines with costly works that were purely environmentally motivated.

The most egregious examples of that are on the new Mannheim-Stuttgart line. Just out of Mannheim this parallels a motorway, which is on the surface. Yet DB has been forced to bury its railway in a 3.34-mile (5.38 km) cut-and-cover tunnel, the Pfingstberg, then landscape the replaced earth with over 100,000 trees. In the next stretch, where the line is in a shallow cutting, a noise suppression ridge has had to be built up between railway and motorway. But at local inhabitants' insistence, it is aligned closer to the

motorway than the railway! (This pacification of objectors also took five years to edge into agreement, incidentally.) At the end of the day, DB reported that all the deviations from most practical lines of route, tunnelling, erection of noise-baffling barriers and so on, to which it had been driven for non-technical reasons, had inflated the capital cost of the first two new line schemes by 10 per cent.

Paradoxically, the country's sharpening 'green' conscience, plus the late-1970s hike of oil prices, fired politicians of all hues to accelerate and expand DB high-speed development. Action included some moves to quicken the passage of DB projects through the planning mill. But more important was specification in successive quinquennial Federal Transport Plans of a rising amount of existing infrastructure adaptation for 125 mph (200 kmph), a process creating *Ausbaustrecke*, or ABS; and of more new line schemes purpose-built for higher speed, these termed *Neubaustrecke*, or NBS for

To placate environmental objections a stretch of the new Mannheim-Stuttgart line had to be buried, hence the creation of the 3.34-mile (5.38 km) Pfingstberg cut-and-cover tunnel. (Deutsche Bundesbahn)

short; plus a great deal more money to execute the proposals. All major DB infrastructure projects, from new lines to electrification, were and still are directly funded by the Federal Treasury.

The 1980 Federal Transport Plan reaffirmed commitment to the Hannover-Würzburg and Mannheim-Stuttgart schemes. Otherwise it was content to nominate six stretches totalling some 68 route miles (1,094 km) for immediate *Ausbau* treatment, and a further 540 route miles (about 870 km) for later attention.

The 1985 Federal Plan went much, much further. It endorsed in principle virtually all the route development schemes that DB had formulated. And it proposed to up Federal finance for DB investment by 25 per cent compared with the previous plan, while at the same time shaving Federal highway investment by 5.6 per cent.

Back on the agenda came the Cologne-Frankfurt area NBS. For DB this was now a priority. Rail competitiveness in the country's biggest travel market, between the Rhine-Ruhr and Rhine-Main agglomerations, was shackled by the enforced restraint of IC speed through the winding Rhine gorge between Bonn and Mainz. And there was now an additional inducement to build. In February 1985 the French and West German heads of state had formally agreed that France's prospective TGV-Nord service from Paris would extend beyond Brussels over upgraded route to Cologne. Three years later their Transport Ministers plus those of the Benelux countries labelled the Cologne-Frankfurt NBS an integral part of the TGV-Nord scheme.

In late 1990, though completion was being forecast in 1995-98, construction had yet to begin. That was partly because of the weight of human and material resources engaged on other NBS and ABS schemes in the later 1980s. But the Cologne-Frankfurt project also excited controversies that took time to resolve.

DB's other NBS schemes, at first envisaged as passenger-only routes kitted for speeds of up to 300 kmph (187.7 mph), were all by now drafted for operation of fast freight as well. That was because the latter-day contraction of heavy industry had cost DB a heavy loss of bulk freight tonnage and consequently a severe haemorrhage of revenue. To compensate, DB must carry more high-rated merchandise freight; and for that it must have faster routes for overnight intermodal and other merchandise freight trains.

The Cologne-Frankfurt NBS could be designed for almost exclusive passenger train use, because two historic main lines thread the Rhine gorge, one on each bank. With the west bank line's intensive IC service transferred to the NBS, that route would be able to process prime freight trains much more expeditiously.

For a while the technology to be applied to the Cologne-Frankfurt NBS was in question, though the ultimate answer was fairly predictable. As described in the final chapter, the German consortium fostering the Transrapid Maglev system badly needed a publicly operating system in its own country to buttress its global marketing. The Cologne-Frankfurt NBS's passenger-only specification presented a made-to-measure opportunity. It is beyond belief that the Bonn Government ever seriously contemplated destroying the continuity of the emergent European high-speed rail network by inserting a Maglev guideway at its core. But political respect for an indigenous technology demanded that the Maglev option be formally debated before its inevitable rejection.

Fixing the line of the Cologne-Frankfurt NBS route took longer. DB naturally pressed for the most direct course: one about 110 miles (177 km) long, from the east bank of the Rhine on Cologne's outskirts through the Westerwald hills, where for some distance it would keep close company with a motorway, to a junction with the Mainz-Frankfurt line at the approach to the Frankfurt Airport station loop. That way DB could slash the Cologne-Frankfurt journey time down to a flat hour, compared with $2^1/2$ hours via the Rhine gorge and Bonn, Koblenz and Mainz. It was July 1989 before the Federal Government steeled itself to adopt this route and rebuff the mighty pressure from Bonn, Koblenz, Mainz and their provincial governments for one of the longer route options that would keep some or all of these cities on a prime IC route.

The other principal projects scheduled in the 1985 plan would improve IC routes between major cities by a combination of ABS upgrading and new line construction where traffic volume justified extra tracks, or where the terrain inhibited worthwhile remodelling of an existing route. One of these NBS/ABS schemes was begun in 1987 over the 193 km (120 miles) between Karlsruhe and Basle. This is the key DB route into Switzerland; besides which it throws off a connection to Strasbourg and France. Its busiest stretch, between Rastatt and Offenburg, sees an average of 270 trains every 24 hours. The other NBS/ABS schemes cover Stuttgart-Augsburg beyond which, as already described, there is long-standing 125 mph capability to Munich; and Nuremburg-Ingolstadt-Munich.

There is no room to detail all the ABS work which, by the start of the 1990s, had already equipped some 400 route miles (640 km) of DB for 125 mph (200 kmph) IC operation. Much more was in progress. Besides curve realignments and installation of LZB, many of the schemes featured installation of one or more additional tracks in places, to provide refuge loops for slower-moving traffic.

In the flatlands of the north, where most of the 125 mph track had been created, DB was by 1990 running British Rail close as practitioners of Europe's fastest start-to-stop timings over historic routes. For example, the standard schedule of the two IC trains each way per hour between Hamburg and Hannover main stations, 110.6 miles (178 km), was 76 minutes, representing an average of 87.3 mph (140.5 kmph). As for the every-other-hour InterRegio (IR) trains serving the principal towns between Hamburg and Hannover, they had to sprint from Celle to Uelzen, 32.5 miles (52.3 km), in just 19 minutes, for a start-to-stop average of 102.7 mph (165.2 kmph). IC and IR were still furnished exclusively by orthodox locomotive-hauled trains in 1990-91, by the way.

The now elderly Class '103' Co-Cos still commanded a substantial share of the IC and IR work in 1990. But from early 1987 the production series of Class '120' Bo-Bo took an expanding part of these duties. The first five prototypes of this marque had emerged

way back in 1980, pioneering Siemens' three-phase ac motor technology — hence the lengthy evaluation of the quintet before a bulk order was placed. The virtue of the technology was that it should make the 84-tonne, 4,400kW continuous, 5,600kW maximum Class '120' Bo-Bo the mixed traffic machine *par excellence*, one as competent in the haulage of 1,500-tonne fast freight or, in multipled pairs, of 5,000-tonne heavy freights, as of 125 mph InterCity trains. So it proved so far as the electrics and electronics were concerned. But at the outset of the 1990s some mechanical parts of the Class '120's' power train were wilting under the stresses of heavy freight tonnage.

Hand-over to traffic of completed sections of the first two NBSs, the Hannover-Würzburg and Mannheim-Stuttgart, began in the spring of 1987. Both were ready for opening throughout four years later. With that, DB's IC timetable was radically rewritten; and one IC route taking in the Hannover-Würzburg NBS was refurnished with new high-speed rolling-stock. Before discussing that, the characteristics of the first two NBSs deserve summary.

The requirement to carry fast freight as well as passenger trains compelled DB to accept more generous curve radii and an easier ruling gradient, 1 in 80, than those of French TGV routes. But on top of that the Hannover-Würzburg line in particular had to be thrust through a tract of mountains and deep valleys without compare on France's TGV routes. Add in the pressures for environmental protection described earlier, and the outcome was a formidable bill for civil engineering.

Of the Hannover-Würzburg line's total length of 327 km (203.1 miles), only 93 km (57.8 miles) are not in tunnel or cutting, or aloft on bridgework. There are 62 tunnels aggregating 116 km (72.1 miles) in length. Four are more than 3 miles long, and this quartet includes what is now Germany's longest, the 10.75 km (6.68-mile) Landrücken tunnel south of Fulda, which terminates a 7-mile climb to the line's summit. Amongst no fewer than 267 bridges are some long and elegant viaducts that sweep the railway across intersecting valleys.

A 4,400kW three-phase ac motor Class `120' Bo-Bo on Nuremberg depot.

The terrain confronting the Mannheim-Stuttgart line was not quite so unfriendly. Nevertheless, of its 99 km (61.5 miles) of new infrastructure, just 4 km (2.5 miles) is precisely at ground level, and it has to thread 28 tunnels with a total length of 29 km (28 miles).

Because of their mixed traffic specification, the NBS routes are studded with a number of `overtaking stations' which, besides crossovers between the two main tracks, have loops. These are the only areas of the NBSs with conventional lineside signalling. The NBSs are equipped with LZB80, the latest refinement of DB's automatic train speed control and protection system (ATP), and all traction expected to travel the NBS frequently has the complementary on-board apparatus. For them, LBZ80 and its in-cab displays serve all signalling purposes on the NBS. The lineside signals apply to any non-LBZ fitted freight traction that finds its way on to an NBS route, and which naturally cannot enter a purely LBZ-controlled section between overtaking stations until the latter is completely clear of other traffic.

The maximum operational speed of DB's latest InterCity train-sets on the NBS routes is at present 250 kmph (155.4 mph), though they are engineered for at least 280 kmph (174 mph). But the prototype from which the design of those units was derived has a much higher mark to its credit.

Late in 1983 the Federal Ministry for Research & Technology came up with DM44 million towards the DM72 million cost of completing the design and construction of a high-speed research train-set which DB and German industry had been studying. It was to be drafted for a maximum speed of 350 km/h (217.5 km/h).

Branded `InterCity Experimental', or ICE, the completed unit of three non-articulated trailers (one of them given over to banks of instrumentation apparatus) and two enclosing power cars was ready for road trials in the autumn of 1985. That, not unintentionally, was the year the country feted the 150th anniversary of its first railway.

The seal-snouted, 78-tonne power cars derived their individual ratings of 5,600kW continuous and a hefty 8,400kW short-term from a three-phase ac asynchronous motor rig based on the Class `120' locomotive's whipped up to 400 kmph (250 mph) or more for 7 km (4.35 miles) on end near Gemünden, and touched 406.9 kmph (252.9 mph) on the 1 in 80 downgrade in the depths of the line's 5.5 km (3.4-mile) Mühlberg tunnel. However, as recorded in another chapter, the French wrested the blue riband back before 1988 was out.

The ICE's May Day 1988 exploit had a domestic as well as an international motivation. Not until late summer 1987 had DB and the Transport Minister extracted Federal Treasury approval to order 41 production series high-speed train-sets. That was the minimum fleet DB needed for its planned 1991 refit of two IC routes, Hamburg-Hannover-Kassel-Frankfurt-Stuttgart-Munich and Hamburg-Würzburg-Munich, taking in the two completed NBS lines. For months previously the purse-holders had dug in around a figure of just 10 train-sets. Why invest billions in rolling-stock with 175 mph capability, they grumbled, for routes it was to share with freight only half as fast? Surely it was economically wiser, and not commercially debilitating, to be satisfied with 125 mph haulage of conventional cars by Class '120s'?

DB held off placing any orders until it got the 41-set consent. By then there was no time left to build, as previously intended, a pre-production prototype for debugging before finalizing the detail of the series. The latter, designated IC-Express, must perforce rely quite substantially on components proven in the IC-Experimental.

Then, at the start of 1988, a furore erupted over the 41-set order's cost. Approval had been based on DB's estimates in its 1986 submission. But those figures took no account of the considerable modifications to the original IC-Express design now found essential to reinforce car interior insulation against the effect of pressure changes in high-speed traversal of the NBS tunnels. Those changes, German industry said, would bump the bill way above the 1986 figure. The ICE's future was yet again clouded.

Both sides came in for a pasting over what one heavyweight Frankfurt newspaper bluntly declared a public scandal. DB was slated for not taking the pressure problem fully on board until it had been exposed by

test running of the IC-Experimental unit; some experts had voiced anxieties on this score more than a decade earlier. At the same time German industry was accused of trying to take a cornered DB for all it could get. The contracts for 41 train-sets were eventually signed for a sum about a third higher than the 1986 figure. But even to hold inflation at that level DB was forced to trim its projected IC-Express format by two trailers, down to 12 flanked by a brace of power cars.

By late summer 1990 the cost of a two-power-car, 12-trailer IC-Express formation stood at DM 51.4 million — around £17.4 million at the exchange rate of that time. Not until then did the Government concede approval for 19 more train-sets needed for a planned hand-over of the Hamburg-Frankfurt-Basel IC route to IC-Express operation. An option on these extra units that had been clipped to the 41-set order had expired in early 1989. But German industry, perhaps moved by DB desperation at the slippage of lead time to 1993, and certainly anxious to keep its own production lines rolling, trustingly started work on the additional power cars in the spring of 1990 before DB was allowed to place a formal order.

The first tranche of ICEs began public service in June 1991 on a Hamburg-Hannover-Frankfurt-Stuttgart-Munich route that embraced both the completed NBS lines. The fastest stretches of their journeys were on the Hannover-Würzburg NBS, where the standard start-to-stop schedule set for the 61.8 miles (99.4 km) from Hannover to Göttingen was 32 minutes for an average speed of 115.8 mph (186.4 kmph). A minute more was allowed in the reverse direction.

The launch day itself was marred by a number of ICE traction and on-train equipment failures (reported in France with just a hint of *schadenfreude*). Largely to blame was the tightness of the manufacturing timescale, which denied DB time both to debug the complex equipment of all the train-sets needed to begin the hourly service, and also to ensure that crews were thoroughly versed in its use. But reasonable reliability had been obtained before the first week was over. I found no ICE seriously adrift of schedule when I spent the last week of the month in Germany.

The power car of a production series IC-Express train-set. (Deutsche Bundesbahn)

Visually and technically, the 78-tonne Class '401' power cars are close kin to those of the IC-Experimental. The outstanding difference is that the continuous rating of each Class '401' power car's three-phase ac asynchronous motor plant has been hoisted to 4,800kW. Other changes include more recourse to microprocessor control of apparatus, and, of course, more effective pressure sealing.

A 1st class saloon of an IC-Express unit. (Deutsche Bundesbahn)

In June 1991 the standard ICE format was two power cars enclosing three 1st class, one restaurant/bistro, one service and six 2nd class trailers. The aluminium-bodied trailers are mounted on MD530 bogies with coil spring secondary suspension. Subsequent builds will probably have air-sprung bogies, but these were eschewed for the first tranche because development work was considered incomplete when the trailer design had to be finalised.

Trailers are the DB standard IC car length of 26.4 m, but their extra width — 3.02 m at the waistline, 200 mm more than the DB norm — is the striking dimension. Couple that with more generous saloon seat area than in a French TGV, 1.2m² as against 0.9m² in 1st, 0.9m² as against 0.6m² in 2nd, and in 2nd there's no sense whatever of riding a ground-hugging jetliner.

Adjoining the 1st class cars is the distinctive Bord Restaurant car. Its passenger spaces, a 24-seat restaurant on one side of a kitchen, and a self-service bistro bar on the other, have a particularly airy ambience because here the vehicle's raised, aerodynamically-faired roof is inset with skylights. Between the Bord Restaurant and 2nd class comes the service car, which for business persons incorporates a four-seat conference room replete with cordless telephone, electric typewriter, photocopier and fax machine. Radio contact between the cordless telephones, the train's public telephone booths and the national network in the long NBS tunnels has been assured by lining the bores with special cables that serve as aerials for relay stations on the ground above.

You don't want for diversions in an ICE. Your seat has a standard terminal for earphones which you can either bring with you or hire for DM6.50 (roughly £2.25) from the conductor. The pure audio offer is six-channel, three for radio, three for on-board tape transmission — one classical music, one rock-pop, one for children. There is a further channel for the video programme, visible only on little flat LCD full-colour screens inset in seatbacks of the smoker areas in the end 1st and 2nd class cars. However, in the first month, when only one hourly repeated tape of tedious travelogue and juvenile cartoons

was on offer, the video was eminently dispensable. It will certainly be absorbing above ground if and when DB fulfils its published intension to transmit live from cameras installed in the power car noses.

In one vestibule of your car are two electronic displays. One alternates details of the ICE's itinerary with its current speed and the time of day. On the other display buttons can be pressed to call up a range of German-language information on DB and ancillary services. This replicates data banked in the service wagon's more elaborate panel, on which rail, hotel and other reservations can actually be booked.

ICE riding was pluperfect on both NBS lines. Equally impressive was the cars' pressure-sealing. Not so much as a feather caress disturbed my sensitive ears as we swept into a tunnel at 250 kmph, or crossed another ICE making the same speed underground. Sound insulation of the car, consequently, was also exemplary. So was its air-conditioning.

Chauvinistic concern for a substantial ICE stake in the next century's European high-speed network was acknowledged early in 1989, when the Federal Transport Minister approved the start of development work on a multi-voltage version. In view of its EuroCity purpose, this project is now labelled with an ECE acronym in some quarters.

At first the IC-M was visualised as four-voltage. By 1991, however, need of voltage versatility had narrowed for the present to two-system. Few feasible or commercially rewarding routes demanding four-voltage complexity and its inevitable limitation of power outputs are visible in the medium-term future. An acceptably proportioned four-voltage power car could be rated at no more than 3,500kW. For maintenance of the 300 kmph likely to be attainable on the next century's high-speed lines, that would restrict a two-power-car set to six trailers.

A 4,000-4,500kV continuous rating is possible in a two-voltage power car, either 15kV 16 ²/₃ Hz ac and 1.5kV dc for through working between Austria/Hungary and the Low Countries (top speed under dc wires would be 220 kmph); or 15kV and 25kV ac for operation into France. So work now centres on a single-power-car, seven-trailer push-pull format, with the driving trailer's leading bogie also motorized to counter risk of aerodynamic uplift at maximum pace in the propelled mode. The six motors of the power car and trailer bogie will have a total rating of 4,800kW.

Two such sets could be multipled to obtain an ICE's seating capacity and still fit within German Hbf platform lengths, though at the cost of amenity duplication because there could be no passenger gangway between them. The planned range of their passenger accommodation and facilities will broadly reproduce that of an ICE. DB is also pondering a single-voltage ICE variant of the concept for *en route* division to a pair of destinations within its own domestic network.

IC-M trailers, like those of the ICEs, will be independent, not articulated. DB deprecates the constraints that articulation imposes on inter-car gangway dimensions and on the use of end-car space immediately above a shared bogie. Furthermore, the Germans point out, the more the axles, the less the load on each disc brake in pulling the train up from top speed, to the benefit of disc life.

The initial IC-Ms will not be TGV-compatible. Their power car design is not to be hamstrung by the SNCF's rigid 17-tonne TGV axleload limit. And trailer design will retain ICE 3.02 m body width, whereas the SNCF's TGV loading gauge stipulates 2.89 m.

The first objective is launch of an IC-M service between Cologne, Brussels and possibly Amsterdam in 1996 or 1997; SNCB and NS both accept the 3.02 m body width. DB expected to have a design completed for placement in December 1991 of orders for two prototypes to be delivered in early 1995, and for subsequent manufacture of a seven-set production series to cover the inaugural Low Countries service. Hopefully the Cologne-Frankfurt NBS will be operational in 1998. For that event a further IC-M sets are to be procured, and the service will start back at Frankfurt instead of Cologne.

DB does propose eventually to develop a multi-voltage IC-M meeting the TGV dimensional specification for through working to Paris, both via Belgium and the TGV Nord, and via Alsace and the prospective TGV Est. For this, no alternative to the two-power-car, six-trailer format is presently discernible. SNCF's intention to design the TGV Est for standard 320 kmph or even 350 kmph operation will aggravate the IC-M power/weight ratio problem.

DB itself has begun an ICE 400 project, to serve which the IC-Experimental is to be prepared for a new research programme. Whether trains can pass each other in a long NBS tunnel at a combined closing speed of up to 800 kmph without a contretemps is obviously a crucial issue. But I have also heard Germans questions whether ICE speed can be lifted to 300 kmph without falling foul of the country's anti-noise pollution statutes.

8
Italy's chequered high-speed story

Italy was the first country in Europe to set about expensive construction of new railways to supersede 19th-century lines that were hopelessly unsuited to the competitive speed market of the 20th century. As far back as 1913 the Italians had embarked on a new *Direttissima* to shorten the distance between Bologna and Florence and eliminate some appalling gradients on the existing railway over the Apennine Mountains. The First World War interrupted the work, but under Mussolini it was pressed to completion in 1934.

A second *Direttissima* was begun after the

A sample of the rugged country traversed by the Bologna-Florence Direttissima *in its passage of the Apennine Mountains.* (Italian Railways)

First World War and finished by the autumn of 1927. This was the coastal route from Rome to Naples. It shortened the run between the two cities from the old inland route's 154.4 miles (248.7 km) to 134 miles (215.8 km), reduced the maximum altitude to be surmounted by 676 feet (206 m), and presented trains with a vastly better alignment. As soon as it was commissioned, the Rome-Naples transit time tumbled overnight from 4 hours 25 minutes to 2 hours 50 minutes.

The Bologna-Florence *Direttissima*, part of the Italian State Railways' spinal trunk route from Milan to Rome, was a titanic engineering operation. The old line had heaved itself up a weary succession of severe curves and gradients as sharp as 1 in 45 to a summit of 2,021 feet (616 m) in the Apennine Mountains at Pracchia. The new line all but halved this climb and markedly flattened the gradients by burrowing the railway under the mountains in the 11.5-mile (18.5 km) Apennine Tunnel, then the second longest in the world, and 29 other tunnels aggregating 23 miles (37 km) in length. The fastest Bologna-Florence time over the old line had been 2 hours 26 minutes; in the final months before the Second World War electric trains were coursing through the mountains to link the two cities in a mere 51 minutes for a start-to-stop average of 70.8 mph (114 kmph). But there was also the hair-raising prestige run

This shot of an `ETR300' `Settebello' train-set on its Rome-Milan run also highlights the curvature typical of so much of the old route until it reaches the Po Valley. (Italian Railways)

staged with a three-car `ETR200' electric multiple unit for the glory of *Il Duce* in July 1939 which I have described in Chapter 3.

Pre-war public service speed standards were gradually recovered after 1945, but not significantly improved. For two decades Italian State Railways made inter-city passenger news chiefly for the elegance of its de luxe Milan-Rome flagships, the three seven-car green-and-grey Class `ETR300' `Settebello' electric multiple units. A four-coach variant of the design, the `ETR250', appeared in 1960 and four of these were built.

The `ETR300s' were built with 100 mph (160 kmph) capability, but at first they had scant opportunity to exploit it. The southern section of the Rome-Milan trunk route pursued such a sinuous course through the hills north of the capital that in the first 90 miles or so (145 km) speed was nowhere permitted to exceed 110 kmph (68 mph). Thereafter, though the alignment was more friendly, signal spacing and braking power fixed the ceiling at 140 kmph (87.5 mph) except over tracts of the broad Po valley beyond Bologna, where the `Settebello' could briefly kick up its heels.

By 1962 Italian State Railways, or FS, knew that it had to overcome the handicaps imposed by nature if its long-haul passenger

traffic (a bigger component of its revenue than of most Western European railways) was to withstand air and road competition. A ten-year plan tabled that year set optimistic sights on average speeds of over 90 mph (150 kmph) as essential to hold off air transport over the longer runs, up to about 625 miles (1,000 km).

Immediate evidence of the railways' ambitions in the early 1960s was the widespread main-line application of coded track circuitry to prepare the ground for a continuous cab signalling system. From the end of the 1960s several hundred locomotives and multiple units were equipped with cab apparatus and inductive pick-ups.

In special tests FS was getting the feel of the higher speed ranges during the 1960s. The favoured test vehicle was usually the pleasingly-styled lightweight inter-city electric multiple-unit that was premiered in 1961. These 60-tonne motor coaches, 87 ft 8 in (26.7 m) in length, classified `ALe601', had all axles powered. First class only, they were designed to associate with a choice of six different trailer types — the Le601 1st class, the Le640 1st and 2nd class composite, the Le680 or Le700 2nd class, the Le480 kitchen-restaurant, and the Le360 kitchen-restaurant-bar. The whole compatible fleet

Above: Front-end of an `ETR300' train-set, showing the passengers' observation lounge with the cab protruding above the roof. (Italian Railways)

Below: One of an `ETR300's' ten-seater lounges. (Italian Railways)

Right: An `Ale601' electric motor coach; one of these has been tested up to a maximum of 155 mph (250 kmph). (Italian Railways)

was air-conditioned and each vehicle was cabbed at each end, trailers as well as power cars, for supreme operational flexibility. Possible permutations of train format were considerable; there would have been nothing to stop a set being fronted by a kitchen to suit some arcane operational requirement.

As early as 1962 one of the first batches of `Ale601' power cars was being worked up to 225 kmph (139.8 mph) in pantograph tests near Grosseto, on the Rome-Genoa main line. In 1968-70 five of the series were fitted up with rheostatic braking and had their gearing modified and power stepped up to 1,000kW to extend their practicable speed range. It was the first pair of this quintet to be altered, ALe601.008 and 010, which at the end of 1968 were opened up to a maximum of 155 mph (250 kmph) under the reinforced catenary of the Rome-Naples line. For 8 continuous minutes the two railcars were held at 240 kmph (149.1 mph) or better. In 1970 21 new ALe601s were delivered with the same characteristics as the rebuilds. These units were handed the cream of Italy's fastest daily services, two *rapidi* each way between Rome and Naples via the *Direttissima*. With the benefit of a 180 kmph (111.9 mph) top speed exceptionally permitted over some 80 km of that route, this pair was timed to cover the 130.5 miles (210 km) in

$1^1/_2$ hours non-stop at an average of 87 mph (140 kmph). Those schedules were eased out later in the decade, however.

Although FS was steadily adding 125 mph (200 kmph) capability locomotives and multiple-units to its traction fleet in the 1970s, the ceiling over most of the system was held at 93 mph (150 kmph). Off the Rome-Naples *Direttissima* the only units with a dispensation to run at 100 mph (160 kmph), over stretches of the Bologna-Milan main line, were the Class `ETR300' electric multiple units. Apart from refurbishing to fit them for the prospective 200 kmph ceiling, the `ETR300s' had been uniquely equipped in 1970 with automatic braking programmers to work in conjunction with the coded track circuitry and continuous cab signalling: in other words, to provide Automatic Train Protection (ATP) coverage. However, the cost of this ATP modification so daunted FS that application to other traction units was deferred until regular 200 kmph (125 mph) working became a practical possibility.

The crippling effect on end-to-end train speed of central Italy's mountainous terrain was patent when the `Settebello' was accelerated to a $5^3/_4$-hour Rome-Milan timing following the revamping of the `ETR300s'. Across the broad Po Valley the southbound `Settebello' timing was screwed up to 1 hour

38 minutes for the 135.5 miles (218 km) from Milan to Bologna, average 83 mph (133.5 kmph), while northbound, when a Piacenza stop was inserted in the itinerary, the 91.2 miles (146.7 km) from Bologna to that point were booked in 65 minutes for an average of 84.2 mph (135.5 kmph). But in sharp contrast the curvature and gradients prevented any better start-to-stop average than 63.7 mph (102.5 kmph) over the 196.3 miles (316 km) from Florence to Rome.

The main line from Milan through Florence to Rome, and the continuation to Naples and Reggio Calabria for the ferry crossing of the Messina Strait to Sicily, is Italian State Railways' spinal chord in every sense, for it bears nearly a third of the system's entire traffic. From the 1950s onward FS had already laid out huge sums for infrastructure improvement to increase its capacity. On the Rome-Florence core, however, no half-measure would close the glaring gap in speed potential between the outer and central sections of the Milan-Naples route. The incessant curvature and gradients inherited from the original builders must be bypassed. Thus, in 1969, with the financial support of a consortium of Italian industry in the shape of ten-year low-interest loans, FS launched construction of its third major *Direttissima* from Rome to Florence.

The new infrastructure was to be expensively engineered throughout for maximum speeds of 250 kmph (155.4 mph), even 300 kmph (186.5 mph). But before the 1970s were very old, FS executives were stressing that they were concerned primarily to enlarge track capacity by creating, in conjunction with the old route, a four-track main line from Rome to Florence. At the peak of the summer holiday season, parts of that inter-city stretch were groaning under more than 100 trains each way daily and, given the mixed character of the traffic, strangulation was threatening. Any rise of maximum speed ceiling would therefore be limited to the possibilities created by a segregation of traffic between old and new lines in such a way as to narrow each route's speed band as straitly as possible.

At that juncture, completion in 1974 was sanguinely forecast. In fact it was early 1977

before so much as a mile of new line was ready for business. By the publication of the first 1978 edition of this book, little more than a third of the *Direttissima* was carrying traffic, and I was then predicting that the residue would not be available until at least 1982. At this writing, in mid-1991, 120.4 miles (193.8 km) of the new infrastructure were operational. But completion of the final 27.3 miles (44 km) would not be affected until early 1992; and how and when the original intention to tunnel the new line from its present northern limit at Rovezzano, on Florence's outskirts, across the city to Prato, on the Bologna main line, would be fulfilled was still conjectural.

Even if they had struck no unforeseen snags, the Italians had taken on some formidable engineering. An operating specification that sought 250-300 kmph (155-186 mph) capability for inter-city passenger trains, and also use of the route by fast freight, required a minimum curve radius of 3,000 m (9,840 feet) and a ruling gradient of 1 in 125. Carving a new line of those characteristics through the terrain's rapidly and often abruptly changing contours north of Rome demanded that in the first 75 miles alone 34 per cent of it must be in tunnel — 17 of them — 15 per cent on bridges or viaducts, and 49 per cent in cutting or aloft on embankment. Amongst that bridgework, incidentally, would be one of the world's longest viaducts, the Allerona, 3.3 miles (5.4 km) in extent, to wing the *Direttissima* across the Paglia river valley.

Two uncovenanted factors made nonsense of a timescale that was pretty exacting had all things been equal. One was the mountains' serious geological resistance to tunnelling, first encountered at its worst in the second lengthy bore north of Rome, the 5.8-mile (9.3 km) Orte tunnel. That set off a massive inflation of costs which was the more troubling because of another malign influence, the financial screws tightened by the 1973 oil crisis. In the second half of the 1970s and in the early 1980s the new line's progress was halting because of hesitant political commitment of funds to fresh phases of the project. As for the geological hazards, they were found so extreme at the

line's northern end that the original alignment and its planned 14.5 km (9-mile) tunnel north of Arezzo had to be abandoned and a new 44 km (27.3-mile) course followed from Arezzo South to Figline. This was the segment of which the last stretch remained to open in mid-1991.

For a decade progressive opening of Rome-Florence *Direttissima* sections had negligible impact on FS *rapido* schedules between Milan and Rome. For one thing, obvious to the observant passenger, the operators were, as predicted, treating the new line as a four-track enlargement of the old, and exploiting the elaborate bi-directional, flying/burrowing junctions between the two — there are eight of them in the completed *Direttissima* — for tactical weaving of out-of-course trains around other traffic. Timekeeping is still somewhat approximate on FS, but in the late 1970s and early 1980s the timetable was even more of a soothsayer's almanac — further justification for applying the new line's benefits to scope for recovery of lost time rather than window-dressing accelerations.

Until 1987, furthermore, only one unit — of which more in a moment — was allowed to travel the *Direttissima* at anywhere near the line's designed top speed. The standard traction of FS's fastest locomotive-hauled *rapidi* in the 1980s, the 4,000kW Class `E444' Bo-Bo, was built with 200 kmph capability. But because at that pace it punished

track it was limited to 180 kmph until, at last, the type's bogies were modified to cure hunting proclivities in preparation for an overdue restructure of the Milan-Bologna-Florence-Rome timetable in the 1987 summer.

Besides discarding the traditional express train designations of *rapido* or *espresso* in favour of `InterCity' for what was now a basically hourly-interval Rome-Milan service, this 1987 recast at last left trailing the previous best timings between the two cities. With two stops it was down to 5 hours 10 minutes, compared with the `Settebello's' prime of 5 hours 35 minutes; and non-stop, by two pairs of trains launched in September that year, to 4 hours 55 minutes, compared with 5 hours 30 minutes by the `ALe601' multiple unit sets in the 1960s. But routeing over the completed stretch of the Rome-Florence *Direttissima*, one must add, had cut the Rome-Milan distance to 364.6 miles (586.6 km), whereas the surpassed timings had been over 391.5 miles (630 km) of wholly historic route.

A quarter-century had passed since that FS development plan of 1962 had wistfully set course for 155 mph (250 kmph) operation. In 1988 the objective was finally attained, by equipment that had itself been over a decade and a half in development.

In 1972 Fiat had rolled out an electrically-powered test vehicle embodying an active body-tilting system which the company had devised. Two years' evaluation of the car on FS tracks were so encouraging that Fiat extended its private venture to construction of two fully-equipped four-car train-sets, one to court interest from RENFE in Spain, the other for trial by FS.

In 1990 the Spanish unit was still on RENFE's books and in occasional use as the railway's Class `443'. But in that country the Fiat tilt-body technology was never contesting a level playing-field with the home-grown Talgo system. Competition apart, furthermore, Fiat's Spanish train-set was from time to time immobilized for long periods by peculiar bureaucratic delays to the passage of spares through Customs.

The Italian unit, formally FS Class `ETR401' but popularly the *Pendolino*, the name now globally associated with the Fiat tilt-body system, saw its first commercial service on the Rome-Ancona cross-country route in 1976. And there it continued in sporadic employment for the next six or seven years. Tracing a sinuous path through the Apennine mountains, this route was much more proof of a tilt-body unit's ability to cut journey

A 4,000kW Class `E444' electric locomotive and a train of the Italian State Railways' latest 1st class Inter-City rapido stock on the Rome-Florence Direttissima. (Italian Railways)

Fiat's first tilt-body test car, the Y.0160, on tangent track and demonstrating its suspension round a curve. (Italian Railways)

times over unfriendly alignments than of the `ETR401's' in-built 250 kmph (155.4 mph) capability. Even so, the frequency of extreme change in the unit's body posture drew com-

plaints of nausea from passengers, more particularly those in rearward-facing seats. These were repetitive enough for FS eventually to make the unit's entire seating

The prototype Fiat `ETR401' Pendolino tilt-body unit.

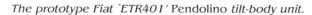

reversible, so that it could be made exclusively forward-facing for each trip.

At the start of the 1980s the `ETR401' was the sole FS equipment with a designed maximum speed of 250 kmph. But if Fiat's impatience for a production order were ever satisfied — and that seemed less likely by the year — most commentators were convinced that the product would be directed primarily to quickening service over routes like Rome-Ancona. Unexpectedly, word spread in early 1985 that FS, flexing newfound decision-making muscle gained from its recent reconstitution as a state corporation released from Transport Ministry bondage, was on the contrary negotiating a deal for a high-speed `ETR401'-based fleet.

As a prologue to its late-May 1985 announcement of the contract, FS took the Italian press for a jaunt in `ETR401'. Outward from Rome the unit took the historic main line to Chiusi, where some of the scribblers reported themselves a mite queasy as the unit heeled this way and that through reverse curvature up to 40 per cent faster than the norm for conventional rolling-stock. The return was over the new Florence-Rome line. And there `ETR401' was spurred to a peak

speed of 255 kmph (158.5 mph).

The order revealed to the press later that day was for just four Rome-Milan train-sets, classified `ETR450'. Tracks were so busy north of Florence, FS said, that there was space for only two high-speed daytime paths each way. Within a year, miraculously, room had been found for a great many more. In 1986 the order was expanded to 11 full-length and four half-length train-sets, though that configuration too was eventually to be revised, for two reasons: one, a decision to standardize train-length; and two, abandonment of catering concentration in a mid-train restaurant bar-car in favour of at-seat service, airline-style, from galleys at various points in the train-set. In 1990 the ultimate format of the `ETR450' fleet had become 15 units, each of nine cars.

The all-1st class `ETR450' reproduces the shape and refines the technology of the `ETR401'. The aluminium-bodied set has four articulated two-car units, electrically and operationally self-contained, each bogie of which is powered on its inner axle by a body-mounted, chopper-controlled 625kW motor driving through a cardan shaft. The ninth car, the one initially planned as a restaurant-bar

The `ETR401' in the course of high-speed trials on the Rome-Florence Direttissima *in 1985.* (FS)

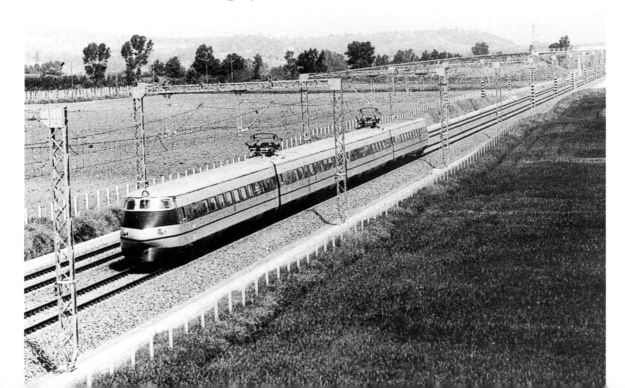

service car but now fitted out for standard seating, is a non-powered trailer. Since a proportion of the cars must be cabbed, some have pantographs, others galleys; and as the preferable train-set position of pantos and galleys does not always coincide, no fewer than seven different car types are represented in an `ETR450's' motored twin-units.

The `ETR450's' active tilt system has a more sophisticated control than that of the `ETR401' prototype. In the latter, each car's tilt mechanism was actuated independently, and reaction to a curve could be abrupt. `ETR450' cars get early warning of imminent curvature: sensors on the head-end car detect the start of a transition curve and measure the speed and extent of change in the track's degree of cant. This data is electronically transmitted to tilt-controlling modules on each car of the set. Relating the received information to its car's position in the train-set, a module commands a preparatory degree of tilt from the vehicle's hydraulic mechanism. In a second phase, as the car reaches the curve, the amount of tilt is precisely regulated by microprocessed signals from a gyroscope and accelerometer system.

Pantographs are mounted on structures separated from the carbodies and attached to the bogie frames, so that their contact with the traction current wire is unaffected by body tilt. The `ETR450' is designed for a maximum body tilt of 10 degrees, but FS is content with 8 degrees, which in general allows a 20 per cent increase of tolerable speed through curves.

In the summer of 1988 the `ETR450s' carried their first fare-paying passengers on a pair of Rome-Milan non-stop services that were publicly non-stop, but included a pause in the Florence area for a crew change. Passed to travel the Rome-Florence *Direttissima* at a full 250 kmph (155.4 mph) and parts of the predominantly straight line over the Po plain from Bologna to Milan at 200 kmph (124.3 mph), the `ETR450s' were set a 3-hour 58-minute schedule for the 364.6 miles (586.6 km). Representing an end-to-end average of 91.9 mph (147.9 kmph), this timing clipped over an hour from the previous best between the two cities. Or theoretically it did. In practice, the `ETR450s' were almost as vulnerable to the eccentricities of FS operation as more mundane traffic.

I took an `ETR450' from Rome to Milan soon after the launch. Compared with the

An `ETR450' train-set. (FS)

An 'ETR450' leaves Florence en route *from Milan to Rome.* (FS)

silky ride of a French TGV-A train's much longer-wheelbase, air-suspension, articulating bogie at 220 kmph (136.7 mph) on historic route as well as at 300 kmph on new TGV track, the coil-sprung 'ETR450' bogies' performance ceded several points. But the smoothness of the tilt system was very impressive. Seated, I was not conscious of any disconcerting sensation. Nor did I have much trouble in keeping my balance when, as we swept through the frequent curves of the ascent to the Apennine Tunnel, I walked the train from end to end. From the earlier description of the tilt control method it will have been apparent that the front cars have less time to adjust to a curve than those further back. Some Italian reports had suggested that this made for much livelier experiences in the leading car, but I found the criticism unwarranted.

By the end of 1990 the Rome-Milan route was the core of 'ETR450' services reaching south to Naples and Salerno, south-east to

Bari, north-east to Venice, and north-west to Turin and (via Florence and Pisa) Genoa. No other railway had yet bought Fiat's tilt-body technology for really high-speed operation, but two had adopted it for service acceleration over sinuous routes, and others were probable purchasers. The confirmed clients were West Germany's DB, for a new design of inter-regional diesel train-set, Class 'VT610'; and Austria's Federal Railway, OBB, for electric inter-city train-sets.

Fiat itself was busy with developments that included a 320 kmph (200 mph) tilt-body train-set employing inverter-controlled asynchronous motor power. Encouragement for this exercise was the uncertainty shrouding the future of the rolling-stock design which had been drafted for a spread of new high-speed FS infrastructure.

The new Fiat venture is known as AVRIL, an Italian acronym denoting a lightweight high-speed unit with independent wheels (*Alta Velocita a Ruote Indipendenti Leggero*).

Running gear development is, as the name indicates, a distinctive feature of the concept. The product of a five-year Fiat R & D programme, it dispenses with bogie frames and conventional heavy axles. Instead, each bogie consists of a central pivot assembly that radiates lightweight legs to four independent wheels, each with its own air suspension, dampers and braking. The inner wheels of each bogie are driven by cardan shaft from a pair of inverter-controlled, asynchronous 200kW traction motors.

AVRIL is conceived as an eight-car train-set formed of two electrically self-contained four-car units. The weight-saving bogie innovation will contribute powerfully to an anticipated tare for the full eight-car train-set of only 310 tonnes. That in turn makes the modest 6,400kW continuous output of the set's 32 motors in total adequate for the high-speed performance promised by Fiat.

In June 1986 FS had published a grandiose *Alta Velocita* (AV) plan. Its immediate objective was a `T' of new 250-300 kmph

A 1st class saloon interior of an `ETR450'.

infrastructure. The vertical would extend the Rome-Florence *Direttissima* north through Bologna to Milan, and south via a Naples bypass (from which a spur would obtain access to that city) to Battipaglia, beyond Salerno *en route* to Sicily. The horizontal arm would head east from Turin through Milan to Venice. At a later date the north-south route would be continued from Battipaglia, not only to Reggio Calabria, the mainland's present ferry terminal for Sicily, but over the prospective Messina Straits suspension bridge to Palermo and Catania in Sicily. And from the vicinity of Cassino, south of Rome, a branch would be driven across country to Foggia and Bari on the Adriatic coast.

Euphoric talk of finishing the new Rome-Battipaglia route by mid-1991 and the extension north to Milan by 1993 accompanied the AV plan's presentation; this despite the certainty that forging a new trans-Apennine route from Florence to Bologna would be as formidable an engineering task as the Rome-Florence *Direttissima*, never mind either the gross inadequacy of then available government AV funding to finish just one of these schemes. Under its new constitution FS was free to bring in private capital. And the private sector, said FS, would be wetting its lips at analysts' calculations of the return on AV investment. By the end of 1987 FS had in fact called for tenders to begin the Rome-Battipaglia civil engineering and itself started the addition of two high-speed tracks to the existing route north of Bologna.

Events a year later ripped this scenario apart. In mid-1988 rumours were rife that some of FS's top brass were creaming perks or even kickbacks from the railway's new freedoms. How come, some were asking, the sumptuous refurnishing of certain senior men's offices? But the expense in question there was trivial compared to the amount involved in the so-called 'golden sheets scandal' that erupted in the following November.

Without proper solicitation of bids, it was revealed, one manufacturer had been amiably granted a contract worth over £50 million to supply disposable bedding for FS overnight services. For that money the entire European sleeping and couchette car fleet should have been covered — and with plenty of change to spare. In the immediate brouhaha the entire FS board resigned, with some of its members under threat of arraignment for corruption, and with its President not long afterward being murdered by persons and for reasons unknown.

At the same time the remorseless rise in FS's massive reliance on state money was agitating the government. Less than one-third of the railway's total costs was being met from passenger fares and freight revenue. So a private sector industrialist with a good rationalizing track record, Mario Schimberni, was brought in to stop the FS rot.

One of his remedies was to shut down FS's recently-formed AV directorate and propose postponement *sine die* of the AV programme. But on that, on the wisdom of retaining the Rome-Naples-Battipaglia component of the AV scheme, and on other issues including the scale of FS workforce cuts, he clashed with the Transport Minister. In mid-1990 Schimberni resigned. On paper the AV network plan seemed to have been preserved intact north of Bologna and south of Rome, but the pace at which it would proceed was for the time being uncertain.

The corollary of that was a dubious outlook for FS's 300 kmph AV network train-set, the 'ETR500'. A development order for this was placed in 1986 with a consortium of Italian industry led by Breda, and an external and internal industrial design commission went to the distinguished Italian auto stylists Pininfarina. The latter was to produce, in my view, the world's most original and dramatic high-speed train outline.

Since it would ply purpose-built high-speed routes, the 'ETR500' would not have body-tilting. Nor would any of its intermediate cars be motored or articulated. The operational plan prescribed end power cars enclosing a variable number of trailers, the formation to depend on seasonal commercial circumstances. The 'ETR500' would be designed for 300 kmph, though initially maximum speed on AV routes would be held at 270 kmph (167.8 mph).

The 'ETR500' power car is a derivative of the latest FS inter-city Bo-Bo locomotive, the 'E402'. In its single-cabbed 'ETR500' form the machine is designated Class 'E404'.

The Class `E402' asynchronous three-phase ac motor 4,250kW Bo-Bo locomotive which has the same traction equipment as an `ETR500's' power cars. (Ansaldo Trasporti)

Steel-framed with a cladding of aluminium and fibre composite, a structure that drops the centre of gravity as low as possible, the 4,250kW `E404' weighs 72 tonnes. Each axle is powered by an inverter-fed, chopper-controlled motor, which is located within the bogie but suspended from the body by a system that keeps a motor's relationship with the bogie stable whatever the vehicle speed or the characteristics of the track. A novel form of flexible drive transmits power from gearbox to axle. Average weight of each aluminium-bodied `ETR500' trailer is about 40 tonnes. FS foresees a maximum consist of 12 trailers between two power cars.

A prototype power car and one trailer, designated ETRX500, emerged in April 1988 for a road test programme which was to have taken in 23.6 miles (38 km) of a line between Modena and Mantua fettled up to permit systematic testing at the power car's full design speed. However, the necessary infrastructure work had been shelved under Schimberni; it was resumed in late 1989, but was unlikely to be finished before 1991. In the meantime ETRX500 was in June 1989 hustled up to a new Italian rail speed record of 316 kmph (196.4 mph) on the Rome-

Florence *Direttissima.*

The second phase of the `ETR500' project was production of a brace of two power car/ten trailer train-sets, designated ETRY500. The aim was to have both available for trial public service by the summer 1990 start of the World Cup football finals in Italy, so that they would get an international travel market exposure as well as domestic sampling. In the event, neither made it to the tracks until later in the year, and their evaluation in commercial service was deferred until the May 1991 timetable changes.

During 1990 the proposed `ETR500' squadron requirement had been scaled down from some dizzy numbers circulating in 1986 to 42 train-sets. But when — or even if — they would be ordered was an open question.

Under Schimberni's successor, Lorenzo Necci, the whole AV high-speed line scheme was returned to the immediate agenda. In March 1991 a mixed holding company, Treno Alta Velocita (TAV), was formed to advance the project. TAV is owned 40 per cent by FS and for the rest by a dozen banks, nine of them Italian, two French and one German, which together put up 60 per cent

The prototype 300 kmph ETRX500.

of the company's starting capital.

In early 1991 the total cost of completing the network was estimated at L30,000 billion (about £13.7 billion). Of that, about a quarter was assigned to high-speed rolling-stock. The Italian government undertook to put up L12,000 billion; the rest would be privately capitalized. A wholly-owned FS subsidiary, Sistav, was created to manage construction and issue contracts on a turnkey basis. The eventual train service would be run by a company known as Comtav, 50 per cent FS-owned.

There was now hope that construction of the Rome–Naples–Battipaglia segment could start in 1992, with completion by the end of 1995 possible. Expectations in early 1991 were that the Milan-Bologna section would take three years to build, Turin–Venice four years and the Bologna–Florence traversal of the Apennine mountains six years.

At the same time a joint stock company embracing Italian banks, Italian motorway operators, the Genoa port and the North Milan Railway (FNM) laid before the Government a proposal to build a new, privately-financed high-speed railway between Genoa and Milan. The signs were that the Government smiled on the scheme.

The Rome–Naples–Battipaglia high-speed line will for the most part parallel the alignment of the country's north-south motorway, the Autostrada del Sol, with Naples being served by a spur. Between Milan and Bologna the two new AV tracks are likely to start at Melegnano, just south of Milan Central, and parallel the north-south motorway to Bologna's outskirts. *En route*, spurs would diverge to service Piacenza, Fidenza, Cremona, Parma and Modena. In mid-1991 a choice had yet to be made from three possible trans-Apennine mountain routes between

Bologna and Florence; the most direct would entail 13 tunnels with an aggregate length of 24.2 miles (39 km) and 18 viaducts.

And what of the 'ETR500'? In the spring of 1991 Signor Necci had been reported so unhappy at its cost that the Breda-led consortium which gave it birth had broken up and regrouped in new alliances. They had been bidden by Necci, it was said, to come up with something cheaper and more likely to attract overseas buyers, so as to give FS the benefit of longer-run costing. But then, inexplicably, a few months later the original consortium was reported to be still in being. And not only that, but expecting any day a firm FS order for a production series of 30 'ETR500' train-sets.

9

Pain, progress and promise in North America

Howard Hosmer may be no name to conjure with outside North America, but it has a niche in US railroad lore. Hosmer was the Interstate Commerce Commission functionary who in 1958 scandalized railroad buffs with a public prediction that within a decade the rail passenger coach would `take its place in the transportation museum along with the stagecoach and the steam locomotive'.

In the event it did come dangerously near to kinship with the dodo. Immediately after the Second World War, North American railroads had enjoyed a deceptive boom in their passenger business which encouraged them to spend big on still more sumptuous and still more extravagantly staffed passenger equipment. But very quickly the airlines got a grip on the medium- and long-haul market, which with the onset of jetliners quickly expanded to a 75 per cent domination. Long-distance road coaches were in there battling, too, but they were puny competitors by comparison. Over the shorter hauls, of course, it was express highway development, an even more rapid growth of automobile ownership and cheap gasoline that bled the railroads of traffic.

Through the 1950s and 1960s the timetables were progressively thinned of the great inter-city trains as managements gloomily totted up the red-ink difference between dwindling revenues and huge running costs

that were escalating rather than abating. By the end of the 1960s nationwide timetables that had offered upwards of 15,000 passenger trains daily in the 1930s were down to a limp listing of under 500; and rail's share of the US passenger market had collapsed to a miserable 7.2 per cent.

But at the same time lobbyists were mounting ever stronger pressure for action to stave off genocide of the inter-city passenger train. Most respected of the voices crying halt was that of the Democratic Senator for Rhode Island, Claiborne Pell, who had been devoting considerable time and energy to what he termed, from the Greek word for a large city, the `megalopolis' problem. Focus of Pell's attention was the increasingly crowded communication lanes, in the air as much as on the ground, in the so-called North-East Corridor of teeming cities that runs from Boston through New York, Philadelphia and Baltimore to Washington.

Pell's work was the inspiration of the High Speed Ground Transportation Act signed by President Johnson at the end of September 1965. The value of the Act was the principle of Federal support for rail revival that it established rather than its munificence. In hard cash it offered only $90 million towards refurbishing the North-East Corridor trunk route — a paltry figure set against the huge Federal investment in air and road facilities: what's more, the operating Pennsylvania Rail-

One of the abortive lightweight essays of the 1950s with which some US railroads sought to cut passenger train operating costs. This is the 'Train X', built by Pullman-Standard in the New Haven Railroad's push-pull version, with a locomotive at each end, that ran between New York and Boston as the 'Dan'l Webster'. (Cecil J. Allen Collection)

road was bidden to hand over to the Federal coffers any profits attributable to the Government share of the improved service.

Three years earlier, shortly before Johnson's advisers had recommended that he take revival of tracked transport seriously and set up an Office of High Speed Ground Transportation, the Pennsylvania Railroad had embarked on an exhaustive study of the economics and practicalities of upgrading its sector of the North-East Corridor, the stretch from New York to Washington. Its findings were negotiated with Washington. The outcome, in April 1966, was agreement to a Federally-sponsored two-year demonstration project to assess public reaction to an intensive high-speed New York-Washington passenger service with new equipment, improved passenger facilities both on the ground and on the move, and the backing of market-orientated fares. At the same time a second demonstration project was agreed on the New York-Boston main line of the New York, New Haven & Hartford RR. This was to employ the United Aircraft Turbotrain that had taken the fancy of Canadian National, of

which more anon. Before long both projects were to come within the same operating orbit following the New Haven's curtain-raiser to the general financial collapse of major railroads in the North-East. By the time the New York-Washington project came to fruition the whole North-East Corridor route was under the suzerainty of the short-lived Penn-Central conglomerate.

There was not too much to complain of in the existing speed-compatibility of the New York-Washington main line. Four-tracked for most of its 226.1-mile (364 km) length, it was straight or curved no more seriously than to a 1,870-yard (1,700 m) radius for 174 miles (280 km) of the 180 miles (290 km) of route lying outside the major metropolitan areas. It was already equipped for intermittent cab signalling, which was considered adaptable to safe operation at up to 125 mph (200 kmph).

Pending delivery of new train-sets, the Pennsylvania decided to exploit the completed trackwork for a yard or two more pace from its existing equipment. Some of the beloved 4,620 hp 'GG1' electric locomotives were regeared for a maximum of 100 mph (160 kmph) — years back, in its development stage, a `GG1' had been pushed up to 115 mph (185 kmph) in tests — and conventional coaches refined for the same speed. About 15 minutes were cut from New York-Washington schedules and for the first time the route was graced with some schedules timed at over 80 mph (130 kmph) start to stop, up to a high point of 85.5 mph (137.6 kmph) between Baltimore and Wilmington, 68.4 miles (110 km) in 48 minutes. But the venerable `GG1s' did not take to this 1968 rejuvenation, nor did the old-fashioned Pennsy catenary. After a succession of breakdowns, chiefly the result of flashovers, the accelerated schedules were discreetly withdrawn.

Worse woes were brewing in the high-speed train-sets to come, however. Trouble had been virtually guaranteed from the start by the Federal Government's insistence on design by committee — a grouping of Pennsylvania men, representatives of the Office of High Speed Ground Transportation and consulting engineers. Then, with no recent native experience of designing high-performance electrified railroad equipment, the committee unwisely essayed an overnight leap ahead to a concept which hopefully would look the Japanese Shinkansen technology proudly in the face. Far too little of the resultant Metroliners' components had been

put through the essential preliminary mill of practical evaluation in the tough railroad environment. Above all, it was soon obvious that the `Metroliners' had been pointlessly over-designed. Such infrastructure improvements as the budget would cover were insufficient to accommodate their maximum performance, even if that had been available trouble-free.

By 1965, when the design committee was appointed, the whole railway world was genuflecting towards Tokyo and Osaka. The New Tokaido line model — which a Pennsy delegation had studied at first-hand — must have strongly influenced the choice of multiple-unit format for the `Metroliners'. Another plus for the concept was that US law allowed a multiple unit to be single-manned, but not a locomotive-hauled train. To spread the bulk of the electric traction equipment and allow its underfloor mounting to maximum extent, each car would be motored; and each would have a driving cab, for maximum operational flexibility in train make-up.

The performance specification set for the `Metroliner' design was staggering. The initial acceleration rate demanded was 1 mph/sec (1.6 kmph/sec), to hustle a train up to 125 mph (200 kmph) in 2 minutes or less, and to 150 mph (240 kmph) in 3 minutes or less on straight and level track; maximum speed capability was to be 160 mph (257 kmph) and a train should be able to maintain

The North-East Corridor in Pennsylvania days: a `GG-1' electric heads the New York-Chicago `Broadway Limited'.

150 mph (240 kmph) up a 1 in 100 gradient. To cope with that specification every axle of each 85-foot (25.9 m) `Metroliner' coach was fitted with a 300 hp (continuous rating) traction motor, capable of a 1-hour output of 640 hp at 100 mph (160 kmph), so that every car in a train would have a short-term punch of 2,560 hp.

When he signed the High Speed Ground Transportation Act in 1965, President Johnson had glibly forecast the debut of 125 mph (200 kmph) trains within about a year. At the end of that year the target date receded to October 1967. But came the autumn of 1968 and there was still no `Metroliner' in public use.

Since the original two-year demonstration project contract had legally expired in March 1968 without a revenue-earning passenger being carried, a joint Government-railroad-supplier task force was deputed to determine why `Metroliners' were not fit to begin public service. Most serious were failures of the traction control and braking systems — in fact, neither Government nor railroad would accept delivery of cars with the original Westinghouse dynamic braking, on the grounds that it fell short of performance specification.

The tripartite task force took refuge in a blanket defence that the project managements had been `overly optimistic with respect to the planning and scheduling requirements of a project of this magnitude

and complexity'. But, it consoled, the major remaining problems of electronic component fallibility, wheel overheating under the air brakes, pantograph bounce at speed and poor riding would soon be unravelled and the trains would be rolling by end-1968.

In the event they started creeping into service early in 1969 as the GE-equipped cars were gradually passed fit for service. And in March, on private test, a `Metroliner' was coaxed up to 165 mph (265.5 kmph) between Trenton and New Brunswick, NJ, over a stretch of now Penn-Central main line (the merger of Pennsylvania and New York Central had been consummated just before the `Metroliners'' long-delayed debut) which had had its current supply arrangements specially stepped up.

Meagre though it was by comparison with the demonstration project prospectus's forecast of hourly New York-Washington frequency, because the Westinghouse-equipped cars were still side-tracked, the 1969-70 `Metroliner' service immediately attracted healthy business. For the first time in years Americans were running on rails at 100 mph (160 kmph) and more. Generally top speed was in the region of 115 mph (185 kmph). But although the governors of the `Metroliners' were supposed to cut off at 125 mph (200 kmph), some claimed they had touched as much as 140 mph (225 kmph).

By 1971 the availability of cars permitted a seven-train service each way daily, and the

In Penn-Central livery, a `Metroliner' hums down the North-East Corridor.

Department of Transportation was prepared to concede that the demonstration had officially started. Northbound 'Metroliners' were on a five-stop, 2-hour 59-minute schedule for the 224.6 miles (361.4 km), and the best southbound timing was 2 hours 50 minutes, but the intermediate running called for some of the fastest point-to-point timings in the world at that time. All seven trains had to cover the 68.4 miles (110 km) from Baltimore to Wilmington in 43 minutes, average 95.4 mph (153.5 kmph) and five the same distance in the reverse direction in a minute more, average 93.3 mph (150 kmph).

Meanwhile, what of the other leg of the North-East Corridor demonstration project, from New York to Boston? To sketch the background there, steps in time must be retraced to developments across the 49th Parallel in Canada.

In the mid-1960s the Federally-owned Canadian National (CN) system suddenly decided that, given refurbished equipment and adept marketing, the Canadian long-haul passenger train had a viable, expanding future. Some 700 inter-city coaches were given an interior revamp and 174 high-quality cars, such as ex-Milwaukee 'Hiawatha' Super-Domes, bought or leased from US railroads that had discarded them in the contraction of passenger service. CN's Montreal-Toronto service was intensified and sharply accelerated. Finally, passenger fares were re-written in a 'Red-White-and-Blue' plan that heavily discounted off-peak rates as an inducement to fill empty seats out of season.

By 1966 CN had boosted its passenger carryings almost 39 per cent compared with 1961, and the average passenger journey was almost the same amount longer in distance. Time, alas, was to justify the sceptics who pointed out that as a result of the discounted fare scheme the revenue from the increased business was a long, long way from overtaking expenses; but in those heady mid-1960s CN was euphorically confident of closing the gap by the early 1970s. To do that, though, demanded more speed.

Since 13.5 per cent of the Montreal-Toronto route-mileage was curved, some of it quite sharply, CN understandably balked at the cost of trying to extract significantly

higher speed from orthodox equipment. Happily, it seemed at the time, an unorthodox answer was in the wings right on cue.

With defence expenditure contracting, several North American aerospace firms had been prompted by Lyndon Johnson's High Speed Ground Transportation programme to dabble in adapting their technology to surface transport. One was the United Aircraft Corporation, which had entered a turbine-powered train-set derived structurally from airframe technology in a design contest sponsored by the US Department of Commerce as a result of the Act. This concept United Aircraft now offered to Canadian National.

UAC's Turbo-train design was based on the premise that reduced resistance was the economical way to gain speed: extra power should be used only to make good what aerodynamics could not achieve. Vital features, therefore, were drastic reduction of weight, aerodynamic drag and mechanical resistance, plus a low centre of gravity and a pendular tilt-body suspension which would win so much pace over curves that there would be no need to aim for extravagantly high speed on straight track.

The Turbotrain version adopted by CN was a seven-car unit, with power concentrated on two four-wheel bogies, one at each end of the set, and the rest of the unit articulated in single-axle junctions between cars (a close-coupled arrangement that usefully eliminated inter-car vestibules). Each single-axle bogie was guided by telescopic arms which were in essence ball-bearing screw actuators; these were to position the bogie, so that theoretically it should always bisect the angle between adjoining cars on a curve. Especially complex was the suspension of the inside-bearing powered bogies, to which the drive from a cluster of very compact, UAC-modified, Pratt & Whitney 400 hp ST-6B turbines in each power car was an intricate web of mechanical couplings and shafts. The power car domes were fronted by driving cabs but mostly occupied by passenger space: a small saloon with revolving chairs for premium-class 'Turboclub' clients at one end of the unit, a less roomy saloon with fixed seats and tables for 'Turboluxe'

A United Aircraft Turbotrain in its original Canadian National livery.

patrons at the other.

UAC built five seven-car, 159-tonne Turbotrains for CN at its own expense and agreed to lease them to CN for eight years. Under the contact UAC also undertook maintenance for the first five years and gave CN an option for subsequent three- and two-year renewals of the deal. For those generous terms, motivated no doubt by eagerness to get in on the ground floor of reborn high-speed railroading, UAC was to pay heavily.

CN had spent a fair amount of money on track strengthening and modification of superelevation on curves — even some modest realignments — before the Turbotrains' public service debut on 12 December

A close-up of a UAC Turbotrain's single-axle articulation. (P.J. Howard)

1969. Nevertheless the newcomers had to be limited to a top speed of 95 mph (153 kmph) instead of their potential 120 mph (193 kmph) out of deference to the Montreal-Toronto route's 240 or so public highway crossings and 700 agricultural or private crossings. Even so, riding did not impress journalists on an inaugural press trip. `Rail nose considerably exceeds that of standard equipment,' wrote one, continuing to allege that curves were a `major problem . . . the many cups of coffee splashing testified to the rough-riding characteristics. The single-axle articulation in practice negotiates curves in a series of short jerks rather than the smooth flowing motion promised in the press releases.'

The Turbotrains had already slipped their intended introduction date of the 1967 summer, to coincide with Canada's Centennial, when they finally took on CN passengers in the winter of 1969. But within just weeks of their launch the Turbotrains had been so persistently lamed by failures, principally of their auxiliary equipment, which plunged the trains into heatless dark, that CN withdrew them and despatched them to UAC for atten-

tion. For the rest of 1969 there was no Turbo service. At last the trains resumed operation in May 1970. But yet again CN found them fault-prone and in mid-February 1971 all five sets were side-tracked once more.

By now UAC, obliged to foot the bills for every alteration sought by CN, was getting nettled. It wasn't having anything like the same bother with the two three-car sets it had been contracted to supply for trial to the US Department of Transportation, and which had been in demonstration public service (not on very exacting schedules) between New York and Boston since the spring of 1969. The aerospace men had a mounting suspicion that CN was ordering its Turbo-trains off the road every time a hinge creaked or an engine coughed. And they said so, publicly. To which a CN vice-president retorted crisply that `the trains never did measure up to the original contract and they haven't yet.'

As with the `Metroliners', but more so, the root of all the problems was inexperience in a rugged railroad operating environment. A great deal of ingenuity and derived technology had been packed into the Turbotrain without extended practical evaluation in rail-

Tray meal service in the `Turboclub' accommodation of a Canadian National Turbotrain. (Canadian National)

A UAC Turbotrain in Amtrak service between New York and Boston.

road conditions. From transmission to suspension and auxiliaries, far too many vital components seemed to have been translated straight from the drawing board to the series production line.

Eventually, after some substantial modification of the gearbox drive and the pendular suspension, plus reinforcement of the sound insulation, CN was pacified and their Turbotrains at last took up untroubled service from the start of 1974. But the schedules they fulfilled in the late 1970s were well short of the 1960s' promise — at best 4^1/$_2$ hours between Montreal and Toronto with three intermediate stops, the fastest intermediate booking being a start-to-stop time of 102 minutes for the 145.2 miles from Kingston to Guildwood, average 85.4 mph (137.4 kmph).

As for the two Turbotrains in the US, favourable public reaction persuaded the Department of Transportation to retain them on the New York-Boston route beyond the original October 1970 terminal date of the demonstration project. But nobody thereafter was writing turbine traction into their visions of a full-scale revival of US inter-city rail speed. Though the French-built Turbolin-

ers which were imported in 1973, then proliferated in 1975-6 by a combination of further orders from France and domestic building under licence, impressed with their reliability, the post-Arab-Israeli 1973 war explosion of fuel prices had destroyed overnight one of gas turbine traction's prime advantages, fuel cost economy. By the end of 1982 both US and Canadian UAC Turbotrains were withdrawn from service. However, a Turbotrain did in March 1976 set an attested Canadian rail speed record of 140.6 mph (226 kmph) on a demonstration run between Kingston and Montreal.

Meanwhile, the US `Metroliners' had come under new management. Confronting a real risk of the inter-city passenger train's extinction, public opinion had mobilized sufficiently to arouse a tremor or two in Washington. After two years of Congressional deliberation and stalling by powerful factions within the Nixon administration, a Federally-financed takeover of all inter-city rail services by a quasi-Governmental operating agency on an approved network was finally ordered by the Rail Passenger Service Act of 30 October 1971. Thus was `Amtrak' born.

For a while the Amtrak management

A Turbotrain leaves Ottawa Union station on a morning run to Montreal in October 1974. (P.J. Howard)

sounded uncertain whether its remit was just to hold a saline drip over the passenger train or to set about transplant surgery. From 1972 onwards, however, it set about positive

redevelopment; and an immediate candidate for attention was the North-East Corridor, where Amtrak was ringing up more than half its revenue, and particularly the New York-

Amtrak's American-built (by Rohr Industries) version of French Railways' RTG gas turbine train-set on 'Empire State Express' service between New York and Niagara Falls, crossing the Mohawk River. (Amtrak)

Washington 'Metroliners'.

The whole fleet was now serviceable and the timetable offered 14 trains each way daily. Moreover, the Department of Transportation had shown that the cars could be perfected. In 1973 it had paid for two of each type to be returned to their respective equipment suppliers, General Electric and Westinghouse, for a long list of nearly 100 modifications. The four rebuilds were shown off to the press in July 1974 on the 22-mile (35 km) demonstration stretch of Penn-Central main line in New Jersey between Trenton and New Brunswick. If the riding was still something less than blissful, the rest of the equipment functioned immaculately and the cars had no trouble in making a top speed of 152 mph (245 kmph).

The high cost of 'Metroliner' refurbishment apart, there was the question of how long the New York-Washington tracks could stand up to high-speed pounding. The 'Metroliners' were very much the minority users, for of the near-1,000 trains travelling the North-East Corridor tracks daily, two-thirds were commuter, nearly 200 freight and a mere 100 or so Amtrak services. Following its official bankruptcy in 1970, Penn-Central had been still more strapped for cash to keep the track in order and within a year or so a 100 mph (160 kmph) limit had to be clamped on the 'Metroliners', enforcing some schedule deceleration and compromising punctuality quite seriously.

Amtrak had always hankered after a thoroughgoing reconstruction of the North-East Corridor into a super-speed railway in the 150 mph (240 kmph) class. By the mid-1970s, however, the prospective costs were so astronomical that the idea had scant chance of endorsement — still less so from a Ford administration with a Secretary of Transportation plainly antipathetic to the whole Amtrak concept.

A new approach of some kind to the North-East Corridor issue became inescapable following the brushfire bankruptcies of almost all the major railroads in the North-East in the early 1970s. To save the situation another quasi-governmental organization, Consolidated Rail Corporation, or Conrail for short, was born in the Railroad Revitalisation and Regulatory Reform Act, the so-called '4R' Act, of 1975, with a mandate to rationalize a heavily duplicated network down to a sensible, economical core.

The '4R' Act's draughtsmen solved the North-East Corridor dilemma by proposing a reversal of roles. Amtrak should buy the route lock, stock and barrel and become the managing operator, leasing out the tracks to Conrail's freight trains and the various regional transport authorities' commuter services. The Ford administration doggedly resisted the idea, but Amtrak eventually won too powerful a support from Congress for the White House to prevail.

Six regional commuter transport authorities retained ownership of segments within their bailiwicks. The rest of the Corridor's route, six stations and assorted maintenance facilities, were knocked down to Amtrak at a price that Penn-Central's creditors and stockholders howled was a gross under-valuation of the assets.

The Ford administration flatly refused Amtrak pleas for funding to transform the Corridor into a Shinkansen. But it conceded a top-up of Amtrak resources sufficient — or so it was thought at the time — to relay track, rebuild life-expired bridges, realign much of the existing route for 125 mph (200 kmph), modernize the signalling, renew the New York-Washington electrification at 25kV instead of the Pennsylvania's 12kV ac, and extend the wires north of New York from the city's suburban network limit at New Haven to Boston. Designated the Northeast Corridor Improvement Program (NECIP), the work began in 1977 and was supposed to be complete in 1981, at a total cost of US$1.75 billion.

In the event, neither the full NECIP nor its time-scale could be honoured. One reason was the project's ill-advised initial remission to incoherent and sometimes acrimoniously divided management by a mix of Federal and rail agencies. By the start of 1981, when the Reagan administration put its feet under White House tables and promptly launched the first of its perennial — but largely abortive — assaults on all public transport subsidy, the prospective NECIP bill was US$2.5 billion. The Reagan men refused to bolster NECIP funding any higher than to US$2.19 billion (though three years later Congress voted to invest a further US$98 million). Anxiety over costs had already forced abandonment of 25kV conversion of the Pennsylvania catenary. Now the more important projection of wires from New Haven to Boston had to be dropped too.

However, by 1982 most of the civil engineering work and track and bridges was complete, and the Federal Railroad Administration could pass some stretches between New York and Washington for a top speed of 120 mph (193 kmph). A gradual acceleration of services between the two cities could begin.

The shape of 'Metroliner' trains had by now changed. The refurbished self-propelled EMU cars had been transferred to New York-Philadelphia-Harrisburg service (by the end of the 1980s they would be stripped of their traction equipment and degraded to hauled vehicles or push-pull control trailers). The 'Metroliner' format had become locomotive-hauled rakes of new motorless cars cloning the EMUs' body design and known as the 'Amfleet' type.

As for the locomotives, Amtrak had imported a Swedish Railways Type 'Rc4' Bo-Bo and a French Railways 'CC21000'-type Co-Co for trials before making a choice. Its existing US-built Class 'E60CP' Co-Cos, essentially derived from a freight design, had proved quite unsuitable for high-speed passenger haulage. The French machine's discomfort on US track may have had some influence on the decision to buy Swedish, but more persuasive for sure was the latter's offer of a 4,600kW output within a weight of only 82 tons (92 US tons). That earned the resultant Amtrak Class 'AEM-7', taking up Amtrak service in the spring of 1980, the tag of 'Mighty Mouse'. The Amtrak fleet was US-built by General Motors to the Swedish design, around the electrical equipment of Swedish traction builders ASEA, which is now part of the ASEA-Brown Boveri (ABB) multi-national conglomerate. The 'AEM-7' design has since been bought by one or two US regional commuter train authorities too.

As the 1990s opened, Amtrak was carrying more passengers between New York and

Washington than any one of the air shuttle operators between the two cities. Furthermore its 'Metroliners' were vying in end-to-end speed with Europe's fastest on historic infrastructure. With 273.5 miles (440 km) of the route now sanctioned for 125 mph (200 kmph), three 'Metroliners' of the hourly train service each way had pinched the New York-Washington journey time down to 2 hours 35 minutes, one to just 2^1/$_2$ hours. The target schedule set at the start of the NECIP had at last been attained. The fastest segment of the route was the 68.4 miles (110.1 km) between Baltimore and Wilmington stops, where the 'Metroliner' timing for 11 trains was 40 minutes, exacting a start-to-stop average speed of 102.6 mph (165.1 kmph). A further 17 services were allowed only 41 or 42 minutes.

Meanwhile, New Englanders were fretting at the widening gap between Corridor speed south of New York and on the largely unreconstructed route north to Boston. In mid-1968 a Coalition of Northeast Governors (CONEG), representing seven states, formed a task force to study the feasibility, applicability and benefits of high train speed to their constituencies. Their objective — which Amtrak shared — was a cut of New York-Boston journey time from the current 4^1/$_2$-5 hours to a flat 3 hours.

Acknowledging CONEG's wish to see what tilt-body rolling-stock could achieve, Amtrak imported from Spain six Talgo Pendular cars and from Canada some LRC equipment — of which more in a moment — for comparative trials in the spring of 1988. The results were passed to CONEG in early 1989, but in 1990 it became clear that, in its negotiations with CONEG and the Federal Railroad Administration on the character and financing of development north of New York, Amtrak was arguing for reinstatement of electrification as the top priority. For that Amtrak at last secured preliminary finance in 1991. Bids for electrification to Boston were likely to be called before 1991 was out.

The LRC (an acronym for 'Light, Rapid, Comfortable') was Canada's last essay in high-speed rail passenger equipment, and, in its earlier years, as ill-starred a product as the UAC Turbotrain. In 1978 the Canadian gov-

An Amtrak `AEM-7' at speed in the North-East Corridor, heading the `Palmetto' over the Bush River near Edgewood, Maryland. (Amtrak)

ernment set up an Amtrak facsimile, VIA Rail, to take over what remained of long-haul passenger operations on Canadian Pacific (CP Rail) and Canadian National (CN) tracks. At the same time the then government put up dollars to accelerate rail service in the coun-try's one populous corridor, the 727 miles (1,170 km) from Quebec through Montreal and Toronto to Windsor, on the US border close to Detroit. Since 1971 a consortium of Canadian companies had been working up the LRC concept, which paired a low-slung

Inside an Amfleet car: this is the premium `Amclub' accommodation. (Amtrak)

2,760kW diesel-electric locomotive with aluminium alloy-bodied trailers equipped with an active tilt-body system. The tilt system comprised essentially a lateral movement-measuring accelerometer on each bogie, and an associated electronic servo valve that actuated the tilt mechanism. Top design speed was 125 mph (200 kmph).

This indigenous product appealed to the newborn VIA management more than the import of a foreign high-speed technology. The government, happy to keep its dollars at home, took VIA's preference on board and supported production of an LRC fleet by Canada's Bombardier company.

The LRCs have never regularly operated at their full design speed. Deliveries began in 1981, but teething traumas held back their full public service debut until June 1982, at a maximum permitted speed of 96 mph (155 kmph). This was because the LRCs shared their tracks with huge freight trains, and nei-

ther the government of the day nor its successors would sanction segregation of VIA's trains and freight where parallel CP and CN routes existed, then foot an estimated C$2 billion bill for some new infrastructure and upgrading of historic line elsewhere that would achieve a reserved 125 mph (200 kmph) LRC route the length of the Quebec-Windsor corridor.

The LRCs did not run untroubled at 96 mph until well into 1985. Twice they were for periods limited to 80 mph (128 kmph), on the first occasion in 1982 because of poor locomotive riding, and later when nagging problems with the tilt system compelled its immobilization. That was during 1983-84, when equipment malfunctions proliferated to the extent that from the end of 1984 to late 1985 the LRCs had to be successively retired to their builders for a retrofit programme of some 200 modifications.

VIA always had a rougher ride than its

Amtrak tested LRC units on the New York-Boston route: an LRC power car in Amtrak livery poses alongside an Amtrak 'FP40H' diesel locomotive. (Amtrak)

Amtrak counterpart. Its best marketing efforts could never drum up sufficient revenue to keep pace with the escalating upkeep costs of its high ratio of outdated traction and rolling-stock, or the punitive terms (until 1986 legislation revised them) on which it rented CP and CN track space and operating and maintenance staff. In the 1980s Amtrak managed year by year to narrow the gap between its revenue and its total costs, so that by 1990, given adequate Federal support for continuing renewal of obsolete equipment, it glimpsed a chance of financial viability by the century's end.

Not so VIA. In the 1980s successive Canadian governments teetered between service cutbacks and capital investment as the key to a reducing VIA deficit. But the Conservative government that won the November 1988 Federal election plumped for savage retrenchment and little else (even though the party's winning platform in a previous election had had expansion of VIA operation as a plank). The following January VIA's train services were halved at a stroke and the agency was told that over the next four years almost 60 per cent of its Federal subsidy would be withdrawn.

That extinguished, it seemed, any lingering hope of realizing the prospectus for a new and dedicated high-speed line between Montreal, Ottawa and Toronto that VIA had researched and published in 1984. But enter, in 1990, the private sector.

Busily establishing a European base by buying up companies or forging alliances, Bombardier had amongst other things acquired from the GEC-Alsthom partnership the North American rights to manufacture and market French TGV technology. In 1990 it announced that, with the full support of GEC-Alsthom, it was seeking partners to build, equip and run a 300 kmph TGV route between Montreal, Ottawa and Toronto at an estimated cost of C$5.3 billion for infrastructure and C$650 million for TGV train-sets.

At the same time, after a decade of proposals, negotiations, back-pedallings, thwarted ambitions and one mortifying fiasco, the US appeared at last firmly on course for inauguration of its first non-Federally financed high-speed service. Since the start of the 1980s a number of states and individuals had been goaded to explore go-it-alone schemes by the channelling into the North-East Corridor of so high a proportion of Amtrak's capital funding, the paltry amount voted in Washington for analysis of potential in other US inter-city corridors, and the commercial success of high speed in Europe and Japan.

The prospects that any of these projects would be fulfilled looked dim when the first to take on a high profile collapsed within three years. In early 1982, with the backing of an encouraging market study by Amtrak, and an engineering feasibility exercise by the Japanese, the American High Speed Rail Corporation was formed to build a Japanese-style Shinkansen line through the heavily-populated Los Angeles-San Diego corridor, with a branch to Los Angeles Airport. Brandishing euphoric traffic forecasts that appeared to guarantee a handsome profit on operation, its founders were confident that raising the construction money in the private sector would be no problem.

But it was, not least because the revenue forecasts were deemed highly suspect. In November 1984 the Corporation had to throw in the towel, unable even to round up the US$50 million it needed to start engineering. This flop was, though, salutary for other promoters of US high-speed schemes. It taught that capital would be signed up only after methodical preparation of the financial ground, including verification of ancillary income potential from associated property development, for instance, as well as the route plan and the technology. And that the assessments of potential market must be really hard-nosed.

It would be tedious to detail all the vicissitudes of the other schemes in the 1980s. Of those that were sustaining credibility in 1991, two were leaning away from wheel-on-rail to the MagLev technology described in Chapter 13. These were the Chicago-Milwaukee-Minneapolis & St Paul, jointly promoted by the Illinois, Minnesota and Wisconsin Departments of Transportation; and a prospective 270-mile (435 km) line from Anaheim, the tourist quarter of Los Angeles, to Las Vegas, Nevada. The latter was sponsored by the California-Nevada SuperSpeed Ground Transportation Commission but would be built and operated by private interests.

Florida's Miami-Orlando-Tampa high-speed venture had looked closest to the starting blocks in 1990. The line of route, partly adopting existing rail alignments, partly adjoining highways, had been fixed by the state's High Speed Rail Passenger Commission; the private entrepreneur — the Florida High Speed Rail Corporation — had been anointed; and with that the type of train had been settled. It would be a version of the ABB Type X2000 tilt-body train-set produced for Swedish Railways (SJ), which is discussed in Chapter 12. As 1990 closed, the Commission looked certain to hand the Corporation a formal build-and-operate franchise in 1991. Inauguration of train service over the first stage of the scheme, the 307.5 miles (523 km) from Tampa to Miami, was anticipated in 1995. At first the trains would run at a maximum speed of 150 mph (240 kmph). But with further refinement of the track and infrastructure there was hope of hoisting pace subsequently to 175 mph (281.6 kmph).

But by early 1991 the Florida project had hit financial rocks. The High Speed Rail Corporation's hope of raising start-up funds from real estate development and other communal benefit along the line of route had been thwarted by recession, a deflated property market and the collapse of US savings-and-loan institutions. No alternative means of raising the money was immediately in sight.

The torch now passed to Texas. There, in May 1991, French TGV technology scored its first clear victory in overseas markets. The prize was the initial 267-mile (430 km) Dallas–Houston segment of a planned 200 mph (320 kmph) railway interconnecting Dallas/Fort Worth, Houston, San Antonio and Austin.

Two consortia were in contention for a franchise from the Texas High Speed Rail Authority to develop this system. One, Texas FasTrac Corporation, was offering German ICE technology. The other, Texas TGV, which promoted French expertise, looked from the start the more soundly-based, quite apart from any merits of its TGV grounding. Led by the big US engineering company Morrison-Knudsen and including TGV's North American licensee, Bombardier, it was backed by several major US and foreign banks and boasted a starting capital of US$1.4 billion.

Texas TGV was unsurprisingly the victor. Pocketing the franchise, though, was only a first step. Until 1994 Texas TGV would be absorbed in detailed design, satisfaction of environmental concerns and raising of funds adequate for construction in full. Texas TGV was also anxious to defuse the determined campaign of one airline, Southwest, against the rail scheme by tying up long-haul air/short-haul rail cooperation agreements with two others, American and Delta. Target year for the Dallas–Houston opening was 1998.

The triumphs of France's TGV

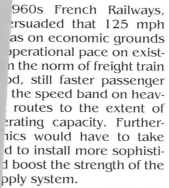

960s French Railways,
rsuaded that 125 mph
as on economic grounds
perational pace on exist-
n the norm of freight train
d, still faster passenger
the speed band on heav-
routes to the extent of
rating capacity. Further-
nics would have to take
d to install more sophisti-
d boost the strength of the
pply system.

capacity was unthinkable
route, the Paris-Dijon-Lyon
e start of routes from Paris
large tracts of south-east
rance, connected 40 per
population. At the rate its
nding in the 1960s its
nents would be choked in
st cases these were in ter-
acking would be formidably
ver, the route's alignments
s a whole did not favour
he higher passenger train
ssential to combat strength-
torway competition for busi-
ris and southern France.

er 1970 SNCF boldly pre-
ch government with a plan
run between the outskirts of
and to be engineered for the

exclusive use of purpose-built high-speed
passenger trains. But though the design of
the new route's infrastructure and of its
rolling-stock would be a thoroughly integrated engineering exercise, the new trains
would be acceptable on historic SNCF main
lines. The core of their operation would be
Paris-Lyon; but they would also be able to
branch off or travel beyond the new line to
provide service from Paris to Dijon, Grenoble, the Riviera, Languedoc-Roussillon and
Switzerland.

This first TGV scheme (*Train à Grande
Vitesse*, or High Speed Train), the TGV-Paris
Sudest, or TGV-PSE, won Ministerial approval
in principle quite smartly, in March 1971. But
it was March 1974 before the Council of Ministers authorized SNCF to start land acquisi-
tion procedures for the new line, and late
1976 before construction could begin.

The main cause of the first two years' inac-
tivity was well-orchestrated opposition from
air and motor industry interests, which persuaded some of the French press that the
scheme was both an extravagance and a certain economic disaster; and even more virulent and certainly more protracted protest
from ecological and agricultural interests
affected by the line's proposed route. Then,
when that had been discounted by proof that
TGV technology would minimize the new
line's environmental disturbance, the government needed in 1973 to reconfirm the

TGV-PSE's traffic projections and economic viability. That year's upgrading of the 1969 estimates found, in fact, that rail passenger traffic between Paris and south-east France was growing substantially faster than was forecast four years earlier.

Unobtrusive projection of a new high-speed railway through central France without coming closer than some 800 feet (240 m) of its tiniest hamlet, let alone any town, was facilitated by the region's low population density. But no less helpful was limitation of the line's use to a single type of high-powered, lightweight and specifically speed-engineered train-set, so that track parameters could be the ideal for that rolling-stock and its designed speed, and not a mixed traffic compromise.

The huge land area of France makes it easier in many regions to find an inoffensive route for a new railway than elsewhere in Europe. But French planning procedures also help. There comes a stage at which, with local and regional authority consultations satisfactorily concluded, the Government stamps a major infrastructure project with a Declaration of Public Utility. Thereafter the scheme is virtually immune to legal objection.

SNCF's 1969 TGV-PSE proposal had been backed by proof from interactive track-and-vehicle research that such a special-purpose line could indulge a minimum curve radius of 4,000 m, only a little more generous than the French motorway norm, and maximum gradients almost as steep — 1 in 28.6 (3.5 per cent) as against 1 in 25. Sessions with France's motorway planners and builders had identified areas where the two modes could share new infrastructure for a considerable distance, thereby sparing both the environment and each mode's construction costs. Two stretches of the TGV-PSE would parallel motorway, but a much greater length of twinned infrastructure was planned for the TGV-Nord from Paris to Lille, the Channel Tunnel and the Belgian border. Of that, more later in this chapter — later than would have been the case had not Britain's Labour government ditched its commitment to a Channel Tunnel in 1974. Until that rebuff the Nord scheme was No 2 on SNCF's TGV agenda.

The gradient and curvature tolerances also allowed the TGV-PSE's infrastructure planners to follow land contours very closely. Consequently the route would be completely innocent of tunnels, even in its negotiation of the Burgundy hills, as well as thrifty in its recourse to embankment and cutting. (One should perhaps interpose that the infrastructure of a French high-speed route is officially termed *Ligne à Grande Vitesse*, or LGV — High Speed Line — but the French rail press is not punctilious about this distinction; I find it simpler to stick to `TGV' as an all-purpose identification of the track, trains and other technology involved.) Whereas the historic Paris-Dijon-Lyon main line profile is basically a very mild climb out of the Seine valley for almost 125 miles (200 km), then a steeper hog's back topped by Blaisy-Bas summit in the Burgundy hills before Dijon, and finally an almost level descent of the Saone valley, the TGV-PSE profile would be jagged, with several peaks flanked by short but steep gradients up to the limit of 1 in 28.5. The new line's summit in the Burgundy hills would be some 915 feet (300 m) higher than the old route's.

To avoid the expense and environmental hassle of driving new track through metropolitan Paris and Lyon, the new TGV-PSE infrastructure was branched off the historic Paris-Lyon by a flying junction at Lieusaint, 29.4 km (18.5 miles) out from Paris Gare de Lyon, and fed back into the existing network at Sathonay, on the outskirts of Lyon. Including a high-speed 9.3-mile (15 km) branch from the new line at Pasilly to the old, for TGV train access to Dijon and Lausanne, 259.2 route miles (417 km) of new double-track route had to be built.

There were just two intermediate stations, at Montchanin-Montceau-les-Mines and Macon. Close to the latter, new and old routes crossed and a flying junction enabled TGVs to switch routes for service of Annecy and Geneva. Both here and at Pasilly the French installed gently tapering turnouts through which TGV trains could diverge from or regain the new line at a speed no lower than 137 mph (220 kmph). In 1989 the Pasilly pointwork was replaced with a new

A TGV-PSE train-set at Dijon, preparing to leave for Paris. (G.Freeman Allen)

design of even longer blades — 58.14 m (190.7 feet) no less — that lifted permissible turnout speed a notch to 230 kmph (142.9 mph); but in trials a TGV comfortably negotiated the divergence at 246 kmph (152.9 mph).

The TGV-PSE was to be engineered for an eventual 300 kmph (186.5 mph), but initially top speed would be 260 kmph (161.6 mph). That was raised to 270 kmph (167.8 mph) in May 1983. Operation at this pace demanded sophisticated Automatic Train Protection, which the SNCF embodied in its TVM300 system of continuous cab signalling for the TGV-PSE. There was no lineside signalling, other than fixed markers, or *repères*, at the

The flying junction at Lieusaint, on the outskirts of Paris, where TGV-PSE diverges from the historic route to the south. In the foreground is an SNCF bi-level suburban electric multiple unit. (SNCF.CAV)

Above: A high-speed crossover between the two TGV-PSE running lines. (SNCF.CAV)

Left: The only lineside TGV signalling — the visual marker of the end of a block section. (SNCF.CAV)

Right: An SNCF Type RTG gas turbine-powered train-set at Calais Ville. (G.Freeman Allen)

start and end of each block section. Coded frequencies actuated automatically by, and transmitted through, the track circuiting, were picked up by inductive coils on the lead car of a train and electronically translated into one of 10 aspects available on the driver's desk signalling display. These aspects, linked to automatic devices checking driver response and initiating braking if that was flawed, covered instructions from freedom to proceed at top speed to warnings of reduction to one of four different speed levels in sections ahead, and then orders to hold pace at the revised level until otherwise advised. In conjunction with the braking power to be built into the TGV train-sets, the system allowed trains to sustain full speed on a headway of three block sections.

Until 1973 a faction within SNCF was still arguing for gas turbine-powered TGV trainsets. Aerospace industry's latest compact and lightweight turbines were powering very successful 100 mph (160 kmph) train-sets recently launched on the Paris-Cherbourg route. That form of traction would relieve the TGV-PSE balance sheet of high fixed electrification costs. Furthermore, electric traction engineers were still unsure that they had mastered efficient current collection by power cars making very high speed.

Indeed, the first prototype train-set to take approximate TGV shape, the articulated five-car TGV001, was turbine-powered. Outshopped in March 1972, the 192-tonne unit had four turbines with a total output of 6,500 hp supplying current to traction motors on all axles through an alternator transmission. By the time TGV001 was retired in January 1978, on the eve of the first pre-production electric TGV-PSE train-sets' appearance, test programmes had submitted it to more than

34,000 miles (54,700 km) running at over 125 mph (200 kmph), of which almost half were covered at more than 160 mph (257 kmph), up to a peak of 198 mph (318 kmph). At the same time a one-off single-unit electric railcar kitted out specifically for research, Z7001, was probing the horizons of electric-powered high speed.

The case for gas turbine traction withered away after 1973. First, the Arab-Israeli war of that year and the subsequent explosion of oil prices savaged the medium's operating economy. Then a research and development programme culminating in tests of a `CC21000' locomotive in Alsace at speeds up to 176 mph (283 kmph) proved that infallible pantograph/overhead wire contact at high speed was attainable. Finally, electric traction technology was advancing so rapidly, and with such containment of cost, that a proposal to build at least some turbine-powered train-sets for operation beyond the new line's limits collapsed. They were

The prototype gas turbine-powered TGV train-set TGV001.

suggested for the service of Grenoble, then not reached by electrification, and Switzerland, to avoid equipping electric train-sets for a third voltage (dual capability was already inescapable: 1.5kV dc for the exit from Paris and entry to Lyon over the historic route, 25kV ac 50Hz ac for the new line). But by the mid-1970s the economics favoured elec-

Z7001, the mobile laboratory that helped to prove the feasibility of electric TGV traction.

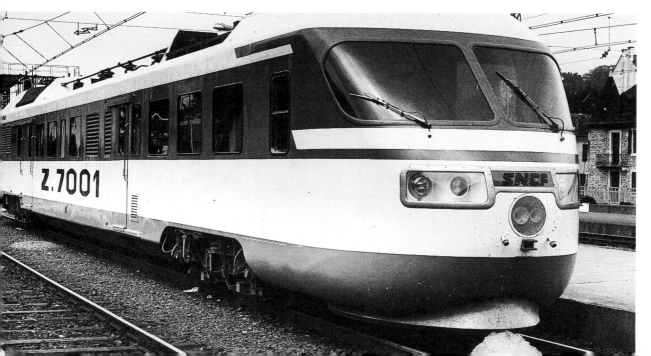

The original articulating bogie and helicoidal suspension of a TGV-PSE unit. (Y.Broncard)

trification to Grenoble; and triple-voltage capability could be built into electric TGV train-sets without overstepping either tolerable cost or the stringent axle-load limits prescribed by the integrated track-train-high speed TGV technology.

The decision to go all-electric was clinched. In late 1976, concurrently with the start of the new line's construction, orders for two pre-production and the first 85 production TGV-PSE train-sets of the eventual fleet of 108 were handed to French industry, led by Alsthom.

Each TGV-PSE train-set was formed of two independent power cars enclosing a unit of eight trailers which was articulated throughout, and the controls were arranged for multiple-unit operation of a pair of sets. Total tare weight of the set was 386 tonnes. The power car weight, 64.5 tonnes, was kept within the 17 tonnes maximum axle-load stipulation by motoring the adjoining end bogies of the trailer unit as well as those of both power cars. On 25kV ac the two power cars together could deliver a continuous 6,450kW from the thyristor chopper-con-

trolled dc motors driving each axle of the six bogies, so that for high-speed running on the new line the TGV-PSE train-set's power/weight ratio was a handsome 22.4 hp/tonne. But on 1.5kW dc the rating was only 3,100kW — perfectly adequate to sustain allowable speeds on historic SNCF infrastructure. Similarly the 2,800kW rating for work under 15kV 16 2/3Hz ac catenary of the nine triple-voltage sets sufficed for permissible pace within Switzerland, where these sets made their debut on a Paris-Lausanne service in January 1984.

For some time SNCF meditated on the application of eddy current braking to the TGV-PSE sets. Prototype equipment had in fact been exhaustively and successfully evaluated on the Z7001 railcar. As hinted in an earlier chapter, the debit of the device is the risk of track deformity from the heat generated by its application unless service headway allows adequate time for rail cooling between trains. That was the constraint that decided SNCF, contemplating 6-minute peak-hour train spacing, to prefer a combination of rheostatic braking on the motored bogies, double disc brakes on all non-pow-ered axles, and the supplement on all axles of electro-pneumatic leather shoe brakes, these last partly to keep wheelrims free of pollutants impairing adhesion.

The original internal layout, furnishing and decor of the TGV-PSE trailers did not do as much as one would have liked to dispel the impression of riding a ground-hugging jet-liner. The worst feature was a cramped buffet-bar, the only source of food and drink for occupants of the 275 2nd class seats and consequently liable to insufferable over-crowding on peak-hour TGV workings. Only 1st class seats had the offer of galley-served, shore-prepared tray meals, which had to be pre-booked at the time of obligatory seat reservation — and which were at first excori-ated by many French travellers for their qual-ity. In 1988, when the design of a much roomier bar-buffet had been adopted for the second-generation TGV-A train-sets, SNCF

began to rebuild all TGV-PSE bar-buffets to the same parameters, at the cost of sacrificing 25 2nd class seats per train-set. Since early TGV-PSE days, too, the tray meal fare in TGV 1st class has been made more enticing.

Along with the late 1980s buffet-bar recon-struction, SNCF also replaced the original suspension of the TGV-PSE trailers' articulat-ing bogies with the later TGV-A pattern. The SNCF had plumped for articulation partly to save weight; partly to keep passenger seats clear of the bogie area and thus standardize ride quality; and partly because adjoining car-ends could be so closely coupled that their connecting vestibule could be spa-cious, easier to seal for effective sound-proofing and air-conditioning, and not least so mounted and sprung that passengers moving between cars would have a com-pletely stable footway, whatever the speed.

The obvious disbenefit of end-to-end artic-

Above: The original buffet-bar of a TGV-PSE set. (SNCF.CAV)

Left: At-seat meals service in the 1st class of a TGV-PSE unit. (SNCF.CAV)

Below: A TGV-A set buffet-bar. (G.Freeman Allen)

ulation, that a defect on one trailer made the entire unit a failure, was in the French view handsomely outweighed by the advantages. That was endorsed by the travelling public as soon as the trains went into full service. At top speed on the new track the ride was excellent, disparity of vertical or lateral movement between adjoining cars almost non-existent. On the other hand, the units' riding on historic infrastructure was generally hard and palpably disturbed by track imperfections. As the 1980s progressed, furthermore, this shortcoming became more manifest. It was completely eliminated in the late 1980s when, along with the buffet-bar construction, SNCF began replacing the original helicoidal-spring secondary suspension of the TGV-PSE trailer sets' Type Y231 bogies with the air suspension of the later TGV-A sets' Type Y237 bogies.

There was a unique addition to TGV-PSE rolling-stock in 1984 — the world's first high-speed mail trains. Persuaded that its overnight mail transfers each way between Paris, Macon and Lyon could be accomplished just as capably by TGV as by air, but at a far smaller operating cost, PTT, the French post office authority, bought two eight-car TGV units plus a four-car spare purpose-built for its traffic. Internally the near-windowless cars were arranged for the exclusive conveyance of parcels and mail loaded in container trolleys. Externally they wore PTT's brilliant yellow livery.

Public TGV-PSE service was prefaced by a spectacular press demonstration of the new technology on 26 February 1981. A TGV-PSE unit curtailed to seven cars, and with its power plant modified to generate a short-term 10,000kW for a train weight of 302 tonnes, stunningly publicized what was to come with a new world rail speed record of 380 kmph (236.2 mph). Public service over two-thirds of the new line began the following September. Two years later the remaining third of the new route was commissioned, along with the opening of a new and, in its architecture, strikingly avant-garde Lyon

The articulating trailer bogie of a TGV-A unit with air suspension; note the axle's four disc brakes. (GEC-Alsthom)

The specially-prepared TGV-PSE unit 16 flashes past a press grandstand at 380 kmph (262.2 mph) near Pasilly on the demonstration of 26 February 1981 before the inauguration of TGV-PSE public service. (SNCF.CAV)

station, Part-Dieu. This was sited to avoid the previous reversal in the city's Perrache station of TGV services calling at, but continuing beyond, Lyon.

Available space precludes a detailed account of the rapid build-up of TGV-PSE patronage; the related loss by Paris-Lyon airline operators of about half of their clientele; and the steady extension of the trains' orbit of service from Paris to take in Grenoble (after electrification to that city), the Mediterranean coast, the Languedoc-Roussillon route from Avignon as far as Montpellier, and Berne and Geneva as well as Lausanne in Switzerland. By 1989 TGV-PSE services were logging 22 million passengers a year, with an average daily count of 55,600 and an average load factor per train of 76 per cent. As a result the high-speed route was returning 15 per cent on the investment in its infrastructure and equipment.

The 1989-90 TGV-PSE timetable showed 11 trains timed to run the 427.2 km (265.5 miles) from Paris Gare de Lyon to Lyon Part-Dieu non-stop in a flat 2 hours for an average of 213.6 kmph (132.8 mph), and three to do likewise over the slightly longer distance, 427.9 km (265.9 miles), in the reverse direction, representing end-to-end average speed of 214 kmph (133 mph). The tightest schedule, though, was set a train calling at Macon, which was required to cover the 363.4 km

(225.9 miles) from Paris Gare de Lyon in 100 minutes at a start-to-stop average of 218 kmph (135.5 mph). As for intensity of service, each weekday between 06.15 and 20.00 Paris Gare de Lyon was dispatching 22 TGV-PSE trains to the service's various destinations, and a few more on Fridays only to accommodate French enthusiasm for `le weekend'.

Inaugurating public TGV-PSE service in September 1981, France's President Mitterand had called for a second TGV project to cater for Brittany and south-west France. The swift TGV-PSE proof of a satisfying pay-off from investment in high speed favoured the project, though analysis showed it would not generate as impressive a return on investment as TGV-PSE. Furthermore SNCF, financially blitzed by the impact of exchange rate fluctuation on the interest it was paying on capital borrowed for TGV-PSE construction, balked at footing the whole bill for a second TGV route. Anxious to please the politically fractious Bretons, the Government agreed to shoulder 30 per cent of the capital cost. The formalities of approval were completed, land acquired, and in February 1985 construction of the TGV-Atlantique, or TGV-A, was begun.

TGV-A is essentially a new exit from the heart of Paris for a swathe of western French destinations from the western tip of Brittany down to Bordeaux and Toulouse. Unlike TGV-PSE, its new infrastructure starts straight from a thoroughly rebuilt and considerably enlarged Montparnasse terminus in the capital. But for survival of the bed for a never-built suburban line, the new tracks' projection into the city would have been dauntingly difficult and costly; even so, SNCF was obliged to bury them in cut-and-cover tunnels that are now surmounted by a 'green corridor' of parks and footpaths. The new line had also to be tunnelled under the Vouvray vineyard beyond its intermediate station at Vendome, at the rim of the Loire Valley.

TGV-A's high-speed route comprises 283 route kilometres (175.9 miles) in the shape of a lateral 'Y'. The fork is at Courtalain, 130.6 km (81.2 miles) out from Montparnasse. From there a western branch extends 51.5 km (32 miles) to a merger with the historic Paris-Brest main line at Connerre, at the approach to Le Mans. The other arm heads south for 86.9 km (54 miles) to the Montlouis area, near the line's bridging of the Loire river, where it too divides. One divergence transfers trains on to the Orleans-Tours main line for service of Tours, while the other avoids Tours and, after 16.9 km (10.5 miles), feeds into the historic Paris-Bordeaux main line.

Like TGV-PSE, TGV-A is engineered for a 300 kmph (186.5 mph) top speed. But unlike TGV-PSE it was regularly operated at that speed from its inauguration, except for a limit of 200 kmph (125 mph) over the first 15 km (6.2 miles) out of Paris Montparnasse, and of 270 kmph (167.8 mph) through two subsequent tunnels. The TGV-A traverses more amiable terrain than the TGV-PSE, so that its ruling gradient is an easier 1 in 40, and that only briefly; the steepest slopes are mostly 1 in 67. Signalling copies TGV-PSE practice and allows a 4-minute headway between trains making the full 300 kmph line speed.

A combination of the TGV's gentler profile and technological advance influenced striking changes in TGV-A train-set design by comparison with the TGV-PSE units. It was now possible to extract twice the power from a

A TGV-A train-set approaches Bordeaux St Jean station. (G.Freeman Allen)

motor and still honour the 17-tonne TGV maximum axle-load limit thanks to perfection of synchronous three-phase ac traction technology, in which a rotor forms the motor's inductor and a stator serves as the armature; thyristors distribute the current in the stator conductors. So, although a TGV-A's articulated rake of trailers was raised to 10 cars, the continuous 1,100kW rating of each synchronous ac motor as against the 535kW of a TGV-PSE's dc motor meant that only the axles of the two TGV-A set power cars needed to be motored. The outcome: a continuous 8,800kW to move 490 tare tonnes of train-set, and a short-term 10,400kW on call.

Internally, a TGV-A set is more stylishly finished than a TGV-PSE. Furthermore, besides conventional saloon seating it offers so-called `Club' 1st class accommodation where an off-centre gangway is flanked on one side by six doorless four-seat compartments, on the other by single seats paired around tables. In the end 1st class trailer there is an eight-seat conference room for business travellers; and in the corresponding 2nd class trailer a section where seats can be removed to create a children's play space. Vital to quality of ride on historic as well as new purpose-built infrastructure is the Type Y237 air-suspension bogie with four longitudinal shock absorbers.

TGV-A sets are also distinguished by a very high-tech, microprocessor-controlled system for monitoring of, and fault diagnosis in, the functioning of a host of the unit's components. As well as reporting to a visual display in the driver's cab, the system can transmit its findings via the train-to-ground radio link to maintenance depots; conversely, depot staff preparing a set for work can radio-activate from the ground some functions, such as the start-up of air-conditioning. However, the very complex TGV-A electronics proved an embarrassment at the start of TGV-A service. For some months sets could not be paired for multiple unit working, and many scheduled services had to be covered by two independent units running at a close headway, before GEC-Alsthom solved the mysteries of

A TGV-A 2nd class saloon. (G.Freeman Allen)

Above: TGV-A `Club' 1st class accommodation with semi-compartments on one side. (SNCF.CAV)

Right: The TGV-A driving cab. (GEC-Alsthom)

Below: The TGV-A 1st class conference room in the leading 1st class trailer of a unit: note the TV screens. (GEC-Alsthom)

the systems' failure to communicate securely throughout a twin-unit formation.

TGV-A service was launched over the Brittany arm in September 1989, over the south-western arm a year later. Journey time savings between Paris and cities such as Nantes, Poitiers and Bordeaux were dramatic, though in terms of city-to-city average speed not up to the TGV-PSE standard between Paris and Lyon because the TGV-A trains completed so much of their journeys on the historic network. However, stretches of that, particularly between Tours and Bordeaux, had been fettled up for TGV-A train-set passage at 200-220 kmph (125-136.7 mph). As a result, the standard TGV-A non-stop schedule for the 352.4 miles (567 km) could be set at only 2 hours 58 minutes. On my first TGV-A trip, held back for 6 minutes at Bordeaux by a late-running connection, we had recouped all the loss by the Paris arrival and consequently averaged a sparkling 122.9 mph (197.8 kmph) start to stop. At whatever speed and on whatever track, curved or tangent, the ride quality was

flawless in its quietness and stability. The city deriving the most from TGV-A 300 kmph was naturally the one nearest the end of the new infrastructure, Le Mans, 125.5 miles (201.9 km) from Paris Montparnasse, which had over a dozen trains each way connecting it with the capital in 54 minutes at a start-to-stop average of 139.4 mph (224.3 kmph).

Before the TGV-A's south-western arm was brought into revenue service, SNCF used the modest and almost straight descent of the newly-completed track from the Courtalain junction to the viaduct over the Loire river to shoot the world rail speed record far beyond its previous mark. And far beyond anything yet achieved by a full-sized passenger-carrying vehicle of the rival MagLev practitioners.

This was the culmination of an R & D programme begun in 1986 to verify how much further TGV technology had advanced the attainable limits of wheel-on-rail speed. In December 1988 TGV-PSE unit No 88, specially rebuilt to test the future TGV-A synchronous motor traction, had already pushed the world rail speed record up to

Main stations served by TGV-A have been extensively modernized in a style with maritime associations, to reflect the service's `Atlantique' title; this is seen in the sail-like shape of the awnings over the Le Mans platforms. (SNCF.CAV)

408.4 kmph (253.8 mph) in the course of 14 sprints exceeding 380 kmph (236.2 mph) and eight up to and marginally surpassing 400 kmph (248.6 mph).

A year later came the three-act thriller starring TGV-A set No 325. For the first act, which reached its climax in December 1989, No 325 was reduced to two power cars and four trailers, one of the latter packed with hi-tech instrumentation apparatus. Otherwise the principal modifications of 325's standard TGV-A equipment were that the power cars' gear ratios were changed and their standard 920 mm diameter wheels replaced by ones of 1,050 mm, so that motors would rotate at 4,000 rpm at 400, not 300, kmph; that transformer and motors were rejigged to put out more power, with the motors uprated from 1,100 to 1,500kW to make a total 12,000kW continuously available (the catenary's current supply was boosted from 25 to 28kV for the programme, too); that brake power was

reinforced; and that a few adjustments and enhancements were applied to the cars' bogies and suspensions.

Set 325 raised the drama's curtain on the last day of November 1989, when it completed the first of what was to be — except for pauses ordered for technical readjustments — a three-sprints-a-day routine between Courtalain and the Loire. The very next day the record recently notched by Germany's ICE was eclipsed with a peak of 442.6 kmph (275.1 mph). After that the pace was stepped up day by day until, on 5 December, No 325, clocking 400 kmph within just 6.25 minutes of a standing start, came within a whisker of 300 mph at 482.4 kmph (299.8 mph) before it had to be braked. It is worth adding that on its ten outings since 30 November, set 425 had travelled in all 337 km (209.4 miles) at 400 kmph (248.6 mph) or faster; and not least that in a manoeuvre to monitor the aerodynamic consequences of TGV trains converging at phenomenal pace, No 325 was made to pass another TGV-A set on the adjoining track at a combined closing speed of 777.7 kmph (483.3 mph)!

SNCF's target was 500 kmph. So for the second act of the drama set 325 was shorn of one its four trailers, trimming its weight to 260 tonnes. Even larger 1,090 mm diameter wheels were fitted to the power cars, and there was fresh aerodynamic titivation.

The second act was timed to start in March 1990 and to close the performance. Unfortunately set 325 did not follow the text. On 5 March a transformer in one power car failed quite catastrophically, allowing high-voltage ac to invade the set's dc circuitry with fairly dire results. SNCF had not publicized the resumption of very high-speed exercises, and characteristically countered rumours of what had happened with a po-faced protestation that new world record attempts were not on its immediate agenda.

In fact, set 325's damage was repaired and a new transformer in place for Act 3 to start early in May. Now the traction current wire voltage was upped to the maximum the French electricity generating authority permitted, 29.5kV. On 4 May 1990 the record was notched up to 485 kmph; and thereby the 300 mph barrier was breached with a speed of 301.4 mph. Between then and 17 May set 325 successfully touched 500 kmph nine times, without any component seriously over-heating beyond specified limits or any unacceptable movement detectable in bodies and bogies.

On 18 May SNCF brass and distinguished guests including the Transport Minister boarded set 325, and around 100 pressmen were ferried to an overbridge near the Loire crossing, at the foot of the racetrack gradient. In mid-morning this press grandstand was alerted. Peering up the straight track, the journalists picked up the twinkle of sparks from pantograph contacts and the trails of dust streaming in the wake of 325. In no time its five cars were a whirr and a flash of blue and silver beneath their feet. Less than half a mile from their viewpoint 325 had just posted a new world rail speed record of 515.3 kmph (320.26 mph).

By the end of 1990 three more TGV lines totalling 550 route kilometres (341.8 miles) were under construction: TGV-Nord; TGV Rhône-Alpes; and TGV-Interconnection. Furthermore, the French Transport Ministry had published a TGV Master Plan that envisaged close on a further 3,200 route kilometres (2,000 miles) of new infrastructure. Completion of this Master Plan would extend new high-speed track to the Spanish border, for end-on junction with a putative Spanish 1,435 mm gauge high-speed line from Madrid and Barcelona (see Chapter 11); from the Lyon region to the Riviera and under the Alps to Italy; through Dijon to Switzerland; from Paris to Strasbourg and across the frontier to a link-up with Germany's high-speed network; from Paris to Normandy; from the present TGV-A extremities to Rennes on the Brittany arm and right down to Bordeaux and Toulouse on the south-west branch; and across country in the far south and north-east to interconnect routes radiating from the Paris hub.

In the spring of 1991 the Government endorsed the Master Plan not merely in full, but with some modest extensions too. This was despite the fact that the majority of the Plan's projects were not calculated to generate the minimum rate of return on investment set by SNCF as a prerequisite for commitment of its own resources.

In January 1991 the Government asked SNCF to begin the processes leading up to a Declaration of Public Utility for the TGV Provence-Côte d'Azur. Tacking on to the end of the TGV Rhône-Alpes (see below) at Valence, this will complete a high-speed route from Paris to the outskirts of Marseilles. However, its path through prized vineyard country has exposed TGV Provence-Côte d'Azur to the most virulent and concerted regional opposition of any TGV project so far. In the 1991 summer protesters were still sporadically blocking existing SNCF main lines in the area with their anti-TGV demonstrations.

Vying for next place on the construction agenda are TGV Languedoc-Roussillon and TGV-Est. The first of these will branch from TGV Provence-Côte d'Azur near Avignon and head south-west via Nîmes and Montpellier

TGV-A sets await duty outside their Paris Chatillon depot. (SNCF.CAV)

to the Spanish frontier at Perpignan. The priority accorded TGV Languedoc-Roussillon may well depend on availability of a firm timescale for Spain's completion of a high-speed route from Madrid through Barcelona to the border (see next chapter). Another factor that may become decisive is rising political concern to see TGV-Est up and running.

TGV-Est will extend from Paris's outskirts via a station near Rheims and another between Metz and Nancy to Strasbourg. Thereafter it will make cross-border connection with Germany's high-speed network, but to what extent by upgraded historic route or new infrastructure, or a combination of both, has yet to be determined. What is certain is that the French are coming to regard TGV-Est as their prime high-speed link with the German system, rather than TGV-Nord's Bel-

gian connection described below.

This book deals essentially with high-speed trains rather than their routes, so discussion of the three more TGV routes under way in 1991 has to be cursory. TGV Rhône-Alpes is a further step towards the Mediterranean coast, a 115 km (71.5-mile) bypass of Lyon, serving that city's Satolat airport *en route*, that will let TGV-PSE services to the Riviera sustain speed until the new line rejoins the historic route at the approach to Valence. Opening throughout was set for 1994.

TGV-Interconnection, as its name implies, is the key not only to a range of cross-country high-speed services within France, but also to some potentially competitive cross-border high-speed routes. Opening for business in 1994-95, this 102 km (63.4 mile) line, engineered for 270 kmph (167.8 mph), will orbit the eastern outskirts of Paris to interlace TGV-Nord, TGV-Est, TGV-PSE and TGV-A. Just beyond its triangular junction with TGV-Nord, TGV-Interconnection will thread a station beneath Paris Charles de Gaulle airport.

TGV Nord is one more vital link in Europe's emergent high-speed inter-city rail network. Starting from Gare du Nord, another comprehensively rebuilt Paris terminus — in this case to cope with still expanding commuter traffic as well as TGV service — the 300 kmph TGV-Nord traces a 225 km (139.8-mile) course to Lille.

At the approach to Lille a triangular junction takes the arm of TGV-Nord 108 km (67.1 miles) to Fréthun, the station on Calais' outskirts that is the gateway to the Channel Tunnel and, beyond that, British Rail. The other arm tunnels under Lille, where TGV-Nord has its own subterranean station close to the city's present main station, then heads for the Belgian border.

TGV-Nord as so far described will open for public service in 1993, the same year as the Anglo-French Channel Tunnel. The seamless continuation of high-speed infrastructure to London, Brussels, Amsterdam and Cologne, to which most of the Governments affected pledged themselves in the 1980s — Britain was the exception — is taking longer.

It would take too much text — and revive too much pain — to recount in full the melancholy history of British Rail's belated acknowledgement that a new Kent Coast-London line was needed to accommodate estimated Channel Tunnel through trains; of the struggle to establish a route for it that combined environmental acceptance with manageable cost; and of the fiasco when, the Thatcher Government obdurately refusing to put up a penny of the cost, BR's private enterprise partners did not fancy the return on their share of the bill and opted out.

However, following Mrs Thatcher's Prime Ministerial resignation in late 1990, there were hints that her successor's administration was probing for loopholes in the Thatcher Channel Tunnel Act's denial of any public money for the project and its British Rail connections. Maybe, it was whispered, land purchase for a new line could be legitimately subsidized, leaving others only with

the railway itself to build and equip. Whatever happened, it was by then a certainty that until the next century the TGV-like London-Paris/Brussels through trains must in England contest track space with BR Network Southeast's intensive regular-interval train service, be content with pace no higher than 100 mph (160 kmph), and be equipped to take traction current from a 750V dc third rail.

Achievement of a new line was set back still further in 1991 when the Government threw out BR's expensively reworked plan for a south London entry to the capital and, largely on political grounds, required a redesigned approach from the east.

In mid-1991 the Belgians had yet to start building their 72 km (40 miles) of new 300 kmph TGV-Nord infrastructure from the French frontier to the Brussels outskirts, or even to settle the alignments of two other stretches aggregating 100 km (62.2 miles) that will complement existing but upgraded track east of their capital *en route* to the German frontier and Aachen. Main causes of the delay were Government unease at the costs, some pockets of ferocious environmental opposition, and not least Belgium's endemic ethnic conflict, in this case inflamed by French-speaking Walloons' wrath at the funnelling of so much rail investment into Flemish-speaking Flanders. However, a positive decision to build was taken in 1991. As a result, 300 kmph TGV-Nord access to Brussels at least should be available by 1995.

Until the next century Dutch access to TGV-Nord too will be over existing tracks, from Amsterdam via Rotterdam and Antwerp to Brussels. But in 1990 a new Dutch Government, environmentally eager to entice travellers off the roads and into trains, blessed financially a 'Rail 21' plan for major expansion of Netherlands Railways' operating capacity. Among new lines scheduled in this plan was a 200 kmph (125 mph) route from Amsterdam's underground Schiphol Airport station via Rotterdam and Breda to Belgium.

It remains to summarize the four types of train that will operate TGV-Nord services. First, the TGV-R (R for *Réseau*, or Network), of which 80 sets were ordered from GEC-Alsthom in 1990. These basically repeat the

TGV-A design, but because their service will include inter-TGV route itineraries via TGV-Interconnection, and they must not be embarrassed by TGV-PSE's 1 in 28.5 ruling gradient, their power cars enclose eight, not ten trailers. For the same reason, dual-voltage (1.5kV dc and 25kV ac) is obligatory; 30 of the first 80 sets will have a third voltage capability, 3kV dc, so that they can work over the historic network of Belgian Railways (SNCB). The only significant criticism one could level at TGV-A trailers, the inadequacy of their pressure sealing against aural discomfort in high-speed passage of tunnels, is put right in the TGV-R cars.

In April 1991 orders were placed for the first 100 bi-level TGV train-sets, each formed of two power cars and eight articulated trailers. Trains of this type are in mind for TGV-PSE as well as TGV-Nord, to accommodate the former route's unchecked growth of demand for peak period capacity. Research has convinced SNCF's design engineers that with recourse to aluminium bodywork and other weight-saving ploys, they can devise a bi-level format that will not infringe the 17-tonne TGV axle-load limit — and what is more, without having to sacrifice inter-trailer articulation. Passage through the train will be at the upper level, from which stairways will lead to the cars' lower decks.

A third train-set type, tagged TGV-PBKA, was not fully designed in late 1990. These would be four-voltage, two power car/eight trailer sets, assigned as their classification acronym indicates for through service between Paris, Brussels, Cologne (*Köln* in German) and Amsterdam. Except under 25kV ac wires, their maximum speed would not need to exceed 200 kmph (125 mph), which simplifies the addition of extra voltages (but equipment of internationally-operating power cars to work infallibly with each railway's Automatic Train Protection is none too easy, one might add). What would pose problems is possible late-1990s scope for a through Paris-Frankfurt service via the future Cologne-Frankfurt high-speed line. That would require a 'PBKF' unit capable of 300 kmph on a diet of German 15kV $16\frac{2}{3}$Hz traction current, as well as 25kV 50Hz ac. But as discussed earlier, French interest in a German connection is veering to the TGV-Est as the key high-speed corridor. That would limit the multi-system need to two ac voltages and frequencies

Lastly, TGV-Nord will host the *Trans-Manche-Super-Trains*, or TMST (Cross-Channel-Super-Trains), providing through London-Paris and Brussels service via the Channel

A model of the bi-level TGV train-set for which the first orders were placed in 1991. (SNCF.CAV)

Tunnel. Derivation of much of their design from the latest TGV rolling-stock was inevitable. Nowhere else was there vehicle and running gear technology thoroughly proven in the regular 300 kmph operation required of the TMSTs on TGV-Nord. Consequently GEC-Alsthom led the Anglo-Franco-Belgian consortium commissioned to build the first 30 train-sets. Of these 14 are BR-owned (and designated Class '373' in BR's scheme), 13 SNCF-owned and three SNCB-owned.

How many TMSTs would be available by the Channel Tunnel's opening in mid-1993 had by late 1991 become uncertain. Construction had fallen seriously behind schedule, partly because the GEC-Alsthom assembly plant at Belfort was overtaxed with other high-speed train contracts, and partly because of problems with the TMSTs' intricate computer systems.

Each 800-tonne TMST consists of two units, each comprising a power car and nine trailers, the latter articulated end-to-end. The extraordinary safety measures imposed on Channel Tunnel operations in general enforced this division of TMSTs into two easily separable units, to simplify withdrawal from the Tunnel in the event of an emergency. Initially this also suited BR's ambitions of later and modest extension of TMST service to the provinces north of London. TMST sets for that were to have the end-trailer of each half-set fitted out as a driving trailer, so that such 20-car sets running beyond London down the East and West Coast main lines could be divided respectively at Peterborough and Rugby to provide independent Paris or Brussels train service for the West Riding, Scotland, the West Midlands and North West England. However, this proposition subsequently hit difficulties of

immunizing the type of signalling system relay used north of London from interference by the ac motor drive of a TMST. Whereas such relays were being replaced between London and the Tunnel, the proposed sparse TMST service north of the Thames could not justify the high cost of substitution north of the capital. Then in 1991 BR recoiled from the expense of redesigning the half-set end trailers with cabs. The half-set concept was dropped in favour of intact 14-car train-sets. Consequently these would serve only two routes north of London: Birmingham–Manchester, and York–Newcastle–Edinburgh.

For reasons already outlined, the 68-tonne TMST power cars have to add third-rail 750V dc traction current adaptability to overhead collection of 25kV ac on TGV-Nord and of 3kV dc in Belgium. To observe the axle-load limits, asynchronous three-phase ac motors, inverter-fed with GTO thyristor control, have to be applied to the neighbouring trailer bogie as well as to both power car bogies. Continuous rating of each power car on 25kV ac is 7,000kW, on 3kV dc 3,600kW, and on BR's 750V dc just 2,150kW.

In 1990 the French Government put up Ffr170 million, and SNCF Ffr95 million, towards GEC-Alsthom's Ffr445 million budget (about £46.5 million at late 1990 exchange rates) for a four-year R & D programme to evolve a third-generation TGV technology. A key objective is to lift standard TGV maximum speed to 350 kmph (217.5 mph). SNCF rates 3 hours as, broadly speaking, the journey duration beyond which inter-city rail starts to yield advantage to air travel. If that judgement is valid, a 350 kmph top speed on TGV routes will raise the inter-city distance at which rail resists challenge close to 1,000 km, or about 620 miles.

11
Spain joins the high-speed club

Spain's national railway, RENFE, is a late-comer to the European high-speed club. For that matter, RENFE did not begin to catch up the advancing North West European technology and standard of operation on a historic network until the 1970s. From the 1940s to the 1960s the after-effects of the country's Civil War and Spain's modest economic strength had denied RENFE resources to upgrade a system that had been built with more concern for minimal cost than progressive quality of service, even by late 19th-century lights. It had also been constructed not to the standard gauge of North West Europe, but to a broad 5 ft 6 in (1,676 mm).

The 1974 oil crisis, alerting the country to the costs and risks of its transport's over-whelming reliance on imported oil, set off a far-reaching rail electrification programme. Then, in the early 1980s, the expansion of intra-European travel and trade, and Spain's anxiety to be part of it within the EEC, prompted formulation of a massive RENFE rationalization and investment plan.

By 1985 infrastructure improvements, especially double-tracking and signalling modernization, had allowed RENFE to launch Spain's first 100 mph (160 kmph) inter-city operation on the triangle of routes connecting Madrid, Barcelona and Valencia. This capability was steadily extended to suitable sectors of other routes, so that by 1991 just over 2,300 route miles (3,700 route km) had been passed for 100 mph working. And in that year RENFE was at work on its first upgrading of existing route for 125 mph (200 kmph), between Valencia and Barcelona.

The 100 mph operation employed a mix of locomotive-hauled trains and RENFE's newest inter-city electric multiple unit, the three-car Class `444.500'. The majority of the locomotive-hauled trains were formed of what was then the uniquely Spanish Talgo rolling-stock.

The Talgo concept was the ingenious 1950s solution of two Spanish engineers, Goicoaechea and Oriel — the `go' of the Talgo acronym — to a lift of speed on what at that time was RENFE's indifferent, often infirm and generally curve-beset main-line track. The Talgo principle centres on very short, very light and very low-slung bodies, each wheeled at one end only and, at the other, piggybacking on their neighbour via a tight, pivoting centre coupling. Each wheel of a pair is an independent stub axle, to make room for an inter-car vestibule between the wheels; and each wheel has its own Talgo-patented suspension. The whole arrangement imparts wheel guidance through curves, which can be negotiated at higher cant deficiency than by orthodox coaches because of the low Talgo centre of gravity.

The first version to go into long-run production was the Talgo III in the mid-1960s.

RENFE'S 160 kmph (100 mph) Class `444.500' inter-city electric multiple unit.

Talgo III cars, of which RENFE was still operating about 390 in the late 1980s, have bodies a mere 34 ft 9¼ in long, and stand only 10 ft 9 in high from rail surface to roof crown.

At the end of the 1970s Talgo introduced a new model which has since become the company's exclusive manufacture for RENFE. This is the Talgo Pendular, so-called because its 43-foot-long monocoque, aluminium-

A Talgo III train-set headed by one of the Krauss-Maffei diesel-hydraulic B-Bs built to the same contours as the low-slung cars.

structured bodies are equipped with automatic body-tilting. Unlike that of Britain's hapless APT, Italy's *Pendolino* or the Swedish X2000, the Talgo tilting system is passive, not active: that is, it reacts to curves and is not driven by on-board curve-sensing and cant-measuring devices. The mechanism basically comprises air bags that are embodied in the secondary suspension above each stub axle. As a curve is entered, rising centrifugal force actuates a controlled flow of air from one bag to its opposite number. Then, as the force subsides on exit from the curve, the air flow is reversed. The passive system limits the extent of a Talgo Pendular car's body tilt to 4 degrees compared, for example, with the 8 degrees maximum possible in the Fiat active system of Italian Railways' Class `450' train-sets.

In 1969 Talgo contrived a means of getting its cars across the gauge break at the Franco-Spanish border without time-consuming exchange of running gear. Stub axles which were laterally movable between foolproof locks were devised, and with them a cat's-cradle-like stretch of trackwork through

which, at the border, a complete train could move at a crawl to adjust each of its axles to a new gauge. So Talgo trains operate internationally as well as within Spain, in both day- and sleeping-car formats, the latter from Madrid and Barcelona to Paris, and from Barcelona to Zurich and Milan.

First sight of a Talgo train-set has one gulping at the prospect of 100 mph in it. When you find that its windows rise little higher than the running boards on conventional cars on an adjoining track, and you recall that each Talgo car weighs 10 tonnes or so, you fear that you might be blown off the track when you pass another train at a combined speed of up to 200 mph (320 kmph). But not so. In my experience 100 mph in a Talgo train on good track is remarkably steady, dinner in its diner untroubled, the passage of other trains unremarkable, and the incongruous single wheel-beat on rail joints well muffled by the soundproofing. I certainly had one of my better on-train nights' sleep in a berth of the Paris-Madrid overnight Talgo.

Talgo Pendular cars are designed for a 125 mph

RENFE Class `269-200' Bo-Bo and Talgo Pendular train-set.

A Talgo III set with adjustable axles in France on a through service from Barcelona in 1974, headed by an SNCF Class `9200' Bo-Bo.

(200 kmph) maximum speed, though up to the start of the 1990s none had been regularly operated at that pace in public service. With scope for wider international use opening up, and including a chance of use over Germany's new high-speed lines, Talgo set about developing a 250 kmph (155.4 mph) model in 1988. Five Pendular cars were set aside as a mobile R & D test-bed, to evaluate and prove various necessary modifications of running gear, suspension, braking and body structure. And at the close of 1988, with a German Federal Class `120' electric Bo-Bo in charge, this rake was hustled up to 291 kmph (180.9 mph) on the new Hannover-Wurzburg line, reportedly with exemplary stability. Talgo subsequently forecast that at the end of 1991 it would roll out a full prototype 250 kmph train-set with all the latter-day prerequisites for international high-speed operation: exemplary pressure-sealing for traversal of tunnels; central control of entrance doors with automatic

protection; improved braking, including electromagnetic brakes; and so on.

Meanwhile, in 1987 the Spanish Government had approved a further huge outlay on RENFE. The programme included not only the upgrading of the Madrid-Barcelona-Valencia triangle for 125 mph (200 kmph), but also construction of three new and lengthy stretches of speed-friendly route to bypass severely curved and graded sectors of key trunk routes. Within a year one of these latter three schemes has been expanded from a 130.5-mile (210 km) substitute for the most restrictive part of Madrid's key route to the south into a brand new route the whole way from Madrid to Seville, 295 miles (475 km). Furthermore it was to be a new route built to Europe's standard 1,435 mm gauge (4 ft 8¹/₂ in), not RENFE's historic 1,676 mm, and the first in Spain to have 25kV 50Hz ac instead of 3kV dc electrification.

Known as NAFA — an acronym for `New Rail Access to Andalucia' in Spanish — this project was quickly under way. The aim was to have the new line operational throughout in time for Seville's grandiose 1992 celebration, with a World Fair, of Christopher Columbus's 1492 discovery of America (for a further mark of which, incidentally, the city and the Andalucian province were largely financing a majestic new Seville station).

That 1992 NAFA target looked mightily ambitious, and not only because the scheme involved complete remodelling of 210 km (130.4 miles) of a historic single line and wholly new infrastructure totalling 250 route

This prototype seat design for RENFE's AVE high-speed train-sets shows the lengths to which passenger information facilities are now being taken: note the digital clock, miniature video screen and push-buttons for audio channel control.

kilometres. Only over the first 15 km out of Madrid's Atocha terminus would 1,435 mm gauge tracks be embedded in existing layouts. Determination to engineer NAFA wherever possible for 250 kmph (155.4 mph) initially, but with hope of 300 kmph (196.5 mph) feasibility at a later date, and elsewhere for 200 kmph (124.3 mph), confronted RENFE with some formidable civil engineering in the route's negotiation of mountainous areas. The parameters were the more demanding because RENFE intended to route fast merchandise freight over the new line. That set 1 in 80 as the maximum tolerable gradient, and the minimum curve radius at 4,000 m. In all, 16 tunnels aggregating 15.3 km (9.5 miles) in length would have to be bored and 24 viaducts with a total length of 8.3 km (5.2 miles) erected. Nevertheless, by the end of 1990 earthworks were largely finished and tracklaying had begun. The NAFA distance from Madrid to Seville would be 99 km (61.5 miles) less than that of the traditional 1,676 mm gauge route.

NAFA's new rolling-stock needs added up to mouth-watering business. It excited no-holds-barred competition not only from French and German industry, but also from the Japanese. Already ensconced in the Spanish rail scene as the basic designer of two modern RENFE electric locomotive types, the Class '269' Bo-Bo and '251' B-B-B, Mitsubishi saw the NAFA orders as a bridgehead to wider-ranging European state-of-the-art traction and train-set contracts.

The contest eventually took on a tag-team dimension. Each national industry had in its corner the highest levels of its Government, the latter hinting none too obliquely at sweeteners or acidities in other areas of its relations with Spain, depending on which way the decisions went. So the outcome smacked as much of political prudence as technical sagacity.

The Japanese got nothing and the spoils were nicely distributed between the French and Germans. A German consortium led by Siemens carried off an order for 75 Class '252' 5,600kW Bo-Bos with 220 kmph (136.7 mph) competence to a design based on German Federal's Class '120' three-phase ac motor type. Of these, the first 20 would be definitely built to 1,435 mm gauge; whether the remainder would be constructed to that or 1,676 mm gauge was left to later decision. A Siemens-led alliance of Spanish and German firms also carried off the order to wire NAFA, and another German firm, SEL, the contract to equip the new line with German Federal's LZB system of ATP and exclusive reliance on in-cab signalling.

Capture of the contract for 24 high-speed passenger train-sets, known as AVE (*Alta Velocidad Español*), was essentially a French triumph, though by now the protagonist company had become the Anglo-French GEC-Alsthom. Design would be almost a replica of French Railways' second-generation TGV-Atlantique units, with each train-set comprising eight articulated trailers flanked by a brace of dual-voltage (3kV dc/25kV ac), 4,400kW asynchronous ac motor power cars. The French and Germans alike had to cede some of the work to Spanish industry, which would not only supply numerous components but also assemble 16 of the train-sets and 45 of the Class `252s'. GEC-Alsthom was also coaxed into taking a controlling interest in two companies of an over-populated Spanish rolling-stock industry crying out for rationalization.

Pending delivery of this new equipment, RENFE modified some of its existing traction for track and rolling-stock research at 200 kmph (125 mph) or more. Four Mitsubishi-design, chopper-controlled Class `269.200' Bo-Bos were rebuilt with new bogies, transmissions, axles and transformers, regeared, and sheathed in new, more aerodynamically-efficient bodywork. Less work was needed on the final series of Krauss Maffei-built diesel-hydraulic B-Bs employed on Talgo train haulage over non-electrified routes. All three series of these machines have stunted, low-slung bodies that precisely reproduce Talgo cross-section. The last eight, RENFE's Class `354', delivered in 1982, pack a 2,340kW (4,000 hp) twin-engine power plant within their compact 80-tonne shape.

Completion of NAFA and public services inauguration of its TGV clones was predicted to halve Madrid-Seville journey times, from 5$^1/_2$ hours to at most 2 hours 50 minutes.

That would represent an end-to-end average speed of 104.2 mph (167.8 kmph). But as well as slashing journey time from Madrid to other southern Spanish centres besides Seville, NAFA was the potential core of a high-speed inter-city passenger service stretching from France's northern shore to Portugal's Atlantic coastline.

To the west, Portuguese Railways (CP) had at last, in 1988, reached agreement with its Government on a forward plan that counterbalanced rationalization or termination of irretrievably loss-making activity with long-overdue, large-scale investment elsewhere. CP could not, amongst other things, aspire to 125 mph (200 kmph) operation on its 25kV ac electrified Lisbon-Oporto main line. This is not only CP's most important inter-city link, but as yet the only trunk in Portugal that can bear technical and operating comparison with main-line practice in North West Europe. CP's first conspicuous move towards Lisbon-Oporto upgrading, in the summer of 1990, was to order 30 mixed traffic electric locomotives with 125 mph (200 kmph) capability. No doubt the wisdom of compatibility with their neighbour's machines swayed the Portuguese to forswear their previous allegiance to Alsthom electric traction technology. Thus the Germans took the business with the Siemens-led consortium's offer of a RENFE Class `252' lookalike.

Close kinship with RENFE's choice was sensible because CP was anxious to plug its inter-city operation into the emergent Spanish high-speed network. Its neighbour's decision to adopt standard 1,435 mm gauge for NAFA — and for a subsequent new high-speed route from Madrid through Barcelona to an end-on junction with French Railways, of which more shortly — set Portuguese planning for this link-up on a new path. There was now a powerful argument for building entirely new, purpose-built infrastructure, instead of adding gauge conversion to comprehensive upgrading and realignment of the existing route, and thereby exacerbating the disruption of its traffic while the work was in progress.

In 1990 consultants were commissioned to evaluate in detail the economics of three schemes that together would create a semicircular 1,435 mm connection with RENFE's evolving standard gauge system. One project envisaged a new line from Lisbon east to Badajoz, with the expectation that RENFE would build a link from Badajoz to its NAFA. The second concerned a new 1,435 mm gauge line from Lisbon to Oporto. The third extended a new line from Oporto east to the frontier at Vilar Formoso, with the objective of feeding into a prospective RENFE high-speed system development in northern Spain.

Impressed by the importance EEC countries were attaching to rail in meeting the rising demand for transport within the Community, the Spanish Government followed the decision to go for standard gauge in NAFA with a request for RENFE to report on the feasibility and cost of wholesale gauge conversion in Spain. That naturally compelled Portugal to ask the same of CP. However, the Madrid Government recoiled at RENFE's figures, the more so in face of a threatening European recession. By 1991 gauge conversion was shelved sine die.

As hinted above, the Spanish Transport Minister had in November 1988 proposed that NAFA be followed by construction of a second new high-speed 1,435 mm gauge line, some 700 km (437.5 miles) long, from Madrid to Barcelona and thence to the French border. Identification of a feasible route was begun, but for two years the project remained a paper outline. Chances of execution looked slimmer as NAFA slid into severe construction cost overruns, and the Government decided that there was an urgent need to invest heavily in Spanish city transport infrastructure and rolling-stock.

But early in 1991 the Transport Minister announced that construction of a Madrid–Barcelona high-speed 1,435 mm gauge line would start in 1993. Unlike NAFA, it would be designed for exclusive passenger train use to limit cost. And whereas the Government had previously contemplated recourse to a degree at least of private sector financing, it would now shoulder the entire capital cost.

This did not satisfy the Government of Catalonia, the province which embraces Barcelona. The national Government had previously rejected Catalan claims that the first priority should be a high-speed line from Barcelona northward to plug into France's TGV network at Perpignan. So the Catalans had set about designing this on their own. But they could not build without permission from Madrid.

That, said the Transport Minister, could be forthcoming if the Catalan Government agreed to take full responsibility for its project, and provided that its financing proposals were demonstrably sound. So there was a possibility in mid-1991 that work would begin on both national and Catalan schemes in 1993. And that by 1998 an uninterrupted high-speed, 1,435 mm gauge route would be operational between Madrid and the French border.

12
Scandinavia, the Alps and the Far East

At the start of the 1990s the only railway-owning country in Western Europe not aiming to run at a 200 kmph (124.3 mph) maximum speed on key routes during the decade was Luxembourg. Denmark's railway, DSB, had the figure in long-term view, but would probably reach no higher than 180 kmph (111.9 mph) before the century faded.

The same ambition was nurtured in at least two Eastern European countries, but with rather less assurance because of their economic traumas. Poland's national system, PKP, had at least taken the first resignalling steps towards its hope of marking the country's 150th railway anniversary in 1995 with 200 kmph operation on the Warsaw-Katowice Central Trunk Route. Distinctly more sanguine was flotation by Czechoslovakia's CSD in 1988 of a scheme to build a new 257 kmph (159.7 mph) high-speed railway between Prague and Brno, though Skoda, the national traction manufacturer, was circulating drafts of new traction and train-set designs to suit the project. Reunited Germany's new high-speed line from Hannover to Berlin was the only scheme certain of execution beyond what had been the Iron Curtain.

In Scandinavia, Sweden's SJ was the pacesetter. In partnership with the country's traction manufacturer ASEA, now part of the ASEA-Brown Boveri (ABB) combine, SJ evolved in the mid-1970s a prototype electric train-set, the X15, with automatic body-tilting. The unit was successfully tested at up to 150 mph (241 kmph) on existing tracks. Government strait-jacketing of SJ investment precluded any series production until 1982, when a more benign Ministerial attitude allowed SJ to invite offers to supply three pre-production six-car train-sets for evaluation in commercial service between Stockholm and Gothenburg.

Fairly swift signature of a contract with ASEA looked a foregone conclusion. But not so. SJ wanted all cars to be tilt-equipped. That included the two inner cars that would be motored with a total output of around 3,000kW, but, because of SJ's comparatively light track structure, within extraordinarily exacting weight and track stress parameters. Neither ASEA nor any other manufacturer could comply with the initial specification. So SJ was compelled to rethink, and the manufacturers to re-bid, until at last, in August 1986, ASEA clinched an order not for three units, but for a full production series of 20 train-sets with an option on 32 more.

In this ultimately accepted design, the X2000, SJ had to accept concentration of traction equipment in a non-tilting, low-slung and lightweight 3,260kW power car, which employs ABB three-phase ac motors under GTO thyristor convertor control. The train-set is reversible, so the end trailer of the five is cabbed. All five have active body-tilting up to angle of 6.5 degrees, for which each bogie has its own electro-hydraulic servo system. Each servo system responds independently and in due time and extent to reference values transmitted by a device on the set's leading bogie that measures lateral acceleration when a curve is encountered. All bogies, including those on the power car, are of the ABB self-steering axle type, which reduces track forces, and thus wheel flange and rail wear.

The first X2000 set took up trial commercial service between Stockholm and Gothenburg at the start of September 1990, but at a maximum speed of 160 kmph (100 mph). Not until 1991 would SJ finish the extensive track upgrading and resignalling of the route that would release the X2000s to run at up to 200 kmph (125 mph). With that licence the tilt-body trains would fulfil their promise to shave about 20 per cent from journey times between the two cities. As they proliferated in following years they would cut still more from previous best travel times between Stockholm and Malmö, and between Stockholm and Sundsvall.

Meanwhile, the Swedish tilt-body technology was making its mark abroad. As described in an earlier chapter, it was the chosen medium for the aborted Tampa-Miami high-speed project in Florida, USA. Beyond the 49th Parallel it was being busily promoted by ABB's Canadian subsidiary as a comparatively inexpensive alternative to Bombardier's TGV proposal for high-speed links in the Quebec-Windsor corridor. A derivation of SJ's X2000 which it tagged 'Sprintor', claimed ABB Canada, could be run at up to 250 kmph (155.4 mph) on existing Canadian track, given some upgrading and also electrification, and thus match projected TGV Montreal-Toronto journey times. But at almost half the cost, because of the TGV scheme's prerequisite of new infrastructure, and in half the lead time from conclusion of a deal to the start of commercial service. In Australia, X2000 technology was in 1990 tapped by the Chief Executive of New South Wales' State Railway Administration as a fallback for accelerated Sydney-Melbourne service, should the extravagant plan for a new high-speed railway between the two cities — of which more later — fall apart.

Much nearer home, the ABB tilt system was

A Swedish State Railways' X2000 tilt-body train-set.

a contender, along with Spain's Talgo and a locomotive-hauled concept from Finnish builders Valmet, for the prototype that Finnish State Railways (VR) planned to buy in 1991 as the precursor of a series order for 200 kmph train-sets to be launched between Helsinki and Turku in 1995. Very likely, too, the Swedish system was in the frame of a Norwegian State Railways (NSB) ambition to spread 200 kmph tilt-body train-set operation to four routes radiating from Oslo by the end of the century. And in 1991 an X2000 of Swedish Railways was borrowed for trials by the German and Swiss Federal Railways.

Mountainous Austria and Switzerland each have only one trunk route with stretches free of inhibiting curves and gradients that are of sufficient length to make development for sustained high speed a worthwhile exercise. But in both countries governments are handsomely supporting huge investment to squeeze more pace from trunk railways, wherever and however possible, as part of over-arching programmes to intensify and otherwise enhance public transport service in the noble cause of environmental protection.

Its 327 km (197-mile) Westbahn, the east-west transversal from Vienna to Salzburg, is the only route where Austrian Federal Railways (OBB) presently has any scope for 160 kmph (100 mph). In 1997, by dint of building stretches of new infrastructure totalling about 68 km (42 miles), by upgrading and curve easement elsewhere, and finally by resignalling, most of the route will have been made operable at 200 kmph.

In 1990 the OBB's fastest traction was the 1989 redevelopment of its 5,000kW Class `1044' Bo-Bo as the Class `1044.2', with a capability of 180 kmph (111.9 mph). The amount of mutually-convenient cross-border locomotive working by the OBB and Germany's DB rises — both are wired at 15kV 16 $^2/_3$Hz ac — and, with an eye to future Austrian locomotive penetration of DB's *Neubaustrecke*, OBB is to build a 230 kmph (142.9 mph) top speed into its next breed of inter-city passenger locomotives. This would be an 82-tonne, 6,000kW Bo-Bo designated Class `1012', with GTO thyristor inverter three-phase ac motor drive. In 1993

OBB would also be taking into service three Class `4012' electric six-car train-sets with Fiat automatic body-tilting, to verify that technology as the most cost-effective tool for substantially faster travel over its winding transalpine routes.

In Switzerland, the Federal Railway's (SBB) numerous schemes for insertion of additional tracks to match operating capacity to a projected 60 per cent inflation of inter-city passenger service include construction of three segments of new 200 kmph infrastructure. The most significant will be between Basle and Berne: one extending 54 km (33.6 miles) between Rothrist and Mattstetten, on the outskirts of Olten and Berne respectively; and the other 34 km (21.1 miles) between Muttenz, the site of a big Basle marshalling yard, and Olten. Completion dates for both are steadily receding to the end of the century, however, driven back by the weight of local objections to the planned alignments, especially between Rothrist and Mattstetten.

The only existing Swiss route sufficiently level and free of curves for 200 kmph is the 25 km (15.5 miles) between Martigny and Sion, on the Rhone Valley main line from Geneva and Lausanne to Brig and the Simplon Tunnel. By 1995 this stretch will have been relaid, rewired and resignalled for 200 kmph.

SBB's new 1990s breed of rolling-stock is designed not only for future 200 kmph and 200 kmph-plus opportunities, but also to extract more speed from other SBB routes without undue punishment of track or vehicle components. The 4,800kW, 81-tonne Class `460' Bo-Bo, embodying ABB's GTO thyristor inverter-controlled three-phase ac asynchronous motor propulsion, has steerable-axle bogies of a design devised by SLM, the Swiss manufacturer assembling the locomotives. Maximum design speed of the Class `460' is 230 kmph (142.9 mph). Another Swiss company, SIG, has perfected a passenger coach bogie which ingeniously combines axle self-steering with a simple passive tilting mechanism that will incline the car body by up to 3 degrees to offset cant deficiency. That is reckoned to permit between 10 and 20 per cent more speed through curves without unnerving passengers.

Above: Austrian Federal Railways' series order for Class `1044.2' was prefaced by the rebuilding in 1987 of an existing Class `1044' Bo-Bo as this one-off Class `1044.5', geared and otherwise modified for a maximum speed of 220 kmph (137 mph). (OBB)

Below: Swiss Federal Railways' one existing main line conducive to high speed is the Rhone Valley, on which the Geneva-Milan `Cisalpin' EuroCity is seen at St Triphon fronted by a Class `Re4/4' IV Bo-Bo blazoned with promotion for the Swiss rail expansion programme, `Bahn 2000'. (John C. Baker)

For many years the Swiss discounted tilt-body technology's ability to prise significant amounts from inter-city schedules over its more tortuous routes. By the end of the 1980s, however, the latest developments in Italy, Spain and Sweden were prompting reappraisal, and in January 1991 the prototype Fiat `ETR401' *Pendolino* unit was imported from Italy for trials over the Lötschberg transalpine route between Berne and Brig. Later in the year, as remarked above, the Swiss evaluated a Swedish X2000 train-set.

On the other side of the globe, the majority of Australia's inter-city railways are essentially freight carriers. Only in the south-east of the continent are sizeable population centres closely enough spaced for passenger trains to have much muscle in a contest with road and more especially air. But even there market size is not such that managements have fancied big spending for higher passenger speed.

Until the mid-1980s the only substantial move for more pace was by the New South Wales administration. At the start of the decade it had local manufacturer Comeng build under licence a modest squadron of diesel train-sets known as XPT, to a design closely based on British Rail's `InterCity 125' HST. However, while the XPTs substantially shortened previous journey times on the itineraries to which they were applied, the limitations of NSW track and route topography pegged their end-to-end speeds well below BR `InterCity 125' standards. Their maximum permitted pace anywhere on NSW tracks was 100 mph (160 kmph). And when, on its commissioning trials, the first XPT set a new Australian rail speed record in September 1981, it was a mere 183 kmph (113.7 mph).

Suddenly, in 1986, a private sector consortium comprising three of Australia's biggest conglomerates, Broken Hill Pty, Elders-IXL and the TNT Transport Group, plus the Japanese construction group Kumagai-Gumi, formed the VFT (Very Fast Train) Joint Venture to build an 870 km (540.7-mile), 350 kmph (217.5 mph) electrified railway inter-connecting Sydney, Canberra and Melbourne. For the rest of the decade the pro-ject revolved around market research, infrastructure and rolling-stock studies, route projections, negotiations with State and Federal governments, and prospecting for the necessary capital.

In the summer of 1989, VFT secured enthusiastic support from Federal Premier Bob Hawke. But the unequivocal word from both Federal and State capitals was that the consortium would not get a dollar of public money. Furthermore, though the Australian business world applauded the project, the antennae of governments in the States to be threaded by VFT were twitching at the breadth and strength of environmental objection that the scheme had aroused. Then, in 1990, Elders-IXL's back crumpled under its weight of debt and it was compelled to seek relief by shedding non-core business enterprises. The other VFT Joint Venture partners insisted that this contretemps left the VFT project unscathed. Nevertheless, scepticism that VFT could fulfil its originally planned opening year of 1995 deepened into doubt that construction would ever begin. Doubt became near-certainty in 1991 when the Federal Government rejected clamour from the VFT group that there should be tax concessions for investors in the project, because of the time that would elapse before they saw any return from an operational railway.

A much surer bet for completion before the end of the 1990s was a new high-speed railway some 410 km (255 miles) long in South Korea's key commercial corridor, between the capital, Seoul, in the north and the city and port of Pusan on the country's south-east coast. Detailed study of a new line to relieve congestion of the corridor's existing railways had been conducted early in the 1980s. The findings were favourable on viability as well as technical feasibility counts; but in 1983 the country's Economic Planning Council, daunted by South Korea's hefty external debt, balked at the size of the new line's appetite for capital.

For the next six years the scheme was on hold, except for further study. The Korean National Railroad (KNR) had to be content with refurbishing the existing Seoul-Pusan line for a 150 kmph (93.2 mph) top speed instead of 120 kmph (75 mph); and with investment in some locally-built and aggressively streamlined train-sets, each enclosing three trailers between a pair of 1,180kW MTU-engined diesel-hydraulic power cars, to make the most of the scope for accelerated service between the two cities.

Then in 1989 newly-elected President Roh Tae Woo put his office firmly behind construction not only of the Seoul-Pusan line, but also of two other new railways: one from Seoul across the peninsula to the east coast, engineered only for 200 kmph (124.3 mph) because of the unfriendly terrain; and from Taejon, near the midpoint of the Seoul-Pusan route, to the south-western port of Mokpo, this aiming no higher than 180 kmph (118.7 mph). Construction on the Seoul-Pusan line, partly government-funded, otherwise by foreign loans, was expected to begin in 1992, with completion targeted for 1998/9.

The new Seoul-Pusan line is to be exclusively passenger-carrying and, of course, electrified. In 1990 the French, Germans and Japanese were vigorously pressing their respective TGV, ICE and Shinkansen technologies on KNR and the Transport Ministry. The South Koreans were envisaging a train formation of no fewer than 22 vehicles — four power cars and 18 trailers — to run at a maximum speed of 300 kmph (186.5 mph), though the infrastructure was still to be designed for 350 kmph. The Seoul-Pusan journey time target was a flat 2 hours, so that the end-to-end average speed would be 200 kmph or a mite higher, depending on the precise distance of the new line's definitive alignment.

South Korea may well be vying with Taiwan for the distinction of operating the first Asian high-speed line outside Japan. In 1990 French Railways' consultancy Sofrerail was handed a one-year contract by the Taiwanese Government to plan a 365 km (226.8-mile), 300 kmph standard gauge railway (the island's existing rail system is of 1,067 mm gauge) down Taiwan's east coast from Taipei, the capital, to Kaohsiung. The crucial word in that sentence is `plan', not `study'. The Government was intending to adopt Sofrerail's completed work as the basis for immediate invitations to tender for construction and equipment of the new line. Sights were set on partial opening by 1996 and deployment of a full service in 1998.

13
MagLev hunts for buyers

Despite France's persistent rolling back of wheel-on-rail's ultimate speed horizon, some continued to forecast that another medium would be the supreme overland inter-city transport of the 21st century. That was Magnetic Levitation, or MagLev, the high-speed development of which was being pursued by the Germans and Japanese throughout the 1970s and 1980s, albeit along different paths.

The basis of MagLev is that electromagnetic reaction between an on-board device and another embedded in its guideway keeps the vehicle permanently levitated when it is on the move. Propulsion and braking are achieved by varying the frequency and voltage of a linear motor system embodied in the guideway and reacting with magnets on the vehicle.

The essential difference between German and Japanese high-speed MagLev technology is that the Germans levitate by magnetic attraction, the Japanese by magnetic repulsion. The German vehicle has on each side an L-shaped skirting that at its base wraps round the edges of the guideway. Within the skirtings are a number of levitation and guidance electromagnets. When these are energized, they are attracted to ferro-magnetic armature rails at the extremities of the guideway. That lifts the vehicle out of contact with the guideway surface and activates the guidance system.

The Japanese technology fits the vehicle with high-power, liquid helium-cooled superconductor magnets and embeds coils of the same polarity in the guideway. The two therefore repel each other; and that keeps the vehicle in suspension above the guideway.

The Japanese technology refines the MagLev method devised by a pioneering US research and development team in the mid-1960s. The Americans' Federally-funded work was terminated in 1975. The US inter-city airline network had become so comprehensive, they were told, that pursuit of new high-speed ground transportation was nugatory. Yet within little more than a decade conviction was spreading that the high-speed train was both a more economical short-haul feeder of international air hubs than the jetliner, and thus an effective alternative to airport runway tailbacks and overcrowded skies. And nowhere more so, ironically, than in the USA.

Present-day experts in MagLev point to two advantages of the Japanese system. One is that it substantially trims the weight of on-board apparatus and thus gross vehicle weight. The other is that whereas the German system requires that the air gap between levitated vehicle and guideway be held steady at only 8-9 mm, the Japanese allows between 10 and 20 cm. The greater Japanese tolerance naturally simplifies construction of the guideway and makes operation less susceptible to any inherent imperfections. The reverse of the Japanese coin at the time of writing is that foolproof protection of passengers from the powerful magnetic fields set up by the superconducting magnets has yet to be assured. This was one reason why, at the start of the 1990s, the German system was closer to commercial realization.

The German technology is marketed under the name of Transrapid by Transrapid International, a consortium of Krauss-Maffei, MBB and Thyssen-Henschel. With finance and sponsorship from the West German Ministry for Research and Technology, a full-scale, 20-mile-long elevated test track in the form of two loops connected by a straight has been erected in Emsland, North Germany, for test and demonstration running of Transrapid vehicles. Over one part of it a top speed of 280 mph (450 kmph) is possible, though up to 1990 the maximum reported on trial runs was 271 mph (435 kmph).

That was in December 1989 by Transrapid's TR06 test train, a brace of articulated three-unit sections, each with a cab at one end. Back in 1985 I had had a chance to travel in TR06 round the half of the Emsland test track which was then completed, though we were then held to a speed limit of 180 kmph (112 mph).

The only blemish on an otherwise satin-smooth ride throughout was a pretty hefty lurch as we came off the loop and sped through the guideway's hugely cumbersome guideway switch — a lumbering flexible steel beam actuated by six motors dispersed throughout its length — to regain the straight section. Loop curvature is generally banked at 12 degrees, so that one was oblivious to centrifugal force. Inside TR06, the only noises of travel were a barely perceptible whine from the electrics; and the merest whisper of a thud, purely aerodynamic, below floor as we swept over the narrow gaps between guideway sections at each support of the elevated structure.

What convinced me even then that MagLev had little inter-city future in Western Europe was not just the considerably greater cost of constructing its elevated guideway than putting down a new TGV route, let alone the sense of beginning a new guided transport system wholly incompatible with railways. It was also the visual obscenity of the elevated guideway in a rural landscape. Erection of the Emsland test track was politically painless because it followed the course of an aborted canal project over land that was government-owned; and because industry was sparse in the area, the locals were prepared to gamble that Transrapid would bring other hi-tech activity in its wake.

The West German Government of the early 1970s had staked its D-Marks on MagLev as the inter-city system of the future. The then Research & Technology Minister had trounced his Transport colleague's case for traditional rail. As a result, a high-speed research programme of that period laid out

Transrapid's TR06 test vehicle on the Emsland test track in North Germany.

more than twice as much seed money for MagLev R & D as for wheel-on-rail. And there was cash, too, for the Emsland test track, whereas a promise of funds to prepare a German Federal line for trials at up to 350 kmph was soon rescinded.

The performance of France's first TGV in the 1980s rewrote the policy. The new Federal Transport Plan of 1985, as already described, put high-speed development of the orthodox railway top of the agenda. Nevertheless, Transrapid International went ahead with development of an improved and lighter-weight vehicle. This is the twin-unit TR07, which Transrapid aspires to operate at up to 500 kmph (311 mph).

But the company's efforts to sell to systems abroad — the prospects were brightest in the USA and South Korea (Seoul-Pusan) — were hobbled by its lack of any publicly-operating Transrapid link in its own country. Transrapid clamour to get one up and running had significant political support. However, that was now tempered by insistence, even by sympathizers, that any indulgence of MagLev must in no way divert resources and traffic from the evolving DB high-speed network.

Once official rejection had formalized universal certainty that Transrapid's bid to provide the international high-speed route from Paris via Brussels to Cologne was a non-starter, the West German Government's 1988 wheel-on-rail preference for its Cologne-Frankfurt high-speed scheme was a foregone conclusion. It had been said that if that decision went against Transrapid, there would be consideration of Hannover-Hamburg (already connected by a twice-hourly inter-city service that is one of DB's fastest), Augsburg-Munich II (Munich's new airport) and Hannover-Braunschweig as route options. But in the event the weight of opinion in the Bonn Cabinet was against processing any of them.

At length, in December 1989, the Research & Technology Minister badgered his colleagues into agreement to a demonstration Transrapid link of just 35 km (21.8 miles) between Cologne and Dusseldorf airports, with the possibility of extension to a further 47 km (29.2 miles) from Dusseldorf

to Essen. But there would be no Federal cash for the project. The capital must come from private industry and the North Rhine-Westphalian provincial government. No way, the latter promptly responded; major transport developments were a Federal responsibility. Simultaneously the environmentalist opposition mobilized. Never mind the visual offence, they protested: they would be pestered by a noise akin to that from low-flying jets. In mid-1991 the scheme had still to get beyond paperwork.

At the start of the 1990s the highest speed so far recorded with MagLev was 517 kmph (321.3 mph), back in December 1979. But that was with a scaled-down, non-passenger-carrying vehicle in the first phase of Japanese research and development. In the 1980s two full-size passenger-carrying vehicles, the twin-unit MLU001 and the single-car MLU002, were built, and with these a test programme taking speed up to 250 mph was conducted on a track only 7 km (4.4 miles) long. Originally managed by Japanese National Railways, the development is now run by the Japan Rail Group's Railway Technical Research Institute.

The objective now is substitution of a 500 kmph MagLev track some 500 km (310 miles) long for the putative second Shinkansen route from Tokyo to Osaka. That, it is forecast, would cut Tokyo-Osaka centre-to-centre journey time down to an even hour.

Realization became likelier in 1990 when, with lush profits from surrounding property in prospect, some high-powered politicking had the alignment of a new 43 km (26.7-mile) MagLev test track fixed roughly at the start of the proposed route — from the western outskirts of Tokyo through the mountains to Yamanashi Prefecture. At the same time a new well-floor articulated vehicle design was on the drawing boards.

Simultaneously the first US inter-city MagLev schemes were edging up to the starting-line. With modern high-speed wheel-on-rail transport limited to the New York-Washington corridor, compatibility of new ventures with the existing rail system was not so pressing a concern as in Europe. Nor, in America's wide open spaces, did the prospect of elevated guideways seem to excite environmental passions. So, despite the already conclusive proof from France that everyday wheel-on-rail public service at 300 kmph (187.5 mph) was reliably and profitably possible, whereas high-speed MagLev had yet to carry a fare-paying passenger, the latter had some weighty political opinion backing it as the more forward-looking choice for the 21st century. Some of this enthusiasm for MagLev had a suspiciously xenophobic ring of anxiety to snub the Europeans by making the US the front-runner in, and manufacturing base of, a different high-speed ground transportation technology.

So in 1990 there was a ludicrous contradiction of policies in Washington. The Bush Administration was on the one hand practising for the last time the annual ritual of the Reagan era, a budgetary effort to withdraw all Federal funding from Amtrak that Congress invariably aborted. On the other, partly motivated by hope of finding a new hi-tech outlet for the contracting US defence industry, its 1991 budget offered dollars for the creation of a National MagLev Initiative. On the latter Congress was in the Bush corner. In mid-1990 various Senators and House members were sponsoring bills to dedicate far greater resources to MagLev development than Bush's Budget had suggested, in one case as much as US$950 million.

Yet, as described in an earlier chapter, proponents of most of the embryonic US high-speed inter-city links still leaned to wheel-on-rail. The exceptions were in Florida, California-Nevada and Pennsylvania, all of them founded on the German Transrapid technology.

Provided that the scheme survived state hearings in 1991, an 18.6 mile (30 km) MagLev link between Orlando, Florida, and the Disney resort complex should be operational in 1995. In Pennsylvania, where Pittsburgh's city hall and industry bosses hanker to establish the US hub of MagLev technology and manufacture, the state's High Speed InterCity Rail Passenger Commission has plumped for MagLev to link Pittsburgh and Harrisburg. But in 1991 this scheme was up against vigorous state political opposition. For the immediate future it was unlikely to aim for more than a 10-mile (16 km) link between downtown Pittsburgh and the city's airport.

By far the most ambitious project is for a 270-mile (435 km) line based on German MagLev technology to connect Anaheim, South California, with the Nevadan gambling capital of Las Vegas. In August 1990 a joint commission of the two states franchised development of this scheme to a consortium comprising Bechtel Corp of the US, the German MagLev company Transrapid, and the Japanese trading agency C Itoh. This trio foresees its enterprise hustling hedonists from the Los Angeles tourist area to Las Vegas in just 75 minutes. And predicts that this first line's appeal will stimulate the spread of a MagLev network through the Pacific Southwest region of the US.

But this is to be a trunk-railway-like operation, with passenger-loaded MagLev vehicles passing each other at high speed. No one has yet tried that. Or even has a layout on which it can be done and proved safe beyond a scintilla of doubt. Small wonder that one of the consortium members, Bechtel, has warned that there is no hope of having the line in revenue service by its projected inaugural year of 1998.

MagLev interests now claim that their high-speed system can tolerate gradients as steep as 1 in 10, compared with the 1 in 28.5 maximum — in short stretches — of France's TGV-PSE. But that will not close the substantial gap in per-mile construction costs between the known bills for a new wheel-on-rail route and the estimates quoted for building a MagLev guideway. Numerous facets of MagLev reliability in regular public service remain to be confirmed, too — not least safety, given the much lighter weight and structure of MagLev vehicles compared with a TGV train-set. And consequently how they will behave should they collide with an unexpected hazard on the guideway: or, as considered above, how two cars will react when they pass each other at high speed.

All things considered, the foreseeable future of high-speed ground transportation is, I believe, firmly based on a fresh advance in wheel-on-rail technology.

Index